Dictionary of Terrorism

Dictionary of Terrorism

David Wright-Neville

polity

First published in 2010 by Polity Press

Polity Press
65 Bridge Street
Cambridge CB2 1UR, UK

Polity Press
350 Main Street
Malden, MA 02148, USA

ISBN-13: 978-0-7456-4301-4 (hardback)
ISBN-13: 978-0-7456-4302-1 (paperback)

A catalogue record for this book is available from the British Library.

Typeset in 11 on 13 pt Scala
by Toppan Best-set Premedia Limited
Printed and bound in Great Britain by MPG Books Group Limited, Bodmin, Cornwall

The publisher has used its best endeavours to ensure that the URLs for external websites referred to in this book are correct and active at the time of going to press. However, the publisher has no responsibility for the websites and can make no guarantee that a site will remain live or that the content is or will remain appropriate.

Every effort has been made to trace all copyright holders, but if any have been inadvertently overlooked the publisher will be pleased to include any necessary credits in any subsequent reprint or edition.

For further information on Polity, visit our website: www.politybooks.com

In memory of my father, Peter. 1923–2009

Contents

Acknowledgements   *page* viii

Thinking about terrorism in late modernity   ix

How to use this book   xxxvii

A–Z of terrorism   1

Bibliography   209

Index   214

Acknowledgements

This book would not have been possible without the assistance of a fantastic team of colleagues and research assistants. At Monash University's Global Terrorism Research Center, I have been guided in particular by the friendship of Dr Pete Lentini and support from other colleagues, especially Waleed Ali, Bill Kelly and Joe Ilardi. Special thanks are owed to Natalie Miletic, without whose painstaking research on the complexities of the Middle East this project would not have been possible. Recognition is also due to the enthusiastic and patient editorial team at Polity, particularly Rachel Donnelly, Louise Knight and David Winters. Finally, thanks are due to all on the home front who helped me through some unexpected hurdles throughout the writing of this book. Of course, any errors or shortcomings are entirely the responsibility of the author.

Thinking about terrorism in late modernity

> Remember that terrorism is a complicated, diverse, and multideter-mined phenomenon that resists simple definition, undermines all efforts at objectivity, forces upon all researchers moral riddles of con-founding complexity, and is as challenging to our intellectual efforts to understanding it as it is to our collective efforts to control it. (Reich 1998:280)

Within the broadly defined field of the social sciences, that area of study known as 'terrorism studies' stands out as an anomaly. It is, as has been pointed out many times, one of the few fields of social science research where there is no agreed definition of the subject of inquiry itself.

This lack of consensus, which has impeded even the United Nations from reaching a standard definition despite almost four decades of effort, poses a particular set of problems for those who draw intellectual comfort from definitional certainty. To what extent can states be guilty of terrorism? Can violence ever be justified in the cause of freedom? These and other questions strike at the very core of political philosophy and it is the failure to excavate beneath the surface level of terrorist violence that looms as one of terrorism studies' major shortcomings.

Unfortunately, this debate is not going to be ended through a single text, even one dedicated to documenting a wide range of ter-rorist issues. Hence, in an attempt to avoid being drawn into the vortex of definitional politics this dictionary uses the definition offered by Martha Crenshaw (1992:71), that terrorism is 'a particular style of political violence, involving attacks on a small number of victims in order to influence an audience'. Clearly, even this definition provides enormous scope for including a wide variety of violent forms of behaviour by state and non-state actors.

State terrorism is particularly problematic, mainly because of the long tradition stretching back to the Treaty of Westphalia in 1648 which conferred upon states the right to use violence to protect their political and territorial sovereignty. Exactly when a state is acting in accordance with this right, or when it is transgressing international laws and norms over the 'legitimate use of violence' is the subject of particularly complex legal and ethical debates. Yet it is clear that states are capable of perpetrating acts of terror that are far greater than those of non-state actors. Research by Rummel (1996) suggests that over the twentieth century, while 34 million people were killed in conventional wars, another 170 million were killed by states acting outside the accepted parameters of inter-state warfare. By comparison, insurgents and other non-state actors using the tactic of terrorism killed around 500,000. In short, across the twentieth century state terrorism was substantially more deadly than non-state terrorism. Moreover, it is state-sanctioned violence against critics of governments or ethnic and religious minorities that often triggers terrorism by non-state actors.

Moving this debate forward through the development of a better understanding of the nature of terrorism requires a multi-disciplinary approach. In particular, the study of terrorism needs to be better grounded across philosophy, political science, sociology, history, anthropology and, of course, psychology. It requires an approach that transcends the uni-dimensional tradition under which it has laboured in the past. Calls for such an approach are long-standing and there are some outstanding examples of the benefits that are generated by its adoption. Bernard Lewis' study of the Assassins (2003 [1967]), Sonn's (1989) study of anarchist terrorism in *fin-de-siècle* France, Esenwein's (1989) exploration of anarchist violence in Spain in the late 1800s, or Phillips and Evans (2008) research into the nexus between political and economic dispossession and terrorism in Algeria all offer excellent insights into the wider social, political and philosophical contexts in which terrorist violence occurs. But accounts of this calibre are few. It is as if the immediacy of the threat of terrorism, and the close nexus between scholarship and policy, discourages complex investigation and explanation in favour of immediate empirical mapping exercises that focus on which terrorist is connected to that terrorist or alternatively describe, borrowing from Arendt (2006 [1963]), the banality of evil. As Gunning (2007) points out, this excessive empiricism contains an instrumental logic that privileges state-centric purposes and the political imperative to find quick solutions to immediate problems. Or, to put it slightly differently, there is a reluctance to talk about terrorism's 'root causes'. This privileging of description over analysis militates against what the anthropologist Clifford Geertz (1973) called 'thick description' – which applied to the study of terrorism involves an ontological approach to understanding the unique cultural, economic, political, philosophical and social circumstances that, throughout history, have shaped the behaviour of different terrorist individuals and organizations.

Terrorism in history

Terrorism is a tactic with a long pedigree that has probably existed in one form or another for as long as humans have organized themselves into hierarchical communities. As Bowden and Davis (2008:xxv) have observed, 'September 11 2001 and the unprecedented attacks on United States soil do not represent Year 1 in the history of terrorism.'

In a much-cited article published in 2001, Rapoport pointed out that terrorism has evolved in waves, each one reflective of the social, political and technological circumstances of the time. Despite the utility of Rapoport's model for understanding the evolution of modern terrorism, it remains the case that the waves into which we divide the evolution of terrorism remain arbitrary. Even so, it is important to note that none of the stages is totally unique; each represents an evolutionary development whereby terrorist groups build on the operational knowledge and techniques developed by their predecessors. Even a cursory glance at the evolution of terrorism demonstrates the extent to which the terrorists themselves are capable of learning from history. Although they might perceive of their own particular struggle through a narrow lens, they typically display a deep knowledge of social structures and the way in which they have impacted on marginal groups that is far beyond that of the ordinary political activist. In other words, terrorism has an educative effect. Each attack, successful or otherwise, provides a set of data that is eagerly sought by other well-organized violence-prone groups to calibrate or re-calibrate their own actions.

At its core, terrorism is a tactic that individuals and groups choose to employ in the service of political goals. Historically speaking, it has not always been the case that terrorists have a clear set of political objectives, in fact in many cases terrorists are more certain about what they are fighting against rather than what they are fighting for.

For instance, the use of terrorism as a tactic against colonialism has been a recurring theme throughout history, yet in many cases those who have resorted to violence have been united by what they collectively oppose rather than by a shared vision of the preferred type of post-colonial society to replace the status quo. Terrorism by Russian anarchist groups such as the Narodniks in the 1870s and 1880s was based on a rejection of what they considered to be the exploitative conditions that existed under the Tsarist government of Alexander II (Burleigh 2008). However, the society they envisioned as an alternative was utopian in the extreme, cast in broad generalizations about egalitarianism and absolute freedom. Referring to nineteenth-century anarchist terrorism in Europe and the United States, Ivianski (2008[1977]:14) writes that it was 'history's thunderous outcry of those crushed beneath the wheels of industrialisation and modernisation'. Similarly, terrorism committed by Marxist groups in Western Europe in the 1960s and 1970s, such as the Baader-Meinhof Gang in West Germany (Merkl 2001 [1995]), the Red Brigades in Italy (Della-Porta 2008) and Action Directe (Dartnell 1995) in France, was grounded in a rejection of capitalism rather than in a clear-sighted vision of the type of society that should replace it. In the contemporary world, the violence perpetrated by al Qaeda also falls into this category. Al Qaeda justifies its terrorism in terms that reject the legitimacy of 'apostate regimes' in the Muslim world and the Western military and economic relations that they believe sustain these governments. Scholars such as Gerges (2005) have referred to this as a two-pronged strategy against both 'near' and 'far' enemies (governments in the Muslim world and the West respectively). However, al Qaeda is substantially more definitive about the type of political regimes they oppose than the type of society they envisage as an alternative (see al Qaeda statements reproduced in Kepel and Milelli 2005). Rather than setting out any sophisticated socio-political alternatives, al Qaeda and its supporters advocate an amorphous vision based on a concoction of obscure literal interpretations of Qur'anic verse coupled with a determination to restore a unified global Islamic Caliphate that will transcend the nation state to encompass the entire global Muslim community. That this vision has no historical precedent – in fact the caliphates of the past were notoriously factionalized and rent by internecine conflict – does not intrude into al Qaeda's imaginary world.

In terms of the recorded history of terrorism, one of the most often referred to in-depth case studies is the account offered by

Josephus (1981) of the Jewish uprising against Roman rule that lasted from 66CE to 70CE in Judea. Resistance to Roman rule coalesced around a sect that has subsequently lent its name to all manner of fanaticism, the Zealots, of which Josephus was a one-time member. Although it is important to contextualize Josephus' account of the uprising as that of a person who eventually turned against the Zealots and lent his support to Roman imperialism, it neverthe-less offers valuable insights into the precursors of resistance and the existential framework that eventually inspired the Zealots' embrace of the tactic of terrorism. The precise details of Zealot tactics need not concern us here, suffice it to point out that they are best remem-bered for the public assassination of Roman soldiers, Greek mer-chants, and Jews thought to be collaborating with the authorities. More pertinent to this discussion is the observation that, even though the mode of attack has evolved, from daggers concealed in the Zealots' clothes to turning aircraft into guided missiles, there are certain continuities that have existed throughout terrorism's long history.

The first is that terrorism is a form of political theatre wherein violence constitutes a carefully scripted performance designed to appeal to different audiences. Those whom the terrorists regard as their enemies – that group whose behaviour they seek to change through fear – constitute the first and most obvious audience. In the case of the Zealots the primary audience was Roman authorities and their supporters, whom they sought to drive from Judea as a step towards establishing an independent Jewish state.

Those who might sympathize with the terrorist cause, but not necessarily be actively involved in committing acts of violence, con-stitute the secondary audience. In this sense, terrorist violence that is designed to appeal to and inspire this secondary audience to 'join the struggle' carries a solipsistic value. For example, terrorism by the Narodniks in nineteenth-century Russia was not only designed to foment fear and precipitate the collapse of the Tsarist government, it was simultaneously intended to inspire other members of the 'down-trodden masses' to join the fight. In the case of Vera Zasulich's 1878 assassination attempt against the despised governor of St Petersburg, there were signs that this solipsistic strategy was working. So popular were Zasulich's actions that a jury acquitted her of all charges (Siljak 2008). More recently, the terrorism perpetrated by the Algerian Front de Libération National (Horne 2006) during the 1950s and early 1960s was aimed not only at ending French colonialism but also at catalysing anti-colonial sentiment, thereby forging a mass movement that Paris would not be able to resist.

A second recurring theme in the history of terrorism is the role played by parallel feelings of alienation, powerlessness and humiliation and an urge for revenge in stimulating a group's embrace of the tactic of terrorism.

As will be discussed more fully below, from a psychological perspective McCauley (2006:16) has pointed out that terrorism is underpinned by deeply rooted feelings of anger, and that anger stems from frustration which in turn flows from a failure to receive expected rewards. In this sense, terrorism is often a violent manifestation of a 'politics of dashed expectations'. A high rate of youth unemployment looms as a significant environmental factor. For instance, throughout the 1990s and early 2000s, countries experiencing significant levels of terrorism also demonstrated high levels of unemployment, especially among young males. Terrorism in Egypt occurred within a social context marked by an unemployment rate of 84 per cent within the 15–29-year-old age bracket (Ikram 2005:245–6). Unemployment was particularly acute among those with an intermediate education (55 per cent of total unemployment), a key area of recruitment into militant and extremist groups. Although the official rate of unemployment in Saudi Arabia is 9 per cent, unofficial estimates suggest it is more than double that figure. Once again it is young people who are especially vulnerable (Hardy 2006). In Jordan, 60 per cent of job seekers are under twenty-five (European Training Foundation 2005:28) In the Gaza Strip, unemployment reached 45 per cent by mid-2007, while on the West Bank it hovered around 25 per cent (Haaretz 2007).

A third historical continuity has been an embryonic relationship between modes of violence and prevailing destructive technologies of the time. Terrorists have always shown themselves to be adept at adapting to new technologies. Just as the Zealots used knives, Guy Fawkes and his co-conspirators used gunpowder, the Narodniks used guns and al Qaeda has used aircraft. Indeed, terrorists' ability to channel their anger in new and technologically creative ways has also been demonstrated by events such as the discovery of plots by mainly British terrorists to destroy trans-Atlantic aircraft using liquid explosives hidden in their shoes and containers marked 'baby formula' (*The Times* 10 August 2006).

Although there are signs that the threshold for violence is changing in that terrorists are increasingly prepared to use modern technologies to kill larger numbers of people (Hoffman 2006), there is often reluctance to utilize new technologies to their full lethal potential. In deciding when and how to strike, terrorists typically apply a kind of 'calculus of violence' by calibrating their desire to terrify their enemies against the danger that being too violent will alienate their community of support. Should terrorists kill too many innocents there is a possibility that potential supporters will regard the act as morally indefensible. For some scholars, it is this logic that militates against the likelihood that terrorists will seek to use chemical, biological or radiological weapons.

A final historical continuity has been the role played by charismatic leaders in catalysing dissent and developing ideologies that facilitate the projection of anger outwards and against real or perceived oppressors. During the second Jewish uprising against the Romans in 132–135CE, this role was played by Shi'mon bar Kokhba, who managed to establish briefly an independent Jewish state, which even minted coins carrying bar Kokhba's name. For the Assassins, a Nizari Shi'ite group dedicated to beating back the influence of the Sunni Caliphate and the Crusaders, this role was played by Hassan-i-Sabah. Nelson Mandela is another example of the power of a leader to generate support for a group across a broad cross-section of the national and international community. The late Velupillai Prabhakaran, the founder and leader of the Liberation Tigers of Tamil Eelam, played a similar role in that he both rallied Tamils within Sri Lanka and also drew the Tamil diaspora into a global network of support. Meanwhile, Osama bin Laden looms as the obvious charismatic figurehead for supporters of al Qaeda and its offshoots. The power of the charismatic leader as a unifying force can also linger well beyond his or her passing. In many cases death can trigger a series of apocryphal stories that sustain a powerful mythology that can resonate for decades, and even centuries, after death.

Bringing society back in

More than eight years after President George W. Bush's declaration of the 'War on Terror', the spectre of terrorism seems more pervasive than ever. In the interregnum since 9/11, high-profile attacks have occurred against commercial and civilian targets across a diverse geographic terrain that includes Britain, Jordan, India, Indonesia, the Philippines, Russia, Saudi Arabia, Spain and Turkey. Coalitions of counter-terrorist intelligence and police services have also thwarted several other major attacks in the UK, Canada and Australia, as well as throughout Southeast Asia and Western Europe. Although generating less international attention, a series of smaller attacks in other parts of the world have simultaneously imposed equally serious economic, social and psychological costs on various developing countries.

Clearly something is happening in the world. Although the media-friendly nature of terrorism has pushed it to the forefront of the daily news, and in many respects led to an exaggerated sense of threat, the fact remains that, as a form of asymmetric warfare, terrorism is emerging as one of several key organizing principles at both the domestic and international levels. While most scholars acknowledge this, little effort has been made to explore how the forces of globalization are shifting the tectonic plates of national politics and, in so doing, creating ructions at the surface level of national and international politics. Expanding the metaphor, very little research involves drilling into the political core to examine how cultural, social and psychological forces are colliding to inspire a growing number of individuals to embrace violence as a mode of political action. To quote Silke (2008:103), 'context matters'.

But even Silke and others like him whose analyses transcend the purely descriptive scholarship that constitutes the bulk of terrorist research – writers such as Crenshaw, Hoffman, Horgan and Sageman – often skirt around the complex interplay between cultural, political and psychological forces. For example, in an account of jihadist terrorism Silke (2008) tends to fall back upon an essentialized notion of Islamic religion as a dominant causal factor. His analysis (like that of Sageman (2008) and others) focuses on psychosocial conditions (age, gender, education, marital status, perceptions of injustice) that drive some young men towards a violent version of religion. But little attention is paid to how these belligerent versions of religion themselves are socially constructed. It is almost as if fundamentalist interpretations of scripture exist as ready-made self-contained repositories for the disenfranchised. But violent versions of religion are not *sui generis*; rather, they exist as categories of belief that are crafted from the artefacts of late modernity. In other words, rational individuals in search of meaning systems that make sense of an increasingly confusing and alienating world consciously craft fundamentalisms. Drawing on Weber, the belief systems that underpin religious and other identity-based terrorist groups usually reflect the rationalization and instrumentalization of religion and culture as tools for resisting a social system that is perceived as exclusionary, unjust and brutal-izing. The same can be said of the justifications for state-sponsored terrorism. As Gough (2008:86) notes with respect to the violence perpetrated by the revolutionary French government in the 1790s, 'the slide towards terror was . . . a political tactic, designed by Jacobin politicians to control sans-culotte violence, and maintain sans-culotte support, by incorporating some of its elements into state policy'.

While over-simplification speaks to the capacity for terrorist vio-lence to solicit emotive rather than objective responses among its audiences, viewing terrorists as supine social agents swept into the maelstrom of violence by wider political or pre-programmed psycho-logical forces sits comfortably with the conservative instincts of the state as well as supporters of the social status quo. To accept that the potential for terrorist violence lies not in the psychotic potential of certain religious traditions but is embedded in the array of highly personal relationships that bind all individuals to the societies in which they exist presages the need to acknowledge the possibility that existing social structures and hierarchies might in fact be part of the problem. Gunning notes correctly that terrorism studies 'tends to accept uncritically the framing of the "terrorism problem" by the state. In short, terrorism studies labour under a "state centric bias"' (2007:368).

Such a view confronts the sensitivities of both conservatives and those policy makers who are uncomfortable with any analysis that risks unsettling political and bureaucratic orthodoxies, let alone established social hierarchies. However, understanding the resilience of contemporary forms of terrorism is not possible without acknowl-edging that a growing number of people perceive the world as an increasingly unjust place, with inequities in the economic, political and social realms and stretching from the global to the local levels. This is clear both in the issues raised in the carefully calibrated rheto-ric of terrorist leaders and in the long lists of grievances that pepper the videos of suicide bombers. More particularly, it is clear in the manner in which terrorist leaders have used these grievances to build large constituencies of both formal and informal supporters.

Terrorism and its root causes

Despite the enormous political energy and economic and military resources directed at reducing the menace of Islamist terrorism since 2001, there are few signs that the threat is diminishing in either its spread or lethality. The failure (and possibly the counter-productivity) of the 'War on Terror' and many of the policies that have fallen under its ambit lies in a reluctance or inability to understand the ontological essence of contemporary forms of terrorism. What follows is a modest attempt to avoid such a shortcoming by offering an explanation of the inner logic of contemporary Islamist terrorism that proceeds from two obvious but often overlooked a priori assumptions: that no one is born a terrorist and that those who eventually become involved in terrorism do so only after passing through an evolutionary progression that involves a complex mix of social, political and psychological forces.

As pointed out by writers such as Horgan (2005) and Richardson (2006), a first step along the path towards terrorism is a (real or imagined) perception of being an outcast and of a corresponding sense that this outsider status is the reason for the repeated disappointments visited upon the individual or their community. For example, in a video recorded prior to his involvement in the 9/11 attacks, Ahmad al-Haznawi al-Ghamidi railed that 'the time of humiliation is over' (Richardson 2006:126), a theme repeated by one of the 7/7 bombers in London, Mohammad Siddique Khan, who used his video to argue that 'until *we* feel security, *you* will be *our* targets. And until *you* stop the bombing, gassing, imprisonment and torture of *my* people *we* will not stop this fight' (BBC 2005). Allegations of oppression and humiliation also informed the video prepared by Khan's 7/7 counterpart Shehzad Tanweer (*The Observer* 2006).

However, a commitment to violence occurs neither suddenly nor easily, and research into the psychological dimensions of terrorism suggests that in the lead-up to the decision to sacrifice their lives and murder others, terrorists such as al-Ghamidi, Siddique Khan and Tanweer have passed through a process marked by increasing levels of alienation and embitterment that is reflected in their simultaneous embrace of militant Islamist ideologies. As McCauley has noted, 'the trajectory by which normal people become capable of doing terrible things is usually gradual, perhaps imperceptible to the individual' (McCauley 2006:19).

In his research into racism and the development of ethnic and cultural sub-communities in France, Wieviorka (2004:290) articulates clearly the powerful reactive logic encoded into recent manifestations of militant Islamist identities. In so doing, he also acknowledges the role of conscious human agency in the shaping of alternative identities:

I have often met young Muslims in France who say two things. In the first instance, they explain that their choice of Islam is personal and deliberate. Second, they consider that Islam enables them to keep going when confronted with a racist society and one in which their living conditions are particularly difficult. In this case, Islam does not keep them apart from society; on the contrary, it is Islam which enables them to be satisfied with limited access to resources, or in any case to bear this while waiting for something better in the future.

Wieviorka's observations help to illuminate the way in which confrontational assertions of religious identity form an important part of a wider search for ontological security by individuals constantly reminded of their outsider status in French society. Faced with daily reminders of their exclusion, in both hard (such as racist violence) and soft (such as cultural invisibility in mainstream media) forms, idealized versions of religion have come to play an important role in providing an alternative sense of community identity. As Kinnvall (2004:759) notes, 'religion, like nationalism, supplies existential answers to individuals' quests for security by essentializing the product and providing a picture of totality, unity and wholeness'. In our contemporary epoch, religion is widely perceived as providing an antidote to the corrosive effects of globalization on once discrete cultures, as well as to the existential pain of exclusion from mainstream society and its cultural, economic and political structures. In other words, religion is consciously moulded by the disenfranchised into a device for addressing a psychological urge to stop being a passive victim and to provide the basis for challenging those forces that are seen to be the principal causes of humiliation, powerlessness and alienation.

In the French case, as in other advanced Western and non-Western societies, a great deal of the sense of exclusion experienced by those who have retreated into sub-national cultural enclaves reflects frustration at repeated failures to access the cultural, economic and social accoutrements of late modernity. Denied access to this aspect of society, they have set about constructing their own world, a place where the need to belong can be satiated and where the excluders from the dominant culture become the excluded. This in turn draws attention to the roots of this exclusion, which rest not in culture or religion per se but in the failure to feel accepted on one's own terms.

Often, those who experience these feelings point to their socio-economic status as evidence of their rejection. For example, a social worker active among some of the Muslim youth who rioted across

France in 2005 opined that the violence 'crystallized the hatred' felt towards French authority by some of the most disaffected and hopeless young men who live in what the government calls 'sensitive urban zones' (*Christian Science Monitor* 2005). Of the 750 zones designated by the French government as in need of special employment and other social programmes, which are also home to the majority of France's Muslim population, unemployment hovers at around double the national average of 10 per cent while average incomes are 75 per cent below the French national average. They are also home to people who, if they are of North African descent, are five times less likely than a Frenchman of white Christian heritage to receive an interview for a job (*New York Times* 2005). Such forms of discrimination have also been identified by employment audits carried out in other Western countries (Sidanius and Pratto 1999:155). For instance, a study carried out in 2004 by the BBC showed that, in Britain, Muslim and African applicants were only half as likely to be invited for job interviews as non-Muslim white candidates, even when they had similar qualifications and experience (BBC 2004).

Such feelings are not unique to contemporary times. Acts of terrorism perpetrated by the Zealots against the Roman occupiers of Judea, as well as by more recent groups as diverse as the Russian anarchists in the 1870s and the Vigorous Burmese Student Warriors of today, contain the same sorts of feelings of alienation and powerlessness in the face of superior political, military and economic forces.

Simultaneous feelings of exclusion, alienation, disempowerment and humiliation are characteristic of almost all the groups and individuals mentioned in this book. Of course there are some exceptions, such as Theodore Kaczynski (the 'Unabomber') and even Ilyich Ramírez Sánchez ('Carlos the Jackal'). In Kaczynski's case it was a deep sense of impotence in the face of the effects on society of new technologies that fuelled his anger and triggered his violence. Unlike most other terrorists, however, Kaczynski was also diagnosed with a mental illness, schizophrenia (Chase 2003). Ramírez on the other hand evolved from his support for secular and socialist causes into being a virtual 'gun-for-hire' (Follain 2000). But even here Ramírez had sympathy for the causes for which he was willing to commit violence. But both these cases signify what is sometimes referred to as the 'lone wolf' phenomenon. More commonly, as is shown below, terrorism is a group activity where a collective experience of alienation and humiliation combines to trigger the urge to lash out against perceived oppressors.

Another contentious issue in terrorism studies is the link between poverty and terrorist violence. Those who question the nexus between relative inequality of both wealth and opportunity and terrorism point out that recent terrorist acts against Western targets have often been carried out by young men from relatively prosperous families and therefore we need to look beyond socio-economic factors for the source of their rage (Maleckova 2005; Weinberg 2006; Laqueur 2004:15–16; Piazza 2006). However, the fact that a small number of migrants in Western countries have overcome the social and cultural obstacles to material success does not mean that others can replicate their achievements. Similarly, that the financial and material success of these successful individuals often comes only after an extraordinary degree of personal effort, including the occasional need to jettison overt displays of cultural difference to appease nervous employers, can also be a source of shame that infects family and community dynamics and which can erupt suddenly into a belligerent re-assertion of these lost cultural traditions.

In modern capitalist societies, environmental factors such as employment status and the quality of one's residential neighbourhood exert a profound influence over a person's sense of well-being and mental health, and in either mitigating or escalating feelings of shame, humiliation and frustration with the core institutions of society (Wilkinson 2004, 2005; Marmot and Wilkinson 2005; Jaynes 2000; Lofors and Sundquist 2007). The issue is therefore more complex than whether or not a person holds a job, or the social status that is sometimes attached to that job. At issue is whether the job concerned is consistent with a person's wider life ambitions. As Victoroff (2009 [2005]:69) notes, arguments that reject the role of poverty in fomenting environments conducive to the emergence of terrorist ideologies focus too much on socio-economic background at the expense of more important causal factors such as economic *prospects*.

Indeed, there is a possibility that successful entrance into an elite profession can even reinforce feelings of shame or humiliation if, as is often the case, a person's employment status does not enhance their capacity to improve the depressed circumstances of other members of their 'in-group'. If a person is gainfully employed but lives within a social context marked by a wider existential crisis – such as limited opportunities to progress one's career, other members of one's family or peer group being unemployed or suffering other forms of social deprivation, living in dilapidated or high-crime areas, or even being exposed to racial taunts at work or in the wider society – then employment can be an important causal factor because it brings into sharper relief the extent of social inequities and can foster in the successful professional a sense of guilt that they have progressed at the expense of their wider 'in-group'. The surprise expressed at news of engineers or doctors being involved in terrorism ignores the point well-made by Elias and Scotson in the 1960s: that when discrepancies in material and cultural power are such that the marginalized feel they cannot escape their lot, they will often use what the dominant groups say about them as raw materials in the crafting of their own separate 'we-image' (Elias and Scotson 1965; Mennell 1994:182). In other words, there is little historical evidence to support the claim that the ability of a small number of individuals from marginalized communities to break into an elite or respected profession will automatically diminish the feelings of shame or anger that also characterize the attitudes of those who miss out on such opportunities because of their race, religion or colour. Nor does career success necessarily attenuate the urge for revenge that can sometimes flow from these feelings.

In the specific case of terrorism by extremist Islamic groups, particularly in Western Europe, it remains the case that the vast majority of the Muslim diaspora exists at the economic and social margins of society and that upwardly mobile Muslims remain the exception rather than the rule. As mentioned above, a plethora of studies point to the higher levels of unemployment and differing levels of employment opportunity among migrant communities in many Western countries. Mason (2000:99–100) points out that unemployment among minority ethnic groups is 'hyper-cyclical' in that it rises faster than white unemployment in times of recession. This underscores the reality that non-white migrants are over-represented in low-paid and low-skilled employment, a pattern of behaviour which has condemned several generations of immigrant communities to a precarious economic existence despite living in some of the wealthiest countries in the world. In a 2002 study prepared by the UK Home Office, it was noted that, while migrants to the UK from 'white' ethnic backgrounds tended to perform as well as or better than the existing population in terms of labour market participation and financial rewards, migrants from 'non-white' backgrounds performed less well than UK-born residents, including those UK-born residents of similar ethnic heritage. Notably, Pakistani and Bangladeshi migrants fared particularly poorly (Haque et al. 2002:4; Saggar 2006). Moreover,

Muslims are under-represented in national and European Union parliaments as well as at grassroots-level councils (Silke 2008:113).

Numerous other studies stretching back to the 1960s have also pointed to both subtle and overt forms of racial discrimination in employment practices in the UK and in other Western economies that sustain race- and ethnicity-based inequities in areas such as skill-recognition and wage-based remuneration (e.g. Daniel 1968; Brown and Gay 1985; Jenkins 1986; Noon 1993; Fetzner and Soper 2004; Bowen 2006). In the latter case, studies have shown that workers from minority ethnic groups in the UK had significantly lower earnings than their white counterparts. Once again, the gap is especially pronounced in the case of Pakistani and Bangladeshi migrants (Mason 2000:102). Overlaying these data are other studies pointing out that unemployment and fear of racial harassment have contributed to significantly lower levels of psychosocial well-being among migrant communities in the UK (Haque et al. 2002:22). Against this background it is not surprising that the Chair of the UK Commission for Racial Equality warned recently that multiculturalism in Britain 'is in danger of becoming a sleight of hand by which ethnic minorities are distracted by tokens of recognition while being excluded from the real business' and where 'the smile of recognition has turned into the rictus grin on the face of institutional racism' (in Brighton 2007:9).

Appreciating the extent of marginalization and frustration generated by these social inequities is essential to understanding the evolution of terrorist identities because it is in such environments that ideologies of resistance and violence most readily take root. As Richardson (2006:126) has observed in the case of bin Laden, 'statements and interviews constantly reassert his desire to redress Muslim humiliation . . . by claiming repeatedly that "death is better than life in humiliation"'. This theme is not particular to Islamist terrorism but has also been a factor in Catholic anger in Northern Ireland, which fed into support for the IRA (Toolis 1995), and among Tamils in Sri Lanka, underpinning support for the Liberation Tigers of Tamil Eelam (Winslow and Woost 2004), as well as in other parts of the world. A similar phenomenon has been documented on the West Bank and Gaza Strip where, in the lead-up to the first Intifada an increase in the proportion of Palestinian men progressing to higher levels of education coincided with rising unemployment rates for college and high school graduates and a reduction in real wages. Atran (2009 [2003]:150) argues that underemployment among graduates also seems to be a factor in al Qaeda's appeal in much of the Middle East.

Often secular and not outwardly pious for long periods of their lives, these young men were not transformed into mass murderers by their sudden conversion to extremist Islamism. Rather than looking for clues for their motives in Islam itself, we need to concentrate instead on the social forces that gradually rendered them open to such a conversion. As noted by Pedahzur, Perliger and Weinberg (2003), the way in which the individual conceives of the relationship between themselves and wider society plays an important part in the decision over whether or not to engage in acts of terrorism. Like others before them, these young men were usually embittered long before their immersion into the terrorist milieu. Indeed, it seems likely that the appeal of the ideology of al Qaedism to the 7/7 bombers and hundreds of others like them lay mainly in its ability to speak to a pre-existing sense of ontological confusion and social alienation. Strip away the religious rhetoric and at the core of the tirades delivered as suicide statements are a set of deeply felt grievances and a pervasive sense of individual and group humiliation. From the point of view of understanding the motivation of the terrorist, it is almost insignificant that these grievances might or might not be imagined. What matters is that for the individual concerned the grievances are real. Hence, there are important similarities between the status of the 7/7 bombers who perceived themselves as representatives of a larger victimized social and cultural group and the attitudes of leftist terrorists in Western Europe a generation earlier, and indeed of terrorist groups stretching back to antiquity.

More significantly, the existence of relative deprivation also points to another factor in the evolution of attitudinal dynamics that render some people open to extremist and violent ideologies. The promise of great wealth and unfettered opportunity is the essence of the neo-liberal dream and forms a core part of the West's mythology about itself. Indeed, it is the appeal of the myth that anybody who works hard and uses their initiative can succeed that has been a key factor in drawing millions of immigrants to Western Europe and the New World. The resilience of this dream has continued to enthral many millions more, particularly those whose immediate environment is so dire that the West looms as a virtual paradise flaunted through the proliferation of Western mass media. However, access to this idealized vision is denied to all but a select few – usually those whose specialized skills are conducive to the drive for even greater levels of economic surplus in the West. Meanwhile, those who lack these skills are either forced to accept a life with few prospects or to access the West through illegal means.

The role of this mythology about the West in sustaining the energy of first-generation migrants is well documented and, until recently, the belief that migration carried with it full access to the privileges enjoyed by native inhabitants was one of the legitimating myths, which Sidanius and Pratto (1999:104) define as the 'values, attitudes, beliefs, causal attributions, and ideologies that provide moral and intellectual justification for social practices'. The significance of the legitimating myths for maintaining peace in ethnically and culturally diverse societies is also clear in places such as the Philippines and Thailand where terrorism by secessionist groups continues to pose major problems. In these cases, indigenous ethnic and religious minorities have lost faith in the ideal of integration and equal rights and, as such, in the mythology that they are part of an organic multicultural nation state. The internalization of these myths by immigrant communities and the first generation of post-colonial minorities explains why, despite their over-representation at the margins of society, they were inclined to support a social system that offered them little genuine prospect of social improvement. However, these myths hold less appeal for second- and third-generation migrants and minority groups who, even if, as has occasionally occurred, they have benefited from the hard work of their parents, are unconvinced that the effort was worth it. Many second- and third-generation children of migrants point out that others not of their background have worked just as hard but have progressed further up the socio-economic ladder or earned greater respect and recognition from mainstream society. For them, this is testimony to the refusal of the system to accept them and reward them. They are often therefore critical of the sacrifices of their parents, which are perceived as naïve, and they are occasionally hostile to a society that they perceive to have rejected them. The shared experience of the failure of the Western secular nationalist dream is what binds them into sub-communities of the frustrated and disenchanted.

The existence of existential crises within diaspora and minority communities is critical to understanding the resilience of terrorist ideologies in the years following 9/11. Of course, this does not mean that all those who experience those feelings will complete the trajectory and evolve into terrorists, a point explored more fully below. For the time being, the argument can be summarized as follows: just as the capacity to love another and to feel pain at the suffering of someone close requires that one first experience love (usually as an infant), so too does the capacity to love and respect society rely upon the experience of being loved and respected by society. Hence, those who express confusion at how young men of middle- and lower-middle-class backgrounds can strike out violently against society are missing the point. As discussed above, the capacity to accumulate a modicum of wealth and material goods should not be confused with the experience of social acceptance, and, rather than focusing upon material wealth as a measure of social integration, attention should be directed at a more complex array of social measures including employment, career progression, visibility in mass culture, and the presence of in-group members in mainstream political and social institutions. As writers such as Gilligan (2000:39) and Elias (1996 [1989]:196–7) have noted, almost all people who kill deliberately hate their own lives as well as those of others.

Terrorism as a process

Recognizing the nexus between ontological insecurity and terrorism constitutes an important step in the crafting of better counter-terrorism policies. However, while a small number of governments appear to have accepted the need to develop more inclusive policies that reduce feelings of marginalization, this approach is still confined to the margins of counter-terrorism policy. Community-based counter-terrorism initiatives are seen widely as a soft option best foisted on to social workers and community leaders so that the bulk of state resources can be dedicated to hard-power initiatives. However, there is a danger that, unless properly calibrated, the use of hard power can intensify the very feelings of alienation that soft-power initiatives are designed to reverse. Underlying this is a tendency among policy makers to view terrorism as a spontaneous phenomenon that is rooted in the madness of its perpetrators rather than the end result of a long process involving incremental increases in alienation and anger and, eventually, an urge to lash out violently.

To paraphrase Horgan, terrorism is a 'process comprising discrete phases' (2005:81), operating at the individual, group and social psychological levels. More importantly, this mix of psychological, social and political forces interacts symbiotically and neither should be considered discrete. In short, these forces conspire in differing ways to elicit different responses among different people. That is, the way in

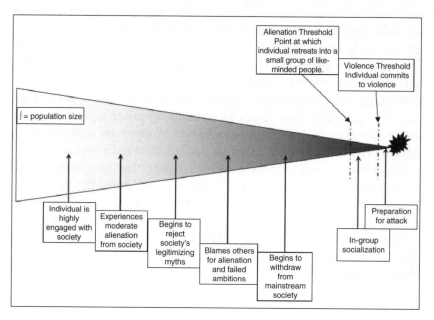

Figure 1   Becoming a terrorist

which one individual responds to a given set of economic, political and social conditions will differ from the way that another person responds to the same set of conditions. The art of terrorist recruiters, however, rests in their ability to identify those individuals whose responses to social forces are roughly similar and to then pull them into a context where in-group socialization standardizes understandings of the outside world and fosters feelings of collective anger and a group urge to respond violently. Put more simply, the causes of terrorism are rooted mainly in what Richardson (2006:14) has called 'subjective perceptions, in a lethal cocktail containing a disaffected individual, an enabling community and a legitimizing ideology'.

This conception of terrorism as a dynamic phenomenon that involves a transitional psychological state before reaching the point of 'acting out' is represented in figure 1. Admittedly, capturing the vast repertoire of personal histories and experiences that have led different individuals to embrace terrorism as a legitimate form of political action is an extraordinarily difficult task. Moreover, the process of becoming a terrorist is rarely a linear progression. Even so, there remain some useful reference points that appear regularly across the variegated life histories of terrorists motivated at different times by a range of different political and ideological goals.

It is understandable that the focus for most police and security agencies, as well as many terrorism scholars, is on the extreme right-hand side of the process – that final stage after a person has committed to violence and when he/she is in the process of planning or carrying out an attack. However, there is a need to avoid seeing this point in the terrorism process as the only area where counter-terrorism policies should be focused. Indeed, a great deal of the resilience of terrorist ideologies in the wake of 9/11 seems to lie in the capacity for hard-power-based counter-terrorism initiatives to reinforce the alienation and anger felt by those further to the left of the diagram (i.e. those either partially or tentatively integrated into mainstream society).

The extreme left of the diagram represents a level of social engagement indicative of most members of society. At this point, despite obvious problems associated with everyday life, few people feel the urge to disengage or to view wider society as inherently hostile to their interests. Everyday frustrations are countered by a deeper understanding that there exist multiple channels for expressing or addressing life's difficulties and for pursuing one's own life choices.

The first step along the path towards becoming a terrorist involves the gradual (and often inadvertent) alienation of an individual from mainstream society. Feelings of rejection and a lack of acceptance, coupled with a steadily intensifying sense of disempowerment (defined as an inability to change one's own circumstances) are common to many people at some stage in their lives. However, in the case of the would-be terrorist these feelings are never redressed through positive socio-cultural affirmation. Rather, the individual feels progressively detached from mainstream society and increasingly frustrated at their perceived inability to do anything about it. Such prolonged exposure to structural forms of violence can eventually result in what some psychologists (e.g. Gilligan 2003; Bandura et al. 1996; Kelman 1973) call the gradual 'death of the self', a psychological state characterized by feelings of intense detachment, an emotional and ethical numbness which inhibits the self-regulatory prohibition against non-self-defensive violence. The likelihood of this occurring is much greater if the individual(s) concerned begin to interrogate critically the legitimizing myths that underpin prevailing social hierarchies. Once the legitimizing myth loses its hold over an individual or community, its ability to keep in check oppositional attitudes and behaviour is simultaneously undermined.

This is essentially what occurs once a person crosses the Alienation Threshold. Although they might still attend work and participate in other public activities, the alienated individual has become embittered and cynical about society's legitimizing myths and may in fact begin to see the social mores that give these myths their public form (such as national holidays, religious celebrations or habitual displays of national pride) as confrontational triumphalism. Estrangement from one's peers and neighbours can be an emotionally wrenching experience, and hence it is not surprising that those individuals who have crossed the Alienation Threshold often search for alternative forms of affirmation by seeking the companionship of like-minded individuals. It is at this stage that alienated individuals can coalesce into alienated groups, a development that underscores the important observation by Crenshaw (2000:409) that terrorism is essentially a group activity.

Of course, not all groups that exist to the right of the Alienation Threshold are violent in practice or in their potential, although they are by definition anti-social. Once incorporated into such a network, the individual derives comfort from being around like-minded people. This dilutes the sense of impotence that manifests when the individual feels that alone he/she was unable to change the system. Where there was once a sense of irrelevance, there is now a sense of importance derived from being part of a larger collective effort against the adversary. The ability of the group to redress the individual's previous sense of powerlessness prompts the individual to associate his/her spiritual well-being with the group. Hence, it is usually within the group that the individual begins to dehumanize the enemy. In the case of the 7/7 London bombers, they seemed to have derived fresh energy from participating in a range of indoor and outdoor activities that focused on physical fitness and which were organized exclusively for this select group. Importantly, it is within this close-knit group that the ideologies that justify violence can take root, providing both a sense of existential purpose and an organizing principle that helps bind the group into a cohesive unit (Horgan 2005:137).

Compared to the sense of helplessness that engulfs the isolated angry individual, in a group environment the individual begins to experience a sense of control, an inflated sense of collective power, and an urge to strike at the enemy. At this point the individual's tendency to self-sanction begins to disintegrate and forms of behaviour that they may have earlier considered to be morally repugnant come to figure as viable or even obligatory acts. Research (e.g. Bandura et al. 1996; Bandura 1990) shows that individuals are prone to acting more cruelly under conditions of group responsibility than when forced to hold themselves individually responsible for their actions. It is at this juncture that an individual can be considered to have crossed a point that in the diagram is signified as the Violence Threshold, after which '[e]ffective moral disengagement creates a sense of social rectitude and self-righteousness that breeds rumina-tive hostility and retaliatory thoughts for perceived grievances. People often reflect hostilely but do not act on their feelings. However, freed from the restraint of moral self-sanctions they are more likely to act out their resentments' (Bandura et al. 1996:366).

Underlying this whole process is a pervasive sense of anger. In political terms, the intensification of anger and solidification of in-group cohesion point to an important part of the terrorist life cycle: the delegitimation of the state and the demonization of its supporters. As Beck (2005:57) has noted, 'wherever consent is withdrawn in rela-tion to power, the control of violence is eroded – either the privatiza-tion of violence sets in, or else the use of the police and the military to tame outbursts of violence can no longer count on the requisite approval'.

The tendency to dissociate terrorism from its structural roots and treat it as a phenomenon that springs only from the maniacal ambi-tions of religious fanatics has prompted governments to respond to the threat by reinforcing some of the very structural attributes that have contributed to the emergence of the problem in the first place. Against this background, policy makers would do well to heed the observation of the criminologist Elliott Currie (1985:19) that: 'we have the level of violence we do because we have arranged our social and economic life in certain ways rather than others'. Applied to the status of Muslim communities in particular, discourses that deny the role of exclusionary economic and social structures in driving the spread of violent ideologies promote a problematic model in which there is only one protagonist, that of Muslims in Western societies who for no discernible reason apart from their own delusions are holding freedom and democracy to ransom. Thus configured, the argument reflects an inter-connected series of fundamental attribu-tion errors; that it is the fault of Muslims themselves that they some-times suffer higher levels of relative depravation and social ostracism; that the majority of Muslims are uncomfortable with Western values and will therefore never exist at ease as part of the broad Western mainstream; that Islam is an inherently violent religion, the core beliefs of which cannot be reconciled with the Western tradition of secular liberalism; and that these religious and cultural impediments to co-existence render all Muslims as potential 'fifth columnists' whose loyalty to their host nations can never be taken for granted.

The same kinds of attribution errors have at times also played a role in societies such as Northern Ireland, Sri Lanka, Turkey and Spain when dealing with their own respective terrorism problems. More importantly, there is evidence that ignoring the interaction between social structures and the emergence of potentially deadly patterns of identity-based anger can be counter-productive and might in fact spread the incidence of terrorism. This is particularly the case in those instances where the state uses collective punishment against those communities from which the terrorists emerge. For example, in the case of Northern Ireland, the actions of the British army and mainly Protestant police forces in Catholic areas had the effect of spreading support for the IRA (Coogan 2002). Similarly, Tel Aviv's policy of destroying the houses of the families of suspected suicide bombers has only worked to deepen anti-Israeli sentiment and boost support for groups such as Hamas (Sarraj and Butler 2002:73). As Horgan notes (2005:50),

> for the same reason that the head-counting of captured or killed terrorists tells us relatively little about the progress of a broad counter-insurgency campaign, shooting terrorists, infringing basic human rights, or corrupting the democratic process will not work because it only feeds into and engages with the processes inherent in political violence by sustaining the legitimization of the imperative strategy of terrorism at all junctures.

To reiterate, there is a real danger that models of terrorism that reduce the phenomenon to the actions of a few mad individuals or to the inherent malevolence of particular cultures or religions risk exaggerating an already dangerous social dynamic by spreading, rather than shrinking, the communities of support upon which terrorists feed. Against this, there is a need to understand terrorism as a complex socially constructed tactic employed by individuals who are motivated by a combination of individual and group psychological processes to act out violently against real or perceived oppressors.

Recurring themes and future trends

It is impossible to predict when, where or how terrorism will impact upon future societies. There is still debate over whether globally active networks such as al Qaeda portend a new era in global terrorist violence or whether they are a passing phenomenon and that smaller, localized terrorist violence will continue to be the norm. What is clear, however, is that even parochial terrorism needs to be understood within the context of a world where national borders are increasingly permeable. The global is intruding into the local at an accelerating pace and, as a result, even those who perceive their oppression as an exclusively local phenomenon can avail themselves of the accoutrements of globalization to fight back. The Internet, the global trade in small arms, the ability to tap into diasporic communities all present new operational benefits to the contemporary terrorist. However, there are several themes that have defined terrorism since Antiquity and which will continue to shape its development into the future.

The first is political frustration. A sense of political impotence in the face of a system of government or a wider set of power relationships perceived to be oppressive and unjust has been a recurring theme in the history of terrorism and will push individuals towards activism and extremism in the future. In a related phenomenon, history also tells us that individuals are more likely to resort to the tactic of terrorism when they perceive their oppressors enjoy a vastly superior conventional military advantage. Non-state terrorism has been, and always will be, a weapon of the weak, a tactic employed when all other avenues for political change are perceived as closed. This aspect of terrorism takes on particular importance in this era of globalization in which the conventional advantage of the terrorists' adversary is increasingly linked to geopolitics. Alliance systems, the international weapons trade and even the spread of secular and materialistic culture can blur the distinction between the local and the global oppressor. This underscores one important distinction between terrorism today and that of the past; in our contemporary era, anger can migrate and, as a result, terrorism is increasingly inclined to break out of the narrow confines of the nation state. In other words, anger at the circumstances in one part of the world can manifest itself thousands of kilometres away. Hezbollah's attacks on Jewish targets in South America in the early 1990s and the attacks of 9/11 are all examples of the migratory potential of contemporary terrorism and they provide a glimpse of its evolution into the future.

A second feature that has been common to terrorism across history is feelings of cultural and social alienation. Significantly, repression by those perceived to be outsiders, as the Romans were to the Zealots, the Sunni caliphates and Seljuks were to the Assassins, and the West is to many in the Middle East, seems to accelerate the progression towards violence. There is a psychological tendency common across all societies whereby individuals tend to be more tolerant of perceived injustices by authority figures within their own 'in-group' than they are of injustices administered by outsiders (Waller 2007). This phenomenon goes some way to explaining why Osama bin Laden and other al Qaeda leaders repeatedly cast the leadership of countries in the Middle East as Western (or US) puppets, why the IRA focused on the presence of the British army and why ETA adopt the rhetoric of an exaggerated distinction between Basque and Catalan cultures. And, once again, globalization can exacerbate this process, especially when associated with the spread of alien cultures and ways of life that either are perceived to upset established hierarchies of power or alternatively are seen to underpin non-representative and oppressive power structures.

Thirdly, while the phenomenon of the lone terrorist, like Leon Czolgosz and Theodore Kaczynski, should not be under-estimated, in a historical sense terrorism has been much more pronounced in cases where there is a clear community of support. In a practical sense, the existence of such a community provides recruits, finance, safe houses and other ingredients needed by any terrorist group if it is to survive the counter-terrorism initiatives arrayed against it. However, at an important psychological level, the existence of a community of support also satisfies critical emotional needs for the terrorist. By providing feedback to the terrorists, by affirming their actions and treating them as heroes, the community reinforces the terrorists' sense of purpose. In fact, in some cases, terrorist violence is almost entirely solipsistic in nature, designed to give hope to an oppressed community. For example there was little chance that the isolated acts of terrorism by the military wing of the African National Congress, Umkhonto we Sizwe, during the 1960s, would weaken South Africa's apartheid government. Rather, as Nelson Mandela noted, their main purpose was to give the African majority a sense of hope, to send a message that somebody cared and was fighting on their behalf (Guelke 2006:217). This aspect of terrorism also partly explains the appeal of Osama bin Laden in many parts of the world; he has developed an image as a modern-day iconic figure, a

Muslim Che Guevara, cocking a snoot at the USA and getting away with it.

Communities of support in any context can be a remarkably fickle phenomenon and so terrorist groups in particular have relied upon charismatic leaders to lock in the loyalty of their supporters. In the case of the Assassins, it was the mythology surrounding the group's founder, Hassan-i-Sabah, which helped maintain group cohesion, while Andreas Baader was critical in this regard in the case of the German Red Army Faction. The contemporary terrorist confronts a substantially new environment generated by the globalization of media and media technologies. In many respects, this represents a double-edged sword for both terrorists and governments. On the one hand, mass media, coupled with new media technologies such as the Internet, allow terrorists to reach a much larger audience than ever before. Al Qaeda's development of its own production house, as-Sahab, which uses carefully selected cable television channels (such as al Jazeera) and the Internet, is an example of the new era in terrorist communication. On the other hand, new communication technologies can blowback on terrorists and undermine their appeal among key audiences, especially if the violence they perpetrate is viewed as disproportionate to the cause for which they are fighting.

As a form of political theatre, terrorists cannot control the way in which audiences respond to the violence they commit as transmitted through the media. Focusing on innocent children killed by terrorist violence, for example, can lead to a backlash and shrinking of the size of the community of support. The 1998 Omagh bombing in Northern Ireland is a case in point: the public backlash when confronted by images of innocent non-combatant casualties forced the Real IRA into issuing a public apology. It also contributed to a fall in public support and a corresponding diminution of its offensive capabilities (Dingley 2009). In a similar vein, the attacks on Shi'a mosques and public gatherings and a series of videotaped beheadings involving al Qaeda's former leader in Iraq, Abu Musab al-Zarqawi, led to unsuccessful efforts by the al Qaeda leadership on the Afghanistan–Pakistan border to rein in their man in Iraq (Fishman 2006). Far from being a charismatic rallying point for al Qaeda in Iraq, al-Zarqawi became a liability and one can assume that his death in a missile attack in 2006 was not mourned by many in the al Qaeda hierarchy. Therefore, although media will continue to be a critical weapon in the arsenals of terrorists and governments, managing its outcomes will become less predictable.

A final continuity relates to terrorists' dependence on technology. The capability of terrorists to implement attacks has always been dependent upon the level of technology available to them. Until recently, terrorists have always tended to calibrate their actions in accordance with a simple equation: to use enough technology to instil terror in the target population, but not too much in order to avoid their supporters turning against them, and their enemies (who by definition have greater conventional military might) responding with such force as to threaten the very existence of the terrorist network itself.

However, some argue that this equation is becoming less important, especially with religiously motivated and globally active terrorist networks, and that terrorists are becoming more murderous in their actions – a trajectory that could eventually lead to the use of chemical, biological or radiological (CBR) weapons (Laqueur 2000, 2004; Hoffman 2006). Adding impetus to this argument is terrorism's status as a form of political theatre that can only survive if there are two kinds of audience – those who can be intimidated (the enemy) and those who can be inspired (the community of support). As with any drama, there is a danger of audience fatigue, and so to remain relevant terrorists need to be willing and able to change the script. For writers such as Laqueur (2000, 2004) this aspect of terrorism carries with it a dynamic of escalation whereby terrorists need to pursue increasingly spectacular events in order to remain relevant and newsworthy. Embracing new technologies of destruction is one way of doing this, and it is for this reason that terrorism has evolved from the use of daggers, poison, gunpowder, bombs or bullets to the use of the artefacts of late modernity itself, aircraft and once-complex explosive devices made easy through instruction manuals carried on the Internet.

Meanwhile, at the level of terrorist psychology, other writers such as Juergensmeyer argue that the revival of religiously motivated terrorism leads terrorists to bifurcate the world into believers and non-believers, with the former charged with doing God's work. This form of Cosmic Warfare, as Juergensmeyer (2003) calls it, overcomes the conventional limits to violence that governed more secular forms of terrorism. Religiously motivated terrorists are inspired to ignore the 'calculus of violence' whereby they calibrate their actions to be just enough to inspire and terrify but not to bring about universal opprobrium. Killing for God transcends this calculus, replacing it with a sense of messianic purpose with few earthly limits.

Those with a more optimistic bent reject these pessimistic scenarios by pointing out that not only are chemicals, biological pathogens and radioactive materials difficult to weaponize, but there is little evidence that even religiously inspired terrorists have jettisoned all semblance of ethical reasoning. Terrorists, including those who use religion to justify their cause, do not generally evince the psychological profiles that would lead them to contemplate mass murder on a national, let alone a global, scale.

Conclusion

Since the attacks of 9/11, terrorism and counter-terrorism have become highly newsworthy and key organizing principles at the domestic and international levels of politics. Although the actions of groups such as the IRA in the United Kingdom, the Red Army Faction in Germany and the Red Brigades in Italy set precedents for dealing with terrorism in the West, the events of 9/11, the Madrid bombings and the London attacks of 7 July 2005 indicate that terrorism has evolved to a new level of lethality and destructiveness. These recent attacks, among others, are also a measure of the extent to which terrorism has evolved from an almost exclusively localized, into a genuinely global, phenomenon. As a tactic employed by those who perceive themselves to be militarily weak and the victims of oppressive or unjust regimes, terrorism has an almost organic quality: it evolves and adapts to the societies in which it takes root. This is especially clear in the way in which today's terrorists cast their grievances, their sophisticated use of media and ability to bend contemporary technologies to their cause. In short, terrorism has always been intimately connected to and shaped by the society in which it occurs. It cannot be defeated, but it can be managed through a combination of hard power *and* policies that address the root causes of the problem.

How to use this book

Listed below is a selection of individual terrorists, terrorist organizations, significant events, techniques, counter-terrorism conventions
and treaties, as well as prominent counter-terrorism organizations.
Of course not every terrorist, organization or event can be included,
and the entries are therefore a product of judgement. This judgement
was based on a balance between offering insights into significant
terrorist events and individuals in history and avoiding losing the
volume's contemporary relevance. In trying to balance the past with
the present, I have deliberately erred in favour of the latter in an
attempt to invest the book with a greater contemporary rather than
historical relevance. This decision reflects the immediacy of the
current threat of terrorism but also the reality that there already exist
some excellent summaries and encyclopaediae on terrorism in
history.

Having selected entries, we are confronted with another level of
subjectivity. Just as terrorism is a notoriously slippery concept to
define, so too are the circumstances and events that surround terrorist activity. Very few researchers in the field of terrorism studies base
their research on primary data – that is, interviews with terrorists
themselves are preciously few. As a result, there is often a high degree
of uncertainty about names, dates and terrorist activities themselves.
The following definitions are therefore inherently contestable – at the
empirical as well as the subjective level. Where a given entry is
clouded by a high degree of ambiguity, I have fallen back on a consensus definition culled from a wide variety of sources.

The suggested readings have been selected not because they offer
a more definitive account of a given entry, but because they will allow
the reader to grasp better the context within which the given event,
terrorist, treaty or organization operates. Sometimes, however, it is
the case that there is simply a lack of relevant English-language refer-
ences on the definition concerned. Where this is the case, suggested
readings have been selected for their relevance as pointers for further
research.

Finally, listings for some terrorist groups carry a note that provides a sample of countries from which they have been proscribed. Listings that include the United Nations refer to those organizations designated by United Nations Security Council Committee 1267, also known as the Al-Qaeda and Taliban Sanctions Committee, as being linked to al Qaeda.

A–Z of Terrorism

7/7

7/7 is a shorthand reference to the date in 2005 when four home-grown terrorists attacked the London public transport system. The attacks killed 52 commuters, while more than 700 were injured. The 4 bombers had assembled at 7.15 a.m. at Luton train station and travelled together to Kings Cross where they separated. Each of the men carried a rucksack containing home-made organic-peroxide-based explosive devices. The first bomb exploded at 8.50 a.m. on a Circle Line train near Aldgate Tube station and was carried by **Shehzad Tanweer**, a 22-year-old university drop-out who lived with his parents and worked in their fish-and-chip shop in Beeston, a suburb of the northern city of Leeds. The second bomb, carried by **Mohammad Siddique Khan**, a 30-year-old former teacher's aid who lived with his pregnant wife and young child in Dewsbury, exploded on another Circle Line train soon after it had left Edgware Road for Paddington. The third bomb, which detonated seconds later on a Piccadilly Line train as it approached Russell Square, was carried by Germaine Lindsay, a 19-year-old convert to Islam who lived with his pregnant wife in the town of Aylesbury. The fourth bomb exploded at 9.47 a.m. at the rear of the top level of a double-decker bus travelling from Marble Arch and was carried by 18-year-old Hasib Hussein, who lived in Leeds with his brother and sister-in-law. Hussein stopped to purchase batteries before boarding the bus, and it is possible that the hiatus between the first explosions and his own attack on the bus was caused by a faulty detonation device, which forced him to change his plans.

Evidence suggests the group was headed by Khan, although less clear is the relationship between the bombers and external terrorist networks. Hours after the attacks, an **al Qaeda**-linked website, Al-Qal3ah, claimed responsibility on behalf of the little-known 'Secret Organization Group of Al-Qaeda of Jihad Organization in Europe' and stated the attacks were 'in retaliation for the massacres Britain is committing in Iraq and Afghanistan'. Two days later, another al Qaeda-linked group, the **Abu Hafs al-Masri Brigades**, also claimed responsibility. This group has a track record of making false claims. On 1 September 2005, Al Jazeera aired a suicide video made by Khan in which he justified the attacks as a defensive act designed to force the British government to stop 'the bombing, gassing, imprisonment and torture of my people ... We are at war and I am a soldier.' Al Qaeda deputy Ayman al-Zawahiri introduced the video, although in his statement Khan makes no reference to al Qaeda. On the eve of the first anniversary of the attacks, Al Jazeera aired a second suicide video made by Tanweer. He also justified the attacks in terms of a defensive act designed to stop Western governments oppressing 'our mothers and children, brothers and sisters from the east to the west in Palestine, Afghanistan, Iraq and Chechnya'. This video is also introduced by al-Zawahiri, although, like Khan, Tanweer makes no reference to the group in his statement. UK security services were aware that the bombers were mixing in extremist circles, although they were not regarded as immediate threats. It is now known that in 2003 Khan visited Pakistan and returned for an extended visit with Tanweer between November 2004 and February 2005. Intelligence sources have surmised that they are likely to have met with al Qaeda figures, although, several years after the attacks, it remains unclear as to how much influence these individuals exerted over the bombers and their plans.

Further reading
House of Commons, *Report of the Official Account of the Bombings in London on 7th July 2005*. London: The Stationery Office, 11 May 2006.
Intelligence and Security Committee, *Report into the London Terrorist Attacks on 7th July 2005*. London: Presented to Parliament by the Prime Minister by Command of Her Majesty, May 2006.
Rai, M., *7/7: The London Bombings, Islam and the Iraq War*. London: Pluto Press, 2006.

9/11

9/11 is a shorthand reference to a set of coordinated attacks against the United States organized by **al Qaeda** and perpetrated by a team of nineteen terrorists on the morning of 11 September 2001. The operation involved the near-simultaneous hijacking of four California-bound aircraft from Boston's Logan airport, three of which were subsequently steered into several iconic US buildings – the twin towers of New York's World Trade Center (WTC) and the Pentagon. A fourth aircraft crashed into a field in Pennsylvania after passengers attempted to wrest back control of the aircraft. According to a key planner of the attacks, al Qaeda's **Khalid Sheikh Mohammed**, the fourth target was Capitol Hill. The operation resulted in the deaths of almost 3,000 people from more than eighty different nations, rendering it the most lethal act of terrorist violence in modern times.

Khalid is generally credited as having conceived the idea of the attacks and as having proposed them to **Osama bin Laden** in 1996. (In 1993, Khalid, along with his nephew, Ramzi Yusoff, had played a key role in an earlier bombing attack against the World Trade Center). The United States government determined that Khalid conceived of the idea of the 9/11 attacks several years earlier, while not an al Qaeda member. A videotape discovered in Afghanistan in November 2001 shows bin Laden admitting to having foreknowledge of the attacks. Bin Laden released his own video just before the 2004 US Presidential elections in which he conceded to al Qaeda's role in the attacks, saying, 'We are a free people who do not accept injustice, and we want to regain the freedom of our nation.'

The hijackers seized control of the aircraft by using box-cutters to kill flight attendants and at least one pilot before taking control of the aircraft themselves. On several flights, mace or capsicum spray might have also been used to control passengers and keep them from the cockpit. Those hijackers designated to steer the aircraft into their targets had prepared for their operation by enrolling in several US flight schools. The first plane to strike its target was American Airlines Flight 11, a Boeing 767-200 wide-body aircraft, which careered into the northern side of the North Tower of the WTC at 8.46 a.m., striking the building between the 94th and 98th floors. The second aircraft, a United Airlines Flight 175, also a Boeing 767-200, struck the South Tower of the WTC at 9.02 a.m., impacting between the 78th and 85th floors. It is this second strike that was captured live by media which had gathered to film the confusion and carnage caused by the first strike. Just over half an hour later, American Airlines Flight 77, a Boeing 757-200, crashed into the Pentagon at 9.37 a.m. Soon after that, at 10.03 a.m., United Airlines Flight 93, a Boeing 757-200, crashed in a field in southwest Pennsylvania just outside the small town of Shanksville, about 250 km northwest of Washington, DC. The ease with which the hijackers thwarted screening processes to smuggle sharp blades onto aircraft, and their ability to circumvent intelligence and security monitoring, led to one of the most dramatic overhauls of the US security bureaucracy in history. Particularly noteworthy was the introduction of a series of reforms designed to streamline interactions between different elements of the US intelligence community, notably the **Federal Bureau of Investigation** and the **Central Intelligence Agency**. The reforms also led to the creation of a mega-bureaucracy in the **Department of Homeland Security**; the introduction of legislation, such as the **USA PATRIOT** Act, designed to boost the state's ability to combat the threat of terrorism by diluting an array of political and legal protections of individual rights; and a corresponding strengthening of the state's ability to intrude into the lives of private citizens. The Bush Administration also used concerns unleashed by 9/11 to approve a plan to monitor, without a warrant, telephone and e-mail communications between the USA and people overseas. The attacks also provided a catalyst for the Bush Administration's decision to invade Iraq, on the grounds that the regime of Saddam Hussein possessed weapons of mass destruction which Baghdad might pass on to terrorists for use against the USA and its allies. Extensive searches in the years following the 2003 invasion failed to find any evidence of either weapons of mass destruction or of links between the Saddam regime and al Qaeda.

Further reading

Fouda, Y. and Fielding, N., *Masterminds of Terror: The Truth behind the Most Devastating Terrorist Attack the World Has Ever Seen*. New York: Arcade Publishing, 2003.

Wright, L., *The Looming Tower: Al Qaeda and the Road to 9/11*. New York: Alfred A. Knopf, 2006.

9/11 COMMISSION

Also known as The National Commission on Terrorist Attacks Upon the United States, the 9/11 Commission was established by an Act of Congress on 27 November 2002 as a bipartisan body charged with producing a 'full and complete account' of the circumstances that led to the **9/11** attacks, as well as of the preparedness of, and immediate response to the attacks by, federal and state authorities. Comprising five Republican and five Democratic members and chaired by former New Jersey Governor Thomas H. Kean, the Commission was also charged with making recommendations designed to ensure that the USA would be better prepared to avoid future attacks. The Commission released the unclassified version of its report on 22 July 2004, the same day that a much lengthier classified report was passed to President George W. Bush. Among the Commission's key findings was that, even though many of the terrorists' preparatory activities had been detected by different agencies within the US intelligence community, notably the **Central Intelligence Agency** and **Federal Bureau of Investigation**, a failure to share information between agencies created operational gaps that were exploited by the terrorists. The final report contained forty-one recommendations in areas ranging from the structuring of domestic intelligence services to the practice of foreign policy. The report also alluded to a general failure by the US intelligence community to adapt to the 'globalizing of terror'. Criticism of the Commission and its report was occasionally vocal, with groups such as the 9/11 Family Steering Committee and the Jersey Girls (a group of 9/11 widows who were instrumental in over-turning the Bush Administration's initial opposition to a commission of inquiry) arguing that it failed to address core issues and covered up a great deal of official malfeasance. A Zogby Poll undertaken in May 2006 showed that 42 per cent of respondents believed that the US government and the 9/11 Commission were complicit in a cover-up.

Further reading
National Commission on Terrorist Attacks, *The 9/11 Commission Report: Final Report of the National Commission on Terrorist Attacks upon the United States (Indexed Hardcover Authorized Edition)*. New York: W. W. Norton and Company, 2004.
Kean, T. H. and Hamilton, L. H., *Without Precedent: The Inside Story of the 9/11 Commission*. New York: Knopf, 2006.

ABU HAFS AL-MASRI BRIGADES
The Abu Hafs al-Masri Brigades are named after the senior **al Qaeda** terrorist Mohammad Atef (also known as Abu Hafs), a former Egyptian policeman and related by marriage to **Osama bin Laden**, who was killed in US air strikes on Afghanistan following the **9/11** terrorist attacks. The group first achieved prominence in August 2003 when an individual claimed the Brigades were responsible for power blackouts across the northeast United States and parts of Canada. Subsequent investigations revealed the blackouts had been caused by technical problems. A few days later the group claimed responsibility for the attacks on the United Nations headquarters in Baghdad, and in November the bombing of two synagogues, the British consulate and a branch of the HSBC Bank, all in Istanbul. In 2004 the group threatened to start their European campaign in Italy as punishment for Rome's failure to respond positively to a truce offered by Osama bin Laden and to withdraw its troops from Iraq. The group also

claimed responsibility for the terrorist strikes on the Madrid public transport system on 11 March 2004 and the attacks in London on 7 July 2005. Both claims are also known to be false. In February 2006 the group issued a statement threatening a 'holy war' against Denmark in retaliation for the publication of cartoons depicting the prophet Muhammad in the Danish newspaper *Jylladens-Posten*. Most of its claims are issued through messages sent to the London-based Arabic-language daily *al Quds al Arabi*. Because so many of the group's claims have been proven to be false, many analysts assess the group to be comprised of little more than a loosely connected array of Internet-based propagandists for al Qaeda-linked causes.

Further reading
Ulph, S., 'Abu Haffs al-Masri Brigades – Fraud or Dissimulation?' *Jamestown Foundation Terrorism Focus* 1(2) 2004.

ABU NIDAL ORGANIZATION (ANO)
Proscribed by: Canada, EU, Israel, UK, USA
Also operating under the aliases 'Arab Revolutionary Brigades', 'Arab Revolutionary Council', 'Fatah Revolutionary Council' and the 'Revolutionary Organisation of Socialist Muslims', the ANO has its roots in the escalating intramural conflict that followed the Arab defeat in the 1967 Six Day War. More formally, it was established by Sabri al-Banna (1937–2002), known to his followers as 'Abu Nidal' (Father of the Struggle) in 1974 when he split from the **Palestinian Liberation Organization (PLO)** following the latter's peace agreement with Jordan, a proposal to set up a separate Palestinian Authority and, by implication, negotiation with Israel. At its peak, the ANO had around 400 members and received tactical, logistic and financial aid from Syria, Libya and Iraq. In the pursuit of its goals, the group carried out attacks in twenty countries, causing several hundred fatalities. One of the group's most notorious acts occurred in December 1985 when ANO members used guns and hand grenades against passengers queued at the El Al ticket counters at Rome and Vienna airports. Eighteen people died and more than 120 people were injured in these near-simultaneous attacks. Libyan intelligence services are alleged to have supplied the weapons used by the terrorists. In 2002 a former senior member of the ANO alleged that Abu Nidal had conspired with Abdullah al-Senussi, the head of Libyan intelligence, to bomb

PanAm Flight 103 which exploded mid-flight and crashed into the Scottish town of **Lockerbie** in December 1988, killing all 259 passengers and crew and 11 townsfolk. Since the height of its activities in the 1980s, the ANO has undergone a slow decline and its last known act was on 29 January 1994 when it assassinated a Jordanian diplomat in Lebanon. From the early 1990s, Abu Nidal lived in exile in Iraq, although in August 2002 the regime of Saddam Hussein announced he had committed suicide. Some intelligence services believe Palestinian gunmen, on orders from Saddam, assassinated him. Others doubt he is even dead. Although the ANO is thought to have some residual supporters in the Palestinian refugee camps in Lebanon, Egypt and Libya closed down the last remaining ANO bases on their territory in 1999.

Further reading

Kameel, B. N., *Arab and Israeli Terrorism: The Causes and Effects of Political Violence 1936–1993*. Jefferson: McFarland Publishers, 1997.

Melman, Y., *The Master Terrorist: The True Story of Abu-Nidal* (trans. Shmuel Himmelstein). New York: Adama Books, 1986.

ABU SAYYAF GROUP

Proscribed by: Australia, Canada, EU, UK, USA

The Abu Sayyaf ('Bearers of the Sword') Group (ASG) was founded in the Philippines in 1991 with the main goal of establishing an Islamic state in the southern regions of the archipelago. By some accounts, Mohammad Jamal Khalifah, **Osama bin Laden**'s brother-in-law who at that time was head of the Manila office of the International Islamic Relief Organization, assisted the ASG's founder, Abdurajak Janjalani. This claim is boosted by the presence within the ASG of a significant number of young men who had fought alongside the anti-Soviet Mujahedeen in Afghanistan in the 1980s. From the outset, the early appeal of the ASG reflected growing frustration among some young Muslims – mainly from the Sulu archipelago – with the failure of a three-decade-long insurgency to address any of their grievances. These ranged from social and economic inequities to the loss of access to ancestral lands. Many of the group's members were formerly with the **Moro National Liberation Front**, which by the 1990s had dropped its demands for independence and settled on an offer from Manila of greater autonomy. In the mid-1990s the ASG also cultivated links with international Islamist terrorists, and in 1995 several members were implicated, with **Ramzi Yousef** and **Khalid Sheikh Mohammed**, in a plot to assassinate Pope John Paul II during a visit to Manila. Other dimensions of this audacious plot, called **Operation Bojinka**, included plans to destroy aircraft flying across the Pacific to the United States. Following Abdurajak's death in a shoot-out with police in 1998, leadership passed to his younger brother Khadafy. A less charismatic figure than Abdurajak, Khadafy (who was killed in a skirmish with the Philippine military in 2006) presided over the gradual disintegration of the group, and by 2001 it had fragmented into a number of competing factions divided along territorial and kinship lines and involved more in organized crime (especially drug smuggling and kidnapping-for-ransom) than in violence with a clear political motive. Operation Balikatan, a joint military exercise launched by the Philippines and United States in the immediate aftermath of 9/11, was partly aimed at freeing several US citizens held hostage by the ASG and eliminating the group once and for all. Despite this, the group continues to play a small but violent role in southern provinces, targeting Christian missionaries and government officials. In 2008 the ASG was implicated in a plot to assassinate Philippine President Gloria Macapagal.

Further reading
International Crisis Group, *The Philippines: Counter-Insurgency vs. Counter-Terrorism in Mindanao* Asia Report No.152. Brussels: International Crisis Group, 14 May 2008.
Ugarte, E. F., 'The Alliance System of the Abu Sayyaf, 1993–2000' *Studies in Conflict and Terrorism* 31(2) 2008, pp. 125–44.
Vitug, M. D. and Gloria, G., *Under the Crescent Moon: Rebellion in Mindanao.* Quezon City: Ateneo Centre for Social Policy and Public Affairs and the Institute for Popular Democracy, 2000.

ACHILLE LAURO HIJACKING

On 7 October 1985 four Palestinians claiming to be from the **Palestinian Liberation Organization** hijacked the Italian cruise ship *Achille Lauro* as it made its way along the Egyptian coast from Alexandria to Port Said. Using 511 passengers as leverage, the hijackers demanded the release of 50 Palestinians being held in Israeli prisons. Endeavours by the terrorists to steer the ship to the Syrian port of Tartus (where they were hoping to seek asylum) foundered when Damascus refused to allow them to dock. The hijackers then headed for Cyprus, but were again refused entry, whence they sought to return to Egypt. Increasingly desperate, the hijackers upped the ante by executing the disabled and wheelchair-bound US citizen Leon Klinghoffer, whose body they dumped overboard. It is believed Klinghoffer was chosen because he was Jewish. The hijackers eventually accepted an offer of safe passage from the Egyptian government but US navy jets intercepted the commercial Egyptian airliner as it flew towards Tunis and forced it to land in Italy. Italian authorities laid charges of kidnapping and murder against the four men, with potential sentences ranging from a few years' to life imprisonment. The leader of the operation, Abu Abbas, fled Italian jurisdiction before his trial and was sentenced *in absentia*. In 1996 he issued an apology for the hijacking and murder of Klinghoffer and called for peace talks between Israel and Palestine. The US government and the Klinghoffer family rejected the apology. In 2003 Abbas was captured by US forces in Iraq. He died in US custody in 2004.

Further reading
Cassese, A., *Terrorism, Politics and Law: The Achille Lauro Affair*. Princeton NJ: Princeton University Press, 1989.

ACTION DIRECTE

Forged from the 1977 merger of two small revolutionary left-wing groups – Groupes d'Action Révolutionnaire Internationalistes ('Revolutionary Internationalist Action Groups') and Noyaux Armés pour l'Autonomie Populaire ('Armed Groups for Popular Autonomy') – Action Directe carried out its first terrorist assault in May 1979 when it attacked the French employers' federation. Justifying its violence as a struggle against imperialism in the name of the proletariat, it was proscribed by the French government in August 1982. A 1984 alliance with the German Red Army Faction (RAF – see **Baader-Meinhof Gang**) led to a joint car-bombing operation against a US air force base in Germany in 1985. Action Directe also expressed solidarity with the **Italian Red Brigades**, Belgium's Combat Communist Cells and various Palestinian groups. The alliance with the RAF also coincided with an increase in Action Directe violence within France itself, including the assassination of René Audran, the manager of

French arms sales, in 1985, and of Georges Besse, the CEO of Renault, in 1986. This latter strike eventually led police to Action Directe's four key leaders, Joelle Aubron, Georges Cipriani, Nathalie Menigon and Jean-Marc Rouillan, all of whom were arrested soon after the attack. The capture and imprisonment of the organization's key leaders led to its rapid decline and the end of its violent activities.

Further reading
Dartnell, M. Y., *Action Directe: Ultra Left Terrorism in France 1979–1987*. London: Frank Cass Publishers, 1995.

ADAMS, GERRY
Born into a strong Republican family in West Belfast in 1948, Gerry Adams first became active in politics in the 1960s. His initial forays were through the Northern Ireland Civil Rights Association, a group dedicated to progressing the rights of Northern Ireland's minority Catholic community. By the late 1960s he was involved with Sinn Fein, the political wing of the Provisional Irish Republican Army (PIRA see **Irish Republican Army (Provisional)**), and in 1971 was interned briefly for illegal political activities. He was jailed again in 1973 for allegedly being involved in planning a series of PIRA bombings in Belfast, an operation known as 'Bloody Friday'. Adams has always denied being a member of the IRA. In 1983 he was elected leader of Sinn Fein and, as the member for West Belfast, became one of the party's first representatives elected to Westminster, although, like the others, such as the hunger striker **Robert ('Bobby') Sands**, Adams refused to take his seat. As a sign of his growing influence within the Republican movement, in 1984 a Protestant paramilitary group wounded Adams in an assassination attempt. In the early 1990s Adams played a key role in steering Sinn Fein and the PIRA towards peace through negotiations that led to the **Good Friday Agreement**.

Further reading
Adams, G., *Before the Dawn: An Autobiography*. Dingle: Brandon Books, 2001.
Coogan, T. P., *The IRA*. New York: Palgrave, 2002.

African National Congress

Founded on 8 January 1912 by John Dube, Pixley Ka Isaka Seme and Sol Plaatje, in its formative years the African National Congress was initially dedicated to non-violent resistance to white minority rule. Its ultimate goal was to achieve racial equality between all of South Africa's races. The commitment to non-violence began to erode with the discovery of diamonds and other resources which led to the introduction of policies that effectively prohibited black Africans from buying, renting or using land in any area except government-designated reserves. This led to mass displacement and the emergence of a black underclass controlled by pass laws that restricted free movement and forbade them from leaving employment on white farms or white-owned mines. The election of the Afrikaner-dominated National Party in 1948 and the introduction of Apartheid as state policy increased the deprivations imposed upon the black population and turned the ANC into a mass movement which, by the 1950s, was engaged in largely peaceful acts of mass defiance against the state. Met with increasingly repressive measures by the authorities, including the massacre of peaceful protestors at Sharpville in 1960, core elements of the ANC went underground and founded a military wing known as **Umkhonto we Sizwe** ('Spear of the Nation' – MK) that commenced a period of armed struggle. In 1961 Nelson Mandela was appointed head of MK, organizing a campaign in which around 200 acts of sabotage were carried out within the first eighteen months of operations. The government responded by introducing the death penalty for sabotage, and detention without trial. After he had been on the run for seventeen months, the **Central Intelligence Agency** alerted South African authorities as to Mandela's whereabouts and he was arrested. He was given five years' imprisonment, but was retried and resentenced to life imprisonment on Robben Island. After international pressure he was released from prison in 1990 and, on 27 April 1994, was elected President in South Africa's first democratic elections. Mandela was only removed from the US State Department's Terrorist Watch List in mid-2008.

Further reading
Holland, H., *The Struggle: A History of the African National Congress*. London: Grafton, 1989.
Mandela, N., *Long Walk to Freedom*. Boston: Little Brown and Company, 1994.

AGCA, MEHMET

Mehmet Ali Agca is the Turkish-born would-be assassin of Pope John Paul II. A petty criminal during his youth Agca received several months' instruction at a terrorist training camp in Syria before returning to Turkey in the late 1970s and establishing contacts with the 'Grey Wolves', an extremist right-wing political group committed to destabilizing the Kemalist regime. In 1979 Agca murdered the editor of a centrist newspaper and was arrested and sentenced to life in prison, but he escaped a short time later and fled to Bulgaria where he deepened existing relationships with the Turkish mafia and Bulgarian intelligence officials. Agca's links with the Bulgarian regime provide the most significant clues into his own political philosophy at the time – he was deeply anti-capitalist and committed to promoting the interests of the Warsaw Pact countries against those linked to the United States. His connection with right-wing elements in Turkey needs to be seen in this light – as part of a larger strategy designed to foment instability in Turkey and undermine its links to the USA and NATO. In early 1981 he travelled to Rome with several Bulgarian accomplices and, on 13 May, fired four shots at the Pope as he crossed St Peter's Square. He was restrained by bystanders and eventually sentenced to life in prison. While incarcerated, Agca accepted overtures from the Pope, whom he met in 1983. Agca claimed that the Pope was targeted for assassination because he symbolized the excesses of global capitalism.

Further reading
Henze, P., 'The Plot to Kill the Pope: A Survey' *Journal of East and West Studies* 27(118/119) 1983, pp. 2–21.
Sterling, C., 'The Great Bulgarian Cover Up' *The New Republic* 129(21) 1985, pp. 16–21.

AIRLINE HIJACKINGS

The hijacking of aircraft has become a hallmark of modern terrorism. Although the first recorded hijacking attempt was carried out by a group of Peruvian revolutionaries in 1931, the tactic became more prominent in the 1960s and 1970s. Until the attacks of **9/11** the objective of most hijacking was to secure political concessions and gain publicity for the terrorists' cause by taking passengers hostage rather than by killing large numbers of non-combatants. To this end, one of the best-known hijackings occurred in 1970 when the **Popular Front for the Liberation of Palestine** seized three aircraft – a TWA flight from Frankfurt, a Swissair flight from Zurich, and an El Al flight from Amsterdam. While the El Al aircraft was flown to Cairo, the other two were flown to Dawson's Field in Jordan where the passengers were released before the aircraft were blown up. The event was captured on news footage and provided a powerful conduit for advertising the Palestinian cause. Other significant hijackings include the March 1970 seizure of a Japan Airlines flight by the **Japanese Red Army**, and the 1976 hijacking of an Air France flight from Tel Aviv by two members of the Popular Front for the Liberation of Palestine and two members of the German Revolutionary Cells. The latter plane was eventually flown to Entebbe Airport in Uganda where it was stormed by Israeli commandos. In November 1996 three Ethiopians seeking political asylum hijacked an Ethiopian Airlines flight en route to Mumbai. The plane eventually crashed into the Indian Ocean after running out of fuel. Although the number of airline hijackings began to decrease from the early 1990s, the number of casualties from each attack has been increasing. This trend is especially clear in the events of **9/11**, which was the first time aircraft had been used as de facto missiles designed to cause mass casualties on the ground. Since then a number of similar plots have been exposed. These include a plan by **Jemaah Islamiyah** to crash a passenger jet into Singapore's Changi Airport, and the **Trans-Atlantic Airline Plot** whereby a number of individuals planned to detonate explosives aboard aircraft flying from the United Kingdom to North America. There are two major international conventions dealing with airline hijackings, the **Tokyo Convention (on Offences and Certain Other Acts Committed on Board Aircraft) (1963)** and the **Hague Convention (Convention for the Suppression of Unlawful Seizure of Aircraft) (1970)**.

Further reading

Jenkins, B., *Aviation Terrorism and Security*. London and New York: Routledge, 1999.

Laribau, T., 'A New Form of Air Warfare' *Air and Space Power Journal* 21(3) 2007, pp. 27–32.

Miller, J. M., 'Conceptualizing the Hijacking Threat to Civil Aviation' *Criminal Justice Review* 32(3) 2007, pp. 209–32.

AL-ADEL, SAIF

Saif al-Adel (b. 1960 or 1963), also known as Mohammad Ibrahim al-Makkawi and Omar al-Sumali, is an Egyptian-born high-ranking military commander in what has been described as the 'al Qaeda hardcore'. Despite his status, very little is known about him. It is thought that in the mid-1980s he served as a special operations colonel in the Egyptian army but, in 1987, he was charged with attempting to revive the outlawed **Egyptian Islamic Jihad** and for being involved in a plot to bomb the Egyptian parliament. Al-Adel fled to Pakistan via Saudi Arabia. Once in Pakistan, al-Adel is believed to have provided explosives training to militants who would later go on to be active al Qaeda members. Al-Adel followed bin Laden and his retinue to Somalia in 1992. Later in the 1990s he was implicated in planning the 1998 **East Africa embassy bombings** and is believed to have been present at a series of high-level meetings in Afghanistan in 1998 and 1999 when the **9/11** attacks were planned. Rumours that he was arrested and imprisoned in Iran in 2003 have not been verified.

Further reading

Burke, J., *Al-Qaeda: The True Story of Radical Islam* (3rd edn). London: Penguin, 2007.

National Commission on Terrorist Attacks, *The 9/11 Commission Report: Final Report of the National Commission on Terrorist Attacks upon the United States (Indexed Hardcover, Authorized Edition)*. New York: W. W. Norton and Company, 2004.

AL AQSA MARTYRS BRIGADES (Also: Al-Shaid Yasser Arafat Brigades)

Proscribed by: Canada, EU, Israel, USA

Despite taking part of its name from one of the holiest sites within Islam – Jerusalem's al Aqsa mosque – the Al Aqsa Martyrs Brigades is a secular Palestinian organization closely connected to the Fatah political party founded by the late **Yasser Arafat**. Although the precise nature of these contacts remains unclear, since the organization's foundation in 2000 there has been extensive movement of members between the two organizations, especially between the Al Aqsa Martyrs Brigades and Tanzim, a more militant faction of Fatah. The adoption of an Islamic theme was inspired in part by a desire to counter the growing influence in the 1990s of Islamist groups such as **Hamas**, whose support among Palestinians on the Gaza Strip and West Bank was growing on the back of decades of corruption and administrative incompetence within Fatah. On the death of Arafat, the group changed its name to Al-Shaid Yasser Arafat Brigades. While militant elements within the organization remain implacably opposed to the existence of Israel, others are committed mainly to gaining control of the Gaza Strip and the West Bank, and the establishment of an independent Palestinian state with Jerusalem as its capital. Organizationally, the Al Aqsa Martyrs Brigades is constituted by a network of semi-autonomous cells that act independently of each other. The group's tactics centred initially on military and settler targets, but in early 2002 suicide bombing was added to the Brigades' arsenal when it launched an attack against a Jerusalem café that killed eleven, and injured more than fifty, Israelis. Since then, suicide attacks have been a common feature of the group's operations. In some cases, it has joined with Islamist groups, such as Hamas to carry out joint operations, including the firing of homemade **Qassam rockets** from the West Bank into Israel.

Further reading

Eshel, D., 'The Rise and Fall of the Al Aqsa Martyrs Brigades' *Jane's Intelligence Review* 1 June 2002.

Frisch, H., 'Has the Israeli–Palestinian Conflict Become Islamic? Fatah, Islam, and the Al-Aqsa Martyrs' Brigades' *Terrorism and Political Violence* 17(3) 2005, pp. 391–406.

AL-BANNA, HASSAN

Born in Egypt in 1906, Hassan al-Banna was the founder of the **Muslim Brotherhood**, which has since grown to become one of the world's most influential Islamist organizations. The son of a respected Imam, al-Banna's religious education began early in life. At sixteen, he moved to Cairo to study at an Islamic college before eventually enrolling in the prestigious Al-Azhar University. Concerned at the decline of Islamic values and the spread of what he considered to be decadent Western values, al-Banna established the Muslim Brotherhood in 1928 as a grassroots movement designed to promote Islamic values, but which eventually developed a more concrete political agenda dedicated to replacing secular regimes in the Muslim world with those based on local Islamic traditions. Al-Banna believed that

the persistence of Western colonialism, the lack of economic development and political corruption that marked Muslim societies at the
time could only be remedied through a stronger embrace of science
and technology within a more rigorous Islamic social framework. In
this sense, al-Banna was a precursor to subsequent but more militant
Islamist thinkers such as **Sayyid Qutb**. Al-Banna was assassinated in
1949. It was alleged, but not proven, that the Egyptian Secret Service
was behind his death.

Further reading
Esposito, J., *The Islamic Threat: Myth or Reality?* (3rd edn). Oxford: Oxford
    University Press, 1999.
Mitchell, R. P., *The Society of Muslim Brothers*. Oxford: Oxford University
    Press, 1993.

AL GHURABAA
Proscribed by: UK
Al Ghurabaa is an offshoot of the militant Islamist organization Al
Muhajiroun, founded in Saudi Arabia in 1983 by the extremist Syrian
cleric Omar Bakri Muhammad. The organization was proscribed in
the UK after senior leaders praised the **9/11** attacks and began to
advocate violence against those considered to have insulted Islam.

Further reading
Wiktorowicz, Q., *Radical Islam Rising: Muslim Extremism in the West*.
    Lanham, Md.: Rowman and Littlefield Publishers, Inc., 2005.

AL ITTIHAD AL ISLAMIA
Proscribed by: Canada, UK, UN
Al Ittihad al Islamia is a Somalia-based organization established in
the early 1990s and dedicated to founding an Islamic state modelled
along Wahhabi lines. Operating mainly from the Ogaden region of
Ethiopia, the group receives funding from wealthy donors in the
Middle East and Gulf states. The group is suspected of having cultivated links with **al Qaeda** and of potentially playing a role in the
1998 **East Africa Embassy Bombings** in Kenya and Tanzania. At the
peak of its influence in the early 1990s, the group is thought to have

had around 1,000 members trained in camps staffed by foreign jihadis.

Further reading
International Crisis Group, *Counter Terrorism in Somalia: Losing Hearts and Minds?* Africa Report No.95. Brussels: International Crisis Group, 11 July 2005.

AL JAMAA AL ISLAMIYAH AL MUQATILAH BI LIBYA
SEE: LIBYAN ISLAMIC FIGHTING GROUP

AL JIHAD
Proscribed by: Canada
Al Jihad formed in 1980 out of two sets of militant Islamist groups that had earlier broken away from the more moderate **Muslim Brotherhood**. The first was a Cairo-based network headed by Mohammad Abdul al-Salam Faraj, and the second a Saidi (northern Egyptian) network headed by Karam Zuhdi. The group kept a relatively low profile until its involvement in the audacious assassination of Egyptian President Anwar Sadat in 1981 thrust it into the international limelight. A subsequent crackdown by security agencies led to the arrest and imprisonment of most of the group's leadership and drove many other members into exile (including to Afghanistan where they played an important role in the anti-Soviet resistance and exerted a growing ideological and logistical influence over **Osama bin Laden**). However, the crackdown also led to a schism, with the Cairo group becoming the **Egyptian Islamic Jihad** (EIJ) and the Saidi group eventually morphing into **al-Gama'a al-Islamiyah** ('Egyptian Islamic Group' – 'EIG'). In 1991 **Ayman al-Zawahiri** assumed leadership of the EIJ and under his influence it gradually subsumed its one-time Egyptian focus to embrace the wider regional and global vision associated with **al Qaeda**.

Further reading
Zeidan, D., 'Radical Islam in Egypt: A Comparison of Two Groups' *Middle East Review of International Affairs* 3(3) September 1999, pp. 1–10.

AL-LIBI, ABU FARAJ
Abu Faraj al-Libi (lit.: 'the Libyan') is the *nom de guerre* of Mustapha al-Uzayti, a senior member of **al Qaeda** who was captured in Pakistan in 2005 and transported to the American holding centre at Guantanamo Bay. In the early 1990s Al-Libi worked as an al Qaeda trainer and later helped to administer the group's camps in Afghanistan. After **9/11** Al-Libi worked as a conduit for messages passed from al Qaeda field officers to the organization's hierarchy. It is believed he replaced **Khalid Sheikh Mohammed** as the principal logistics person in al Qaeda after the latter's capture in 2003. He is also thought to have been the principal organizer of the failed 2006 **Trans-Atlantic Airline Plot** and two assassination attempts on former Pakistan President Pervez Musharraf.

Further reading
Campbell, D., 'Pakistan Says al Qaeda Link to Plot Found' *The Guardian* 17 August 2006.
Sengupta, S., 'Pakistan Reports Arrest of Senior al Qaeda Leader' *The New York Times*, 5 May 2005.

AL-MANAR
The Beirut-based satellite television station Al-Manar TV (lit.: 'the Beacon') was founded in Beruit in 1991 and is a key element of **Hezbollah**'s propaganda arm, broadcasting to an estimated global audience of up to 15 million. Offering a variety of entertainment and political commentary, the station is a key element for the promotion of Hezbollah's political ambitions and ideology, both within Lebanon and to a wider audience across the Middle East. Criticism of Israel and the promotion of the Palestinian cause constitute a large part of Al-Manar's programming. Critics of Al-Manar argue that it is funded in part by Iran, a claim that the station's management and Hezbollah strongly reject. Al-Manar has been proscribed as a terrorist entity by several countries including France, Germany, Spain and the United States. It has been denied broadcasting licences in Australia, Canada and other parts of the world.

Further reading
Dallal, J. A., 'Hizballah's Virtual Civil Society' *Television and New Media* 2(4) 2001, pp. 367–71.

AL-MAQDISI, ABU MUHAMMAD

Abu Muhammad al-Maqdisi is the *nom de guerre* of Isam Mohammad Tahir (b. 1959), a Palestinian writer best known as the inspiration for the first leader of **al Qaeda in Iraq, Abu Musab al-Zarqawi**. Born in the Palestinian territories but raised in Kuwait, al-Maqdisi emerged in the 1980s as a highly influential theorist of Islamist resistance who has inspired a range of radical groups from the Middle East to Southeast Asia. His ideology is based on a rigid interpretation of Qur'anic texts and emphasizes an uncompromising devotion to Allah in all facets of life. His influence has been propagated through books and pamphlets and, more recently, via a militant Islamist website maintained by al-Maqdisi until his arrest in Jordan in May 2005. Since his incarceration the website has been maintained by his followers.

Further reading
Wiktorowicz, Q., 'The New Global Threat: Transnational Salafis and Jihad' *Middle East Policy* 8(4) 2007, pp. 18–38.

AL-MASRI, ABU AYYUB

Al-Masri (b. 1965) assumed the leadership of **al-Qaeda in Iraq** less than a week after the death of **Abu Musab al-Zarqawi** in June 2006. Before assuming the leadership role, al-Masri had responsibility for strategic planning, intelligence, recruitment and ideology. With respect to the latter, he is particularly well suited as he has a strong reputation for being well versed in Shar'ia law. Born in Egypt, he joined the **Egyptian Islamic Jihad** (EIJ) in the early 1980s, and in subsequent years became a close disciple of **Osama bin Laden**'s deputy, **Ayman al-Zawahiri**. Following the merger of the EIJ and **al Qaeda** in 1986, he travelled to Afghanistan and trained at al Farouq camp where he specialized in the construction of explosives, notably truck and roadside bombs. His known aliases include: Abu Hamza al-Muhajir ('the Immigrant'), Youssef al-Durairi, Yusuf al-Dariri.

Further reading
Brooke, S., 'The Preacher and the Jihadi' in *Current Trends in Islamist Ideology* Vol. III. Washington, DC: The Hudson Institute, 2006.
George, M., 'The Legend and Legacy of Abu Mussab al-Zarqawi' *Defence Studies* 7(3) 2007, pp. 338–57.

AL QAEDA

Proscribed by: Australia, Canada, India, Israel, Russia, UK, UN, USA
For a group that has become synonymous with terrorism in the early twenty-first century, there is a surprising level of debate between scholars and terrorism watchers over the precise nature of al Qaeda. However, there is general agreement on several core issues, the first of which is that the term 'al Qaeda' (Arabic for 'the base') was appended to the organization not by its leaders but by US officials investigating the 1998 **East Africa embassy bombings**. The second is that al Qaeda had its origins in Afghanistan in 1988 when **Abdullah Azzam**, the Palestinian-born leader of Maktab al-Khidamat, an organization established to recruit fighters for the anti-Soviet struggle in Afghanistan, convened a meeting that included **Osama bin Laden** (whose status until this stage had been built on the way he had used his wealth to fund the anti-Soviet resistance) and senior leaders of the **Egyptian Islamic Jihad** (including **Ayman al-Zawahiri**). Following Azzam's assassination in 1989, bin Laden assumed leadership of the group.

The next stage in al Qaeda's evolution occurred against the backdrop of Iraq's 1989 invasion of Kuwait. Convinced that the Afghan Mujahedeen had proven their mettle and should play a key role in expelling Iraqi forces, bin Laden approached the Saudi government with such a proposal. Angry at being rebuffed by Riyadh, and infuriated at the Saudis' subsequent decision to allow the USA to establish military bases on Saudi soil, bin Laden's criticism of the Saudi regime grew increasingly strident. He was eventually expelled from the country in 1992, finding sanctuary in Sudan.

It was on the return to Afghanistan from Sudan in 1996 that al Qaeda began to assume a more concrete form. In ideological terms, bin Laden and other leaders announced that their long-term goal was to drive all foreign military forces, and purge all Western cultural influences, from Islamic lands. Justifying this agenda in scriptural terms, as acts of self-defence, bin Laden issued a fatwa (religious ruling) effectively declaring war on the United States and its allies, including those in the Arab world. Despite bin Laden and other colleagues lacking the religious credentials required to issue such a ruling, on 23 February 1998 bin Laden and the leaders of other groups, working under the title the World Islamic Front for Combat against Jews and Crusaders, issued a second fatwa. This second document emerged as the clearest statement of al Qaeda's

aims to that point. The fatwa claimed it was the individual responsibility of all Muslims, whenever practical, to kill Americans and
their allies. The goals were to liberate the al Aqsa Mosque (in Jerusalem) and the holy sites of Mecca from the control of 'infidels and
apostates' and to drive back the mechanisms of military and cultural
control in Muslim lands. This declaration signalled the beginning
of a more systematic campaign of global terrorism by the network
of groups that had coalesced around bin Laden. On 7 August 1998,
al Qaeda launched near-simultaneous truck bombings against the
US embassies in Kenya and Tanzania, which killed more than 220
and wounded many hundreds more. Almost all of the victims were
Africans. Then, on 12 October 2000, al Qaeda terrorists drove a
small boat laden with explosives into the USS *Cole* while it was at
anchor in Aden harbour, with the loss of 17 lives and 39 injuries.
However, it was the attacks of **9/11** that cemented al Qaeda's status
in history.

Operation Enduring Freedom, the US-led invasion of Afghanistan
in the wake of the 9/11 attacks, quickly destroyed al Qaeda's network
of training facilities, killed or captured key leaders, scattered its fighters, and toppled its hosts in the Taliban regime led by Mullah Omar.
Since that time al Qaeda has become a more decentralized organization, with its key leaders constantly on the move along the difficult
mountainous terrain that marks the border between Afghanistan and
Pakistan. Bin Laden's status as al Qaeda's leader remains intact,
although by 2002 his power was mainly symbolic and rested in his
ability to inspire resistance among the remnants of the network and
a new and emerging generation of radicals in many parts of the
world. Through a clever use of the media, enhanced by the establishment of its own production houses such as **as-Sahab**, al Qaeda's
leaders, especially bin Laden and al-Zawahiri, but also younger
spokespeople such as the US-born convert **Adam Yahiye Gadahn**,
produce a stream of video- and audio-taped messages designed to
maintain their profile and tap into a range of grievances across a
variety of societies. Individuals with clear links to the upper echelons
of the movement remain active in Iraq through **al Qaeda in Iraq** (also
known as 'al Qaeda in Mesopotamia' and 'al Qaeda of the Jihad in
the Land of the Two Rivers') and in North Africa through **al-Qaeda
Organization in the Land of the Islamic Maghreb** which formed in
late 2006 out of a merger between al Qaeda and the Algerian Group
for Preaching and Combat. According to French officials, al Qaeda's

spread to Algeria, Morocco and Tunisia is designed not only to take the fight to North Africa, but to provide easier access to European targets for al Qaeda-trained personnel.

Al Qaeda's ability to forge links with groups in other parts of the world and to use a variety of media to tap into new constituencies imbues it with a high degree of operational resilience. For this reason al Qaeda, or groups and individuals inspired by it, is likely to remain a key player in global terrorism for many years.

Further reading

Bergen, P., *The Holy War, Inc: Inside the Secret World of Osama bin Laden*. London: Weidenfeld & Nicolson, 2001.

Burke, J., *Al-Qaeda: The True Story of Radical Islam*. London: Penguin, 2004.

Kepel, G. and Milelli, J.-P., *Al Qaeda in Its Own Words*. Cambridge, Mass.: The Belknap Press of Harvard University, 2008.

Wright, L., *The Looming Tower: Al Qaeda and the Road to 9/11*. New York: Alfred A. Knopf, 2006.

AL QAEDA IN IRAQ (Tanzim Qa'idat al-Jihad fi Bilad al-Rafidayn)
Proscribed by: Australia, UN, USA

Among the myriad problems that have plagued Coalition efforts to pacify and stabilize Iraq since the US-led invasion of 2003, groups such as Tanzim Qa'idat al-Jihad fi Bilad al-Rafidayn (also known as 'al Qaeda in Iraq', 'al-Qaeda in Mesopotamia', the 'al-Zarqawi network' and 'al Qaeda of the Jihad in the Land of the Two Rivers') have been especially difficult to contain. Drawing support from the Sunni triangle, which stretches north from Baghdad, and volunteers from places such as Yemen, Saudi Arabia and elsewhere, al Qaeda in Iraq has been responsible for a large number of post-invasion terrorist attacks in the country. Its targets are US and other Western military personnel, but also Shi'a Muslims who have been singled out in an attempt to foment sectarian tensions that would unite the Sunnis and further complicate governance. The group emerged in 2003 under the leadership of **Abu Musab al-Zarqawi**, a long-time extremist who until 1999 was imprisoned in Jordan. In 2004, al-Zarqawi pledged allegiance to **Osama bin Laden** which in turn led bin Laden to urge resistance fighters in Iraq to follow al-Zarqawi. However, the relationship was not always comfortable as al-Zarqawi rebuffed al Qaeda orders to halt attacks on Shi'ite cultural sites because of the deleterious impact they were having on al Qaeda's reputation in the Middle East and elsewhere. After the death of al-Zarqawi in 2006, Abu Hamza al-Muhajir (real name believed to be **Abu Ayyub al-Masri**) assumed the leadership of al Qaeda in Iraq; however, the group soon splintered into a highly decentralized movement. Estimates suggest the group consists of up to several thousand loosely affiliated fighters. It has perpetrated some of the worst terrorist attacks inside Iraq and in the region more generally. In 2002, the group assassinated US diplomat Laurence Foley in Jordan. In 2003 it bombed the UN headquarters in Baghdad, killing twenty-two people, including the UN special envoy to Iraq, and prompting the UN to withdraw most of its personnel from the country. That same year the group attacked the Shi'ite Imam Ali Mosque in Najaf, killing an estimated eighty-three people. In 2006 the group bombed another Shi'ite mosque in Samara, causing severe damage to one of the holiest shrines in Shi'a Islam. This attack triggered a surge of sectarian violence, while a number of car bombs and mortar attacks perpetrated by the group in Sadr city that same year killed hundreds and further inflamed sectarian violence. By the late 2000s a surge of US forces in several Sunni-dominated provinces resulted in a series of setbacks for the organization.

Further reading
Tonnessen, T. H., 'Training on the Battlefield: Iraq as a Training Ground for Global Jihadis' *Terrorism and Political Violence* 20(4) 2008, pp. 543–62.
Hafez, M. M., 'Jihad after Iraq: Lessons from the Arab Afghans' *Studies in Conflict and Terrorism* 32(2) 2009, pp. 73–94.

AL QAEDA ORGANIZATION IN THE LAND OF THE ISLAMIC MAGHREB
Proscribed by: Australia, UN
On 11 September 2006, **Ayman al-Zawahiri** announced a merger between **al Qaeda** and the Algerian Group for Preaching and Combat (GSPC) and the formation of Al Qaeda Organization in the Land of the Islamic Maghreb. Although the GSPC had previously expressed support for al Qaeda, the formal merging of the groups marked a new development. It represented a particular success for al Qaeda, which for several years had been trying to forge a coalition of like-minded groups, in Algeria, Morocco and Tunisia in particular. Al Qaeda's efforts in the Maghreb are motivated by a

desire to expand its influence into a region rife with social and political grievances, and which is therefore assessed to be receptive to its messages. Although operating under the al Qaeda umbrella, it is senior GSPC personnel who exercise a leadership role at the regional level.

Further reading
Marret, J.-L., 'Al Qaeda in the Islamic Maghreb: A "Glocal" Organisation' *Studies in Conflict and Terrorism* 31(6) 2008, pp. 541–52.
Steinberg, G. and Werefels, I., 'Between the "Near" and the "Far" Enemy: Al-Qaeda in the Islamic Maghreb' *Mediterranean Politics* 12(3) 2007, pp. 407–13.

AL QAEDAISM

'Al Qaedaism' refers to the complex mix of political, religious and cultural beliefs – especially as articulated by **Osama bin Laden** and **Ayman al-Zawahiri** – that provides the fulcrum on which al Qaeda the organization hangs its tactics and strategies. The salience of the term rests in its ability to explain the resilience of the al Qaeda brand despite the damage inflicted on its structural coherence by the US-led invasion of Afghanistan in 2001 and parallel counter-terrorism initiatives in other parts of the world. In other words, despite disruption of the organizational structures of al Qaeda, the group has been consistently able to rejuvenate itself by attracting fresh financial and human resources. This is because the political and spiritual messages that define the organization continue to proliferate and find new and receptive audiences in different parts of the world. Those who are inspired by these messages need not have formal contact with a clearly demarcated hierarchical organization to act in its name. Rather, al Qaedaism provides both a political and a pseudo-religious basis upon which individuals can self-radicalize and, in some cases, forge home-grown terrorist groups which act in al Qaeda's name, but without necessarily having any connection to the formal al Qaeda network.

Further reading
Burke, J., 'al Qaeda' *Foreign Policy* 142 May/June 2004.
Gray, J., *Al Qaeda and What it Means to be Modern*. London: Faber, 2004.

AL-SHARIF, FADL

Egyptian-born Sayyed Imam Al-Sharif (also known as 'Dr Fadl' and Abd Al-Qader bin Abd Al-Aziz; b. 1950) is a major intellectual figure within **al Qaeda** and other organizations committed to violent **jihad**. His book, *The Essentials of Making Ready for Jihad*, was used extensively as a training manual in al Qaeda's camps in Afghanistan when al-Sharif was rumoured to be one of the group's senior leaders. Although he was once close to **Osama bin Laden**'s deputy **Ayman al-Zawahiri**, the two fell out over doctrinal issues in the 1990s. The use of violence against civilians was a particular point of contention between the two men. Al-Sharif opposed mass casualty attacks, arguing they were counter-productive and at odds with Qur'anic scripture. Contrary to al-Zawahiri and bin Laden, Al-Sharif argued for the gradual infiltration of government structures and a 'take over from within'. Soon after leaving al Qaeda, Al-Sharif moved to Yemen where he returned to practising medicine and the study of theology. In 2004 al-Sharif was deported to Egypt where he was sentenced to life in prison for his involvement in terrorist attacks in that country during the 1980s. It was in prison that Al-Sharif wrote *Rationalizing Jihad in Egypt and the World*, which condemned the use of violence in the name of jihad. The tract attracted widespread condemnation among his former counterparts in jihadist circles.

Further reading
Wright, L., 'The Rebellion Within: An al Qaeda Mastermind Questions Terrorism' *The New Yorker* 2 June 2008.

AL-ZARQAWI, ABU MUSAB

As one of the most well-known figures in contemporary Islamist militancy, Abu Musab al-Zarqawi (b. 1966), whose real name is believed to have been Ahmed al-Khalayleh, had been active in militant groups for two decades before his death in Iraq in June 2006. Al-Zarqawi was raised in the Jordanian town of Zarqa. By his late teens he was involved in petty crime, for which he was arrested. It was during this period that he first began to embrace a militant form of Islamism. He travelled to Afghanistan in the late 1980s but arrived too late to participate in combat against the Soviets. Even so, he spent time in a terrorist training camp outside Peshawar where his extremist ideas were set in stone. In 1994 he was imprisoned in Jordan for being a member of a banned organization, and after his release from prison in 1999 returned to Afghanistan where he set up his own training camp near the town of Herat. It was around this time that he established a Sunni resistance group called Jama'at al-Tawhid wa'al-Jihad that was responsible for a number of terrorist attacks in Jordan and Iraq. In October 2004 al-Zarqawi pledged allegiance to **Osama bin Laden** and **al Qaeda** and changed the name of his organization to Tanzim Qa'idat al-Jihad fi Bilad al-Rafidayn (sometimes called **al Qaeda in Iraq**). Under this label, al-Zarqawi and his followers carried out numerous bombings against UN, US and Coalition forces as well as Shi'a holy sites. The targeting of the latter reflected his declaration of 'all-out war' against the Shi'a and an attempt to foment sectarian conflict. However, this tactic appears to have drawn criticism from the al Qaeda hierarchy, especially **Ayman al-Zawahiri** who is reported to have written to al-Zarqawi urging him to stop the targeting of Shi'a because it was having a deleterious impact on support for the insurgency from the wider Muslim community. From an even more gruesome perspective, it was al-Zarqawi's use of kidnapping – whereby he snatched foreigners and Iraqis working for the Coalition, decapitated them, and posted the deaths on the Internet – that cemented his notoriety.

Further reading

Fishman, B., 'After Zarqawi: The Dilemmas and Future of al Qaeda in Iraq' *The Washington Quarterly* 29(4) 2006, pp. 19–32.

Napoleoni, L., *Insurgent Iraq: Al-Zarqawi and the New Generation*. New York: Seven Stories Press, 2005.

Tonnessen, T. H., 'Training on the Battlefield: Iraq as a Training Ground for Global Jihadis' *Terrorism and Political Violence* 20(4) 2008, pp. 543–62.

AL-ZAWAHIRI, AYMAN

Widely recognized as one of the most senior leaders of **al Qaeda**, Ayman al-Zawahiri is a key advisor to **Osama bin Laden** and the organization's key ideologist. He was born into a wealthy and well-educated Cairo family in 1951; his grandfather was a prominent Imam, his father a professor, and another family member the first Secretary General of the Arab League. Under the influence of an uncle who was the Grand Imam of Cairo's al-Azhar University, al-Zawahiri joined the **Muslim Brotherhood** when he was just fifteen. Despite being arrested for being a member of the Brotherhood, which at that time was banned in Egypt, al-Zawahiri went on to study medicine, graduating in 1974. But university studies did not attenuate his growing militancy, and when the Muslim Brotherhood publicly renounced violence al-Zawahiri co-founded a violent splinter group called Islamic Jihad (see **Egyptian Islamic Jihad**). The writings of the militant Islamist **Sayyid Qutb** exercised a major influence on the development of al-Zawahiri's thought at this time. In the early 1980s al-Zawahiri travelled to Pakistan and worked in a Red Crescent clinic, helping wounded Afghan refugees. In 1981 he returned to Egypt where he was arrested in a sweep of militant Islamists following the assassination of President Anwar Sadat, spending the next few years in prison. The crackdown on Islamists contributed to the fracturing of Islamic Jihad into a number of competing factions, with al-Zawahiri leading the largest of these sub-groups. After his release from prison, al-Zawahiri returned to Pakistan where he provided medical assistance to wounded Afghan soldiers and Mujahedeen. It was during this period that al-Zawahiri met bin Laden, and by the early 1990s both men were in exile in Sudan. This period was critical in al-Zawahiri's development as a terrorist. He became an ardent advocate of the importance of attacking the 'near enemy' – which to him was the Egyptian government – before attacking the 'far enemy', most notably Israel and the United States. In 1998 al-Zawahiri agreed to fold his faction of Islamic Jihad into a new group, the World Islamic Front for Combat against Jews and Crusaders, or al Qaeda – a decision that some observers say was formalized in 2001. This also provided a clear indication of a gradual shift in al-Zawahiri's notion of how best to achieve al Qaeda's aims, from attacking the 'near enemy' to attacking the 'far enemy' whenever possible. To this end, al-Zawahiri sanctioned the 1998 **East Africa Embassy bombings**, the attack on the USS *Cole* in Aden harbour in 2000, and finally the attacks of **9/11**. Following the 2001 US-led invasion of Afghanistan, al-Zawahiri fled and, by the late 2000s, was thought to be moving constantly along the Afghan–Pakistan border region. The stresses of being one of the world's most hunted men has not stopped him from publishing his memoirs, *Knights under the Banner of the Prophet*, or from taking the lead from bin Laden in appearing in a number of al Qaeda video and audio messages.

Further reading
Al-Zayyat, M., et al., *The Road to al-Qaeda: The Story of Bin Laden's Right-Hand Man*. London: Pluto Press, 2004.

Mansfield, L., *His Own Words: A Translation of the Writings of Dr. Ayman Al Zawahiri*. New Jersey: TLG Publishers, 2006.

ANARCHIST TERRORISM

The predominant form of terrorist violence at the turn of the nineteenth century was that committed by Anarchist and Marxist groups. Through their adaptation of new technologies of destruction – handguns and bombs in particular – various Anarchist groups had an impact on societies as diverse as Argentina, France, Italy, Spain and the United States. In the latter case, the 1901 assassination of President William McKinley by the Anarchist **Leon Czolgosz** was especially significant in its impact on American society at that time. Despite a general embrace of the concept 'propaganda by the deed' there was no single Anarchist agenda that united various groups; on the contrary, Anarchist organizations were notoriously prone to splits and divisions. However, recurring themes among Anarchist leaders such as Johann Most, Emma Goldman, Mikhail Bakunin and Paul Brousse was resistance to the centralization of power in the hands of political and industrial elites and the 'liberation of the people' from the imperative to behave in accordance with the dictates of the economic and political status quo. By the 1930s the threat of Anarchist terrorism had faded, its appeal overtaken by the rise of nationalism, fascism and totalitarian forms of Marxism.

Further reading

Jensen, R. B., 'The Evolution of Anarchist Terrorism in Europe and the United States from the Nineteenth Century to World War I' in Brett Bowden and Michael T. Davis (eds.) *Terror: From Tyrannicide to Terrorism*. St Lucia: University of Queensland Press, 2008, pp. 134–60.

Kassel, W., 'Terrorism and the International Anarchist Movement of the Late Nineteenth and Early Twentieth Centuries' *Studies in Conflict and Terrorism* 32(3) 2009, pp. 237–52.

Miller, M. A., 'The Intellectual Origins of Modern Terrorism in Europe' in Martha Crenshaw (ed.) *Terrorism in Context*. University Park: The Pennsylvania University Press, 1995, pp. 27–62.

ANIMAL LIBERATION FRONT

The original Animal Liberation Front (ALF) was established in the UK in 1976 after a split in the Hunt Saboteurs Association. According to the **Federal Bureau of Investigation (FBI)**, a US branch of the ALF was established a few years later, although it was not until the group initiated a multi-million-dollar arson attack on a California animal laboratory in 1987 that it was listed by US authorities as a terrorist organization. Since then, groups using the ALF label and professing a commitment to its guiding principles have spread to other Western countries. The ALF justifies its actions through a philosophy of ethical equivalence, arguing that the distinction between human and animal rights is arbitrary and a key source of cruelty. Its activities centre on freeing or 'rescuing' animals from vivisectionist facilities, and imposing financial costs on companies and premises involved in animal experimentation – primarily through sabotage and property damage caused by fire bombings. Popular targets include abattoirs, furriers, pharmaceutical companies and butchers' shops. In August 2003 ALF activists successfully released 10,000 mink from a fur farm in Washington State. Activists work anonymously, either in individual operations or in small **cells**. These cells are not hierarchically structured, although there are ethical guidelines by which all members are expected to abide. These include an obligation to live a vegetarian or vegan lifestyle. The ALF divides its aims into short- and long-term goals. In the short term, it seeks to save as many animals as possible and to render legal animal abuse unprofitable and socially unacceptable. Over the long term, the ALF aims to drive companies that rely on animal exploitation (including many farms) out of business and to change public consciousness so that animal exploitation is ended for all time. The organization is committed to non-violence and activists are required to avoid harming humans, whom the organization regards as another species of animal. However, more extreme elements of the movement have been charged with targeting scientists who work at research laboratories by vandalizing family homes, making death threats against family members, and engaging in sustained campaigns of public harassment.

Further reading
Best, S. and Nocella, A. J. (eds.) *Terrorists or Freedom Fighters? Reflections on the Liberation of Animals.* New York: Lantern Books, 2004.

Monaghan, R., 'Animal Rights and Violent Protest' *Terrorism and Political Violence* 9(4) Winter 1997, pp. 106–16.

ANSAR AL-ISLAM
Proscribed by: Australia, Canada, UK, UN, USA

Ansar al-Islam is a Sunni Islamist terrorist organization based in the Kurdish region of Northern Iraq. Founded in late 2001 by the exiled Kurdish Islamist Mullah Krekar (also known as Faraj Ahmad Najmuddin) out of a merger between smaller Islamist groups, its long-term goal is to establish an independent Kurdish state based upon a strict interpretation of Qur'anic law. In the short term, it has dedicated itself to driving US-led forces from the region and, to this end, it has cooperated with other Islamist terrorist groups. According to US intelligence reports Ansar al-Islam has also received logistic and perhaps material support from **al Qaeda**-linked groups. The group has fewer than 500 members and has focused many of its attacks on the secular Patriotic Union of Kurdistan, which it sees as a rival for the support of the Kurdish people of the region. In 2004 Iraqi authorities arrested Mullah Krekar soon after his return from exile in Norway, and he was replaced by Abu Abdullah al-Shafii (also known as Warba Holiri al-Kurdi).

Further reading
McKiernan, S., 'Kurds in the Way? The Complex Relations between *al-Qaeda, the United States, Turkey, and Iraqi Kurds' Harvard Political Review* 30(1) Spring 2003, pp. 34–5.
Schanzer, J., 'Ansar al-Islam: Back in Iraq' *Middle East Quarterly* 11(1) 2004, pp. 41–50.

ANSAR AL-SUNNAH
Proscribed by: Australia, UK, UN

Based in northern and central Iraq, Ansar al-Sunnah is a radical Sunni organization dedicated to driving out US and allied forces from Iraq, toppling the post-invasion secular government, and establishing Iraq as an Islamic state. Made up of fighters from a range of different militant groups, some of which pre-date the US-led invasion of 2003, Ansar al-Sunnah members are known to have cooperated with **al-Qaeda in Iraq** (Tanzim Qa'idat al-Jihad fi Bilad al-Rafidayn), the al Qaeda-linked organization headed by the late **Abu Musab al-Zarqawi**. However, following al-Zarqawi's death, the two groups increasingly came into conflict. Ansar al-Sunnah has been responsible for a number of suicide bombings targeting US and allied forces and has released video recordings of the execution of several of its hostages.

Further reading
Fishman, B., 'Using the Mistakes of al Qaeda's Franchises to Undermine its Strategies' *The ANNALS of the American Academy of Political and Social Science* 618 2008, pp. 46–54.

ANTI-TERRORIST OPERATIONS COORDINATION UNIT OF FRANCE (UCLAT)

UCLAT is the French anti-terrorist unit established to coordinate the activities of various departments of France's wider counter-terrorism structure. The 1980s and early 1990s saw a number of terrorist attacks in France carried out by several different groups. In the 1980s Iranian-backed members of a **Hezbollah** cell targeted supporters of the former pre-revolutionary Iranian regime. These attacks led to a series of changes in the way the French authorities organized their counter-terrorism regime. But these changes were further enhanced in 1995 and 1996 when the Algerian **Armed Islamic Group** (GIA) carried out a series of bombings in Paris. In responding to these threats it was found that excessive bureaucracy militated against effective counter-terrorism cooperation. For example, even within the National Police there existed the French Secret Service (the DST), the General Intelligence Service (RG) and the National Anti-terrorism Division (DNAT). Overlaying these was the External Intelligence Service (DGSE), which fell under the mandate of the Ministry of Defence, while the Gendarmerie and Paris' Judicial Police maintained their own counter-terrorism investigation and intelligence functions. UCLAT emerged as one of several attempts to coordinate actions between these bodies by facilitating greater intelligence sharing and other operational functions. In 2006 all of the aforementioned bodies were centralized in one location to make UCLAT's role easier.

Further reading
Chalk, P. and Rosenau, W., *Confronting 'the Enemy Within': Security Intelligence, the Police, and Counterterrorism in Four Democracies.* Santa Monica: Rand Corporation, 2004.
Gregory, S., 'France and the War on Terrorism' *Terrorism and Political Violence* 15(1) March 2003, pp. 124–47.

ARAB CONVENTION ON THE SUPPRESSION OF TERRORISM

Adopted by the Council of Arab Ministers of the Interior and the Council of Arab Ministers of Justice at a meeting in April 1998, the

Convention is a preliminary statement that commits members of the League of Arab States to 'promote mutual cooperation in the suppression of terrorist offences, which pose a threat to the security and stability of the Arab Nations and endanger their vital interests'. There are four core tenets to the convention:

1.   A commitment to the 'highest moral and religious principles' to protect innocent lives as set out in Shar'ia law
2.   A commitment to the humanitarian heritage of an Arab nation, a heritage that the signatory states agreed is antithetical to all forms of terrorism
3.   A deeper commitment to the principles that underpin the Pact of the League of Arab States, the UN Charter and all the other relevant international convents
4.   Not withstanding these preceding tenets, an affirmation of the right of peoples to combat foreign occupation and aggression by armed struggle in order to liberate their territories and secure their right to self-determination.

The fourth principle reflects mainly the reluctance of Arab nations to adopt any measures that might be seen to undermine the armed struggle of various Palestinian groups. It is this refusal to classify as terrorism acts of violence in the name of self-determination that has also placed Arab nations at loggerheads with the USA and other Western states within forums such as the United Nations.

Further reading
'United Nations Treaty Collection: Conventions on Terrorism'. Available at http://untreaty.un.org/English/Terrorism.asp (accessed 13 September 2008).

ARAFAT, YASSER

Yasser Arafat was born Mohammed al-Raman Abd al-Raouf Arafat al-Qudwa al-Husseini ('Yasser' was a nickname) on 24 August 1929 in Cairo, the sixth of seven children. His father was a textile merchant of mixed Palestinian and Egyptian ancestry while his mother was from an old Palestinian family from Jerusalem. Following the death of his mother in 1933, he was sent to live with relatives in Jerusalem, at that time within the British mandate in Palestine. In 1950 he graduated with an engineering degree from the University of King Fuad 1 (now Cairo University). During this time he read widely on Zionism and Arab nationalism and throughout the 1950s immersed himself in Palestinian politics, becoming head of the General Union of Palestinian Students. After settling in Kuwait and working as a teacher, he gradually formed a close-knit group of fellow Palestinian exiles (including several members of the **Muslim Brotherhood**) and eventually formed **Fatah**, a reverse acronym for the Arabic term 'Harakat al-Tahrir al-Watani al-Filastini' ('The Palestinian National Liberation Movement'). The exact date of the group's founding is a matter of dispute, although it is generally given as 1959, which was the year Fatah was first mentioned in Palestinian media. In 1962 the group moved from Kuwait to Syria to take advantage of the latter's proximity to Israel and to access a greater number of Palestinian refugees. The move was successful, in part because of Fatah's ability to encourage defections from other Palestinian resistance groups by offering higher salaries. Fatah's objective was to serve as a vanguard movement for armed struggle against Israel and in this context Arafat oversaw a steady increase in terrorist violence. In later years Arafat's commitment to terrorism waned, and on 14 December 1988 he publicly accepted United Nations Security Council Resolution 242 formally acknowledging Israel's right to exist and renounced all forms of terrorism, including state-sponsored terrorism. Although welcomed in some circles, it was roundly condemned as a sell-out in others, and it added to the growing appeal of emerging non-secular Palestinian terrorist groups such as **Hamas**. In 1990 Arafat alienated other potential supporters in the USA and Saudi Arabia, but also many in the Arab public, when he openly supported the invasion of Kuwait by Iraq. However, by 1993 he had successfully negotiated the Oslo Accords with Israel, which granted the Palestinian territories of the West Bank and Gaza Strip a degree of autonomy in return for recognition of Israel. In 1994 he was awarded the Nobel Peace Prize along with two Israeli Prime Ministers, Yitzhak Rabin and Shimon Peres. Throughout the rest of the 1990s Arafat struggled to maintain his authority as alternative groups outside Fatah, such as Hamas and Islamic Jihad (see **Palestine Islamic Jihad**), but also factions within his own organization, sought to undermine him. His credibility was further diminished by allegations in the late 1990s that he had misappropriated millions of dollars in aid pledged to help the Palestinian people, and by his marriage in 1995 to Suha Tawil, a former private secretary thirty-four years his junior. Arafat died on 11 November

2004 at a French military hospital in Paris. According to French doctors the cause of death was a 'blood and liver disease', although precise details from the autopsy were released only to his immediate family. Speculation in some Palestinian circles that Israeli agents poisoned him remains unproven.

Further reading

Arafat, Y., 'A Discussion with Yasser Arafat' *Journal of Palestine Studies* 11(2) 1982, pp. 3–15.

Rubin, B. and Colp, R. Judith, *Yasser Arafat: A Political Biography*. Oxford: Oxford University Press, 2005.

ARMED ISLAMIC GROUP (Groupe Islamique Armé – GIA)
Proscribed by: Australia, Canada, UK, UN, USA
Established in 1992 by Mansour Meliani following the Algerian military's decision to nullify the outcome of a national election in which the Islamic Salvation Front (FIS) won the majority of votes, the GIA dedicated itself to the overthrow of the secular and military-backed administration. Constituted mainly by former members of the FIS, the GIA was involved in a bloody war of attrition wherein both the GIA and Algerian military used extreme violence to coerce the civilian population to bend to their respective wishes. The bloodiest actions took place south of the capital Algiers, which the GIA referred to as 'the liberated zone' but which others have referred to as 'the triangle of death'. From 1994 to 1996 the GIA also targeted French interests, hijacking an Air France passenger jet and carrying out a series of bombings in Paris and Lyon in an effort to end French support for the government in Algiers. Regular changes in leadership and concessions on both sides, including the return of national elections, contributed to a reduction in GIA violence and, by the early 2000s, hard-core members began drifting towards groups linked to **al Qaeda**. These recalcitrantly militant individuals and groups targeted Westerners and many went on to form the **al-Qaeda Organization in the Land of the Islamic Maghreb**.

Further reading

Hafez, M. M., 'Armed Islamist Movements and Political Violence in Algeria' *Middle East Journal* 54(4) 2000, pp. 572–91.

Turshen, M., 'Militarism and Islamism in Algeria' *Journal of Asian and African Studies* 39(1–2) 2004, pp. 119–32.

ARMY OF GOD

Formed in the mid-1980s as a loose network of underground Christian fundamentalist anti-abortion activists, the Army of God has been responsible for a spate of violent acts, including murder, across the United States. Members believe not only that the use of violence is a legitimate mode for preventing abortions, but that they have a mandate from God to do so. Indeed, the Army of God Manual claims the group to be 'a real Army' with 'God as Commander-in-Chief'. The first public mention of the group occurred in the context of the 1982 kidnapping of an Illinois doctor and his wife by three anti-abortion activists, but the idea of a network of activists who considered themselves part of a larger underground army appears to have solidified only in the mid-1980s when a Supreme Court judge received a death threat signed by the group, which was followed by a number of arson attacks on abortion clinics and the American Civil Rights Union. The group's activities are governed by a manual which describes how members might best achieve their aims of ending abortion, with tactics ranging from blockades and arson to acid attacks and other acts of violence. In the months after the **9/11** attacks, envelopes containing white powder and a letter that read 'You have been exposed to anthrax. We are going to kill you. The Army of God' were sent to more than 160 women's health clinics across fourteen US states by an Army of God supporter, **Clayton Lee Waagner**. The powder was not anthrax but the intent was clear: to terrorize individuals involved in providing abortions. The Army of God Manual is also noteworthy for its strong opposition to homosexuality and its suspicion of government, two positions that open up the possibility of connections with other extreme right-wing groups in the USA. Some notable individuals associated with the Army of God include the Reverend **Michael Bray**, **Eric Rudolph** and Scott Roeder, the latter responsible for the fatal shooting of a Kansas doctor accused of performing late-term abortions.

Further reading

Juergensmeyer, M., 'Christian Violence in America' *The Annals Of The American Academy Of Political And Social Science* 558(1) 1998, pp. 88–100.

ARMY OF THE RIGHTEOUS
SEE: LASHKAR-E TAYYIBA

AS-SAHAB
A hallmark of **al Qaeda**'s tactics has been its preparedness to embrace new media technologies to communicate its messages to different audiences; as-Sahab, a TV, video and sound-recording facility, represents the most sophisticated of these efforts. Using a combination of digital recording technologies, an informal network of volunteer camera people, and the Internet and new band widths, as-Sahab (Arabic for 'the Cloud') has evolved into al Qaeda's principal production unit for statements prepared by **Osama bin Laden** and **Ayman al-Zawahiri**. Its autonomy allows al Qaeda to circumvent censorship laws in Middle Eastern and Western countries, while simultaneously reducing its dependence on private Arabic-language media outlets. Apart from video and audio statements by senior al Qaeda personnel, most of as-Sahab's outlet is comprised of video footage of insurgents fighting allied forces in Iraq, especially successful attacks on US forces, but also of alleged human rights abuses against Muslims.

Further reading
Brackman, J. M., 'High-Tech Terror: Al Qaeda's use of New Technology' *Fletcher Forum of World Affairs* 30(2) 2006, pp. 149–64.
Weimann, G., *Terror on the Internet: The New Arena, the New Challenges*. New York: The United States Institute of Peace, 2006.

ASAHARA, SHOKO
Born Chizuro Matsumoto (1955), Shoko Asahara was the founder and leader of the religious cult **Aum Shinrikyo**, a group responsible for a 1995 sarin gas attack on the Tokyo subway system. Raised in poor circumstances, Asahara contracted infantile glaucoma at a young age and, as a result, he has been legally blind for most of his life. In 1977 he failed to gain entry to Tokyo University, Japan's most prestigious higher education institution, subsequently turning to traditional Chinese healing and yoga. In 1982 Asahara was arrested for selling fake 'traditional remedies' and was bankrupted by a ¥200,000 fine. In 1984 he attracted a small cabal of followers and established a formal group called Aum Shinsen no Kai that emphasized enlight-

enment through yoga. In 1989 he changed the group's name to Aum Shinrikyo ('Supreme Truth'). Asahara's claims became progressively more outlandish, and after a trip to India in 1987 he claimed to have achieved 'perfect enlightenment' and developed superpowers that allowed him to levitate and time-travel. It was also at this time that Asahara's ideology began to develop a more apocalyptic dimension. Fusing elements of Buddhism, Christianity and Hinduism with a healthy dose of ideas culled from science-fiction literature and the writings of Nostradamus, he developed a messianic cult with himself at the apex as the reincarnation of the Hindu god Shiva. In 1990 Asahara involved his organization in the national Japanese elections, predicting he would win in a landslide. After his party failed to win a single seat, he denounced the poll as a fraud and both Asahara and his group began to express deeper hostility towards the state. The 20 March 1995 sarin gas attack launched on the Tokyo subway system by members of Aum Shinrikyo were widely interpreted as being designed to unleash a wave of panic that would eventually spread throughout Japan and further afield, toppling governments and ushering in a new political and social order. On 27 February 2004, Asahara was convicted of organizing and sanctioning the sarin attack – which killed 12 and injured over 1,000 – and was sentenced to death.

Further reading

Lifton, R. J., 'Aum Shinrikyo: The Threshold Crossed' *Journal of Aggression, Maltreatment & Trauma* 9(1–2) 2004, pp. 57–66.

Reader, I., *Religious Violence in Japan: The Case of Aum Shinrikyo*. Honolulu: University of Hawaii Press, 2000.

ASBAT AL-ANSAR

Proscribed by: Australia, Canada, Russia, UN, USA

Established by Hisham al-Shraidi in 1986, Asbat al-Ansar ('League of Partisans') is an extremist Sunni group based mainly in Palestinian refugee camps in Southern Lebanon. Its key objectives are to beat back Western influence, establish Lebanon as a fundamentalist Sunni state, and to destroy the state of Israel. A rival group assassinated al-Shraidi in 1991, after which leadership of Asbat al-Ansar passed to Ahmad Abdul al-Karim al-Saadi (also known as Abu Mihjin). After the 2003 US-led invasion of Iraq, Asbat al-Ansar cadres joined the

Sunni-based resistance. Meanwhile, **al Qaeda in Iraq** is known to have trained Asbat al-Ansar members in Lebanon's Bekaa Valley. The group has also been implicated in rocket attacks on Israel, a plot to assassinate a former US ambassador to Beirut, a rocket-propelled grenade attack against the Russian embassy in Lebanon, and a series of violent strikes against Western fast-food outlets.

Further reading
Cordesman, A. H., *Arab–Israeli Military Forces in an Era of Asymmetric Wars.* Stanford: Stanford University Press, 2008.

THE ASSASSINS
Operating in the eleventh and twelfth centuries in an area that now corresponds roughly to the Iran–Iraq border, the Assassins (or Hashashin) were from the Ismaili (Nizari) sect of shi'a Islam. They emerged after a schism within the Fatimid Empire and were motivated mainly by a fear of cultural and political annihilation in the face of their opponents within the caliphate, the growing power of the Seljuk Turks, and occasionally the Christian Crusaders. Founded and led during their early years by the charismatic leader Hassan-I-Sabah, the Assassins quickly developed a reputation as astute political operators whose use of terrorism was always methodically planned and efficiently executed. Their preferred *modus operandi* was to secrete themselves into the retinue of their targets, almost always high officials, before stabbing their victim to death. The tactic was combined with a strategy of religious conversion, focusing in particular on the populations living around key Seljuk fortresses. This strategy eventually allowed the Assassins to beat back their enemies and, in the opinion of some scholars, establish a de facto state. The main group was finally destroyed by the arrival of the Mongol armies led by Hulagu Khan in 1256, while in 1273 a Syrian branch eventually succumbed to Mamluk Baibars.

Further reading
Bartlett, W. B., *The Assassins: The Story of Islam's Medieval Secret Sect.* Stroud: Sutton, 2001.
Lewis, B., *The Assassins: A Radical Sect in Islam.* London: Phoenix, 2003.

ATTA, MOHAMMED

De facto leader of the nineteen men who carried out the **9/11** terrorist attacks in the United States, Mohamed Atta (1948–2001) was born in Egypt and was raised in a religious middle-class Egyptian home shared by his lawyer father, mother and two sisters – one a medical doctor and the other a university professor. After obtaining a degree in architecture from the University of Cairo, Atta travelled to Germany in 1992 where he obtained a Masters degree in urban planning. It was while studying in Germany that Atta began attending the Al-Quds Mosque where he embraced a radical form of Islam. It was around this time that he was also introduced to others involved in the planning of the 9/11 attacks: Marwan al-Shehhi, Ziad Jarrah and Ramzi Binalshibh, the latter not participating in the attacks but later arrested in Pakistan and handed over to US authorities. Atta joined these men and others on occasional trips to Pakistan and to **al Qaeda** camps in Afghanistan, where, in late 1999, he met with **Osama bin Laden** and other top al Qaeda leaders such as the principal planner of the 9/11 attacks, **Khalid Sheikh Mohammed**. In June 2000 Atta and al-Shehhi enrolled in an accelerated pilot programme at a South Florida flying school. In mid-2001 he travelled to Spain where he met with Binalshibh to discuss final details of the plot. On the morning of 11 September 2001, Atta and fellow hijacker Abdulaziz al-Omari flew to Boston from Portland, Maine, where they boarded American Airlines Flight 11 armed with box cutters. Shortly after take-off, Atta and his team seized control of the aircraft and at 8.46 a.m. he and his co-pilot crashed the Boeing 767 into the North Tower of the World Trade Center.

Further reading

9/11 Commission, *The 9/11 Commission Report: Final Report of the National Commission on Terrorist Attacks upon the United States*. New York: W. W. Norton, 2004.

McDermott, T., *Perfect Soldiers: The 9/11 Hijackers: Who They Were, Why They Did It*. London: HarperCollins, 2005.

AUM SHINRIKYO

Proscribed by: Canada, EU, USA

Aum Shinrikyo ('Supreme Truth') is the organization started by **Shoko Asahara** in 1984 and first named Aum Shinsen no Kai ('Group of Gods' / 'Supreme Beings'). The prefix 'Aum' is an acronym chosen by Asahara because it represented the first letters of the Sanskrit words for 'creation', 'maintenance' and 'destruction' – all key concepts to Asahara's philosophy, as well as that of the group that he headed. Within Aum Shinrikyo, it is possible to identify a process of gradual embitterment and alienation from mainstream Japanese society. In particular, Asahara's repeated failures to be elected to parliament inclined him towards conspiracy theories and a desire for a wholesale destruction of the established order. From its original 15 members in the early 1980s, by the early 1990s Asahara had managed to expand the membership in Japan to around 10,000, among whom there were several hundred hardcore supporters. At the heart of this expansion was the recruitment of mainly young professional Japanese from the country's leading universities, but also several hundred scientists with skills in areas such as biochemistry, genetics and medicine. However, the end of the Cold War and the collapse of the Soviet Union also saw the group expand into Russia and other countries. By the mid-1990s it is estimated to have signed-up 35,000 foreign members, mainly in Russia, but also in Germany, Taiwan and the United States. By this time it had also accumulated an estimated US$1 billion in assets, mainly through the obligation for members to commit a portion of their earnings to the organization. Under Asahara's leadership, the organization also ventured into the corporate world, especially real estate. It was the purchase of a sheep farm in Western Australia in the early 1990s that allowed the group to first experiment with poison gases. The significance of this was made clear on 20 March 1995 when Aum Shinrikyo members launched a sarin gas attack on the Tokyo subway system, killing 12 commuters and injuring more than 1,000 others. The aim of the attack was to set in motion the social and political dynamics that Asahara believed would bring about his prophecy of the end of the world and the dawn of a new era. Throughout the period leading up to the sarin gas attack, Aum Shinrikyo demonstrated a steadily increasing intolerance of dissent within its own ranks and a determination to eliminate or silence external critics, usually through kidnapping and murder. In 2000 the group's new leader, Fumihiro Joyu, changed the organization's name to Aleph and moved to distance it from Asahara, who is now described as a 'founder' rather than 'supreme leader'. Joyu also apologized for past actions and condemned acts of terrorism. However, Joyu's actions have opened wide schisms, and a faction headed by Tatsuko Muraoko and Asahara's biological children opposes him.

Further reading
Juergensmeyer, M., *Terror in the Mind of God* (3rd edn). Berkeley: University of California Press, 2003, pp. 103–18.
Lifton, R. J., *Destroying the World to Save It: Aum Shinrikyō and the New Global Terrorism*. New York: Owl Books, 1999.

AXIS OF EVIL

Attributed to President George W. Bush's speech-writer David Frum, the term 'Axis of Evil' first appeared in the President's State of the Union Address on 29 January 2002, four months after the attacks of 9/11. In the Administration's view, the Axis was constituted by: North Korea, which Bush charged with amassing missiles and weapons of mass destruction while starving its citizens; Iran, which Bush charged with both pursuing the development of similar weapons and exporting technologies of war to enemies of the USA; and Iraq, which the Administration alleged had plotted to develop anthrax, nerve gas and nuclear weapons while brutalizing its citizens. For Bush,

> states like these, and their terrorist allies, constitute an axis of evil, arming to threaten the peace of the world. By seeking weapons of mass destruction, these regimes pose a grave and growing danger. They could provide these arms to terrorists, giving them the means to match their hatred. They could attack our allies or attempt to blackmail the United States. In any of these cases, the price of indifference would be catastrophic.

While the combative tone of the term appealed to conservatives in the USA, it made many US allies uncomfortable, with many fearing it could place the named countries on a more defensive footing and reduce the scope for diplomatic solutions. This discomfort increased when the concept was used to justify a series of US proposals and policy initiatives that included the 2003 US-led invasion of Iraq. Early into Bush's second term, the phrase faded and then disappeared completely from the Presidential lexicon.

Further reading
Cummings, B., Abrahamian, E. and Ma'oz, M., *Inventing the Axis of Evil: The Truth about North Korea, Iran, and Syria*. New York: New Press, 2004.
Peña, C., 'Axis of Evil: Threat or Chimera?' *Mediterranean Quarterly* 13(3) 2002, pp. 40–57.

AZZAM, ABDULLAH YUSUF

Born in Palestine, Abdullah Yusuf Azzam (1941–89) was a highly influential Sunni theologian best-known for his logistic support for the Afghanistan Mujahedeen in the struggle against Soviet occupation. As a young man in Palestine he grew cynical over the socialist credentials of the **Palestinian Liberation Organization (PLO)** and envisioned instead a Pan-Islamic movement that would transcend national borders, which he viewed as a device for keeping Muslims divided. In the early 1970s Azzam commenced studies in Islamic theology at al-Azhar University in Cairo, where he came into contact with other prominent Islamist thinkers including **Ayman al-Zawahiri**, who would later become **al Qaeda**'s second-in-command. It was Azzam who coaxed a young **Osama bin Laden** to Afghanistan in the early 1980s, and for the next few years he became an important mentor to the al Qaeda leader. However, with the withdrawal of Soviet forces in 1989, Azzam and bin Laden had a falling-out over where the next site of resistance ought to be. Azzam's most influential text, *Join the Caravan*, encouraged Muslims to embrace a conservative version of 'pure' Islam and to cooperate against external aggression and Western imperialism. Unknown assailants in Pakistan assassinated Azzam and his two sons in November 1989.

Further reading
Bergen, P., *The Osama bin Laden I Know: An Oral History of al Qaeda's Leader*. New York: The Free Press, 2006.
Wright, L., *The Looming Tower: Al Qaeda and the Road to 9/11*. New York: Alfred A. Knopf, 2006.

BAADER, ANDREAS

One of the founders and early leaders of the German Red Army Faction (also known as the **Baader-Meinhof Gang**), Andreas Baader was born in Munich on 6 May 1943. The son of a professor of history, Baader had a difficult youth and was often in trouble with the authorities for acts of delinquency. He was initially drawn to left-wing student politics by a thirst for excitement but drifted quickly towards the underground leftist movement because – according to some scholars – of the possibility that membership might allow him to realize a desire to act out violently against a society that he had come to despise. In 1968 Baader and his girlfriend Gudrun Ensslin were convicted and sentenced to prison on the charge of bombing a department store. In 1970 the journalist **Ulrike Meinhof** helped Baader escape from the prison library and, along with several comrades, they spent several years on the run, during which time they formed the Baader-Meinhof Gang. He was recaptured in June 1972 along with fellow group members Jan-Carl Raspe and Holger Meins. After the longest and most expensive trial in German history, Baader and his accomplices were sentenced to life in prison. In September 1972 several gang members attempted to force the release of Baader and ten fellow gang members by kidnapping a German industrialist, Hanns Martin Schleyer. Meanwhile, Baader's connection to Palestinian groups was evinced by the 1977 hijacking of a Lufthansa flight by four members of the **Popular Front for the Liberation of Palestine** in an attempt to force Baader's release. While Schleyer was murdered by his captors, the hijacking was ended when German GSG 9 Special Forces stormed the plane and released the passengers and crew. Later that day Baader committed suicide in his cell, as did Ensslin and Raspe. A fourth member, Irmgard Möller, attempted suicide but survived. Supporters of the group claimed the deaths, like that of Ulrike Meinhof several months earlier, were the result of extrajudicial executions. However, there is little evidence to support this allegation.

Further reading

Kellen, K., 'Ideology and Rebellion: Terrorism in West Germany' in Walter Reich (ed.) *Origins of Terrorism: Psychologies, Ideologies, Theologies, States of Mind.* Washington DC: Woodrow Wilson Center Press 1998, pp. 43–58.

Varon, J., *Bringing the War Home: The Weather Underground, the Red Army Faction, and Revolutionary Violence in the Sixties and Seventies.* Berkeley: The University of California Press 2004, pp. 196–289.

BAADER-MEINHOF GANG (Also: German Red Army Faction)
Defining itself as a 'communist urban guerrilla group', the Baader-Meinhof Gang (later called the Red Army Faction) was one of Germany's most violent post-war leftist organizations and operated from 1970 until 1993. Emerging out of a post-war German environment rich with anti-establishment intellectual foment, the Baader-Meinhof Gang was established in 1970 by Andreas Baader, his girlfriend Gudrun Ensslin, Horst Mahler, Irmgard Möller and several others.

The group eventually evolved into the German Red Army Faction (RAF). Contrary to popular opinion, Ulrike Meinhof's role in the group was always secondary to that of Baader, Ensslin, Mahler, Raspe and several others. Her name was appended to the group by media, mainly because of her existing profile as the editor-in-chief of the moderately influential left-wing magazine *konkret* and for the key role she played in helping Baader and others escape from prison in 1970. The group engaged in a series of violent acts, particularly bombings and kidnappings, and were responsible for thirty-four deaths. They also forged a temporary alliance with similar groups such as **Action Directe** in France. Along with other groups with a similar ideological orientation at this time, the Baader-Meinhof Gang also played a role in internationalizing terrorism. It had loose links to groups such as the **Japanese Red Army** and the **Popular Front for the Liberation of Palestine**.

Further reading

Merkl, P. H., 'West German Left-Wing Terrorism' in Martha Crenshaw (ed.) *Terrorism in Context*. University Park: The Pennsylvania State University Press, 2001 [1995], pp. 160–210.

Red Army Faction, *The Urban Guerrilla Concept* (pamphlet edition), Kersplebedeb, April 2005.

BABBAR KHALSA

Proscribed by: Canada, EU, UK

Babbar Khalsa is one of a number of Sikh organizations committed to the establishment of a separate Sikh homeland – Khalistan – in the Punjab region of India. Founded in 1978 after a number of Sikhs were killed in clashes with members of the Nirankari sect, it was most active in the 1980s when it was implicated in the murder of Nirankari leaders and in the 1985 bombing of Air India Flight 182 from Montreal to Mumbai. An offensive against Sikh militants launched by the Indian government in the early 1990s led to the capture and deaths of a number of senior Babbar Khalsa officials, after which the group's influence began to wane. Since then the group has been responsible for sporadic acts of terrorism, including the bombing of New Delhi cinemas in 2005. Like its contemporary, the **International Sikh Youth Federation**, Babbar Khalsa receives funding and support from the Sikh diaspora in Europe and North America.

Further reading
Major, A., 'From Moderates to Secessionists: A Who's Who of the Punjab Crisis' *Pacific Affairs* 60(1) 1987, pp. 42–58.
Razavy, M., 'Sikh Militant Movements in Canada' *Terrorism and Political Violence* 18(1) 2006, pp. 79–93.

BALI BOMBINGS

There have been two significant terrorist attacks on the popular Indonesian resort island of Bali. The first and most deadly occurred on 12 October 2002 when a series of bombs were detonated at different points on the island. While one of these bombings – a small device near the US consulate in the up-market area of Sanua – was probably meant as a diversion, two larger devices carried by suicide bombers were detonated in the popular tourist area of Kuta Beach. The first and smaller of the attacks occurred at Paddy's Bar. The second attack occurred when a mini-van packed with explosives detonated in the street outside the Sari Club near to Paddy's Bar. This second attack was almost certainly designed to maximize carnage by taking advantage of the chaos caused by the first bombing as people crowded into Kuta's narrow streets. In total, 202 people died from the blasts. Australia, with 88 dead, suffered the largest number of casualties. This was followed by Indonesia (38), Britain (24), the USA (7) and Germany (6). The remainder were from seventeen countries spread across five continents. The attacks initiated an extensive forensic investigation involving officials from Indonesia, Australia, the UK and the United States. The ensuing manhunt led to the arrest of more than thirty people, most of whom were linked to the group **Jemaah Islamiyah** and its spiritual leader Abu Bakar Bashir (also Abu Bakar Ba'asyir). Several weeks after the attacks, **Osama bin Laden** claimed they were in retaliation for the US **War on Terror** and for Australia's role in 'liberating' East Timor from Indonesia. Despite this claim, there is little evidence that **al Qaeda** played any role in the attack. In April 2003, Amrozi bin Haji Nurhasyim ('Amrozi') was the first person arrested when he was charged with buying the explosives and mini-van. This was followed soon after by the arrest of Mukhlas ('Ali Ghufron'), who was charged with chairing preparatory meetings, sanctioning the choice of targets and raising funds for the operation. In 1989 Mukhlas (Amrozi's older brother) had travelled to Pakistan and then to Afghanistan, admitting during trial that he had met Osama bin Laden, although he denied bin Laden was involved in the plot. A third person arrested was a computer expert, Imam Samudra, who was charged with being the ring-leader of the plot, of chairing planning meetings and sanctioning the choice of targets. Samudra proved especially adept at manipulating publicity after his arrest. In 2004, he published from prison a best-selling autobiography, 'I Fight Terrorists', in which he justified the attacks. In August 2003 an Indonesian court sentenced Amrozi, Mukhlas and Samudra to death by firing squad. After a series of failed appeals and threats of retribution by the accused and their supporters, they were eventually executed in November 2008. Others involved in the plot, notably Idris (born Jhoni Hendrawan) and Samudra and Amrozi's younger brother Ali Imron, were spared the death penalty and given life sentences after expressing remorse for their actions. The second terrorist attack occurred on 1 October 2005 when three suicide bombers struck at popular eating spots in Kuta and nearby Jimbaran, killing 20 and injuring around 130. The majority of the dead (15) were from Indonesia, mainly Hindu Balinese. Also killed were 4 Australians and 1 Japanese citizen. Although connections to Jemaah Islamiyah are less clear-cut than in the case of the first Bali bombings, Indonesian police are certain that the group was involved.

Further reading

Conboy, K., *Second Front: Inside Asia's Most Dangerous Terrorist Network*. Jakarta: Equinox Publishing, 2005.

International Crisis Group, *Indonesia Backgrounder: How The Jemaah Islamiyah Terrorist Network Operates* Asia Report No. 43. Jakarta and Brussels: International Crisis Group, 11 December 2002.

BALUCHISTAN LIBERATION ARMY

Proscribed by: Pakistan, UK

Formed around 2000 and made up of a collection of Baluchi tribes in an area stretching from eastern Pakistan to Afghanistan and Iran, the Baluchistan Liberation Army (BLA) has the stated goal of establishing an independent Baluchi state. Operating mainly from southern Afghanistan, the BLA has claimed responsibility for dozens of bombing and mortar attacks against infrastructure such as railroads, Pakistani military personnel and individuals suspected of spying for the government in Islamabad. According to the Pakistani government and some Western observers, the BLA receives covert funding from the Indian government.

Further reading

Bansal, A., 'Baluchistan: Continuing Violence and its Implications' *Strategic Analysis* 30(1) 2006, pp. 46–63.

Fair, C. and Chalk, P., 'United States Internal Security Assistance to Pakistan' *Small Wars and Insurgencies* 17(3) 2006, pp. 333–55.

BASQUE FATHERLAND AND LIBERTY
SEE: EUSKADI TA ASKATASUNA – ETA

BEHEADING

Although terrorists' use of beheading has recently been associated with groups acting in the name of Islam, the practice has a long pedigree in both Islamic and non-Islamic cultures. It has been a particularly prominent tool in the arsenal of state terrorism. For example, the apostle Paul was beheaded in Rome during the anti-Christian persecution by the emperor Nero, while, 1,500 years, later St Thomas More was beheaded when, as Lord Chancellor, he refused to sign the Act of Supremacy which would have made King Henry VIII the head of the Catholic church in Britain. And several hundred years later, during the French revolution, the neo-Jacobins used the guillotine to secure the more efficient – and publicly spectacular – execution of counter-revolutionary forces. This latter point on the dramatic power of beheading has been a constant throughout history. Whether used as an instrument of state or non-state terrorism, the act of beheading carries a powerful imagery that enhances the act's ability to influence or coerce the audience. In the contemporary context, unlike killing through bombing or shooting, where the potency of death can be anonymized by the carnage of a blast (in which it is usually difficult to distinguish human remains from structural detritus) or the immediacy of death by shooting, death by beheading can be a drawn-out and intensely personal event. Video-taped and broadcast over a multitude of uncensored websites, the beheading of the US journalist Daniel Pearl in February 2002, as well as other Americans, Turks, Bulgarians, a Nepalese, Korean and Egyptian and scores of Arabs, by **al Qaeda**-linked groups in Iraq almost inevitably included the victims' pleas for mercy as well as the traumatic vision and guttural sounds of death. There is nothing anonymous about the act of beheading, even though the murderers themselves might be hooded. For al Qaeda, the trauma of the act is widely believed to have been counter-productive in that it turned more people away from the organization than it inspired. Since the 2006 death of al Qaeda's former head in Iraq, **Abu Musab al-Zarqawi,** the incidence of beheading has waned.

Further reading
Lentini, P. and Bakashmar, M., 'Jihadist Beheading: A Convergence of Technology, Theology, and Teleology?' *Studies in Conflict and Terrorism* 30(4) 2007, pp. 303–25.

BEIRUT BOMBINGS

On 23 October 1983, near-simultaneous truck bombings occurred at the US and French marine barracks in the Lebanese capital of Beirut. A suicide bomber drove the first truck into the building that housed the US marines, killing 241 servicemen and 1 Lebanese civilian and injuring around 70 more. Several minutes later and 6 kilometres away, another explosives-laden truck was steered into the building that housed the 3rd Company of the 1st French Parachute Infantry Regiment, killing 58 French personnel and 4 Lebanese citizens. Several militant Shi'a groups claimed the attacks, which occurred amidst a violent civil war, although suspicion still falls upon **Hezbollah**, which at that stage was consolidating itself as a major military actor. Individuals associated with the group had charged that, rather than acting as an unbiased Multinational Peacekeeping Force, the US and French were in fact partisan participants in Lebanese politics. The USA, it was alleged, were assisting pro-Israeli forces while the French were cooperating with Maronite Christian groups. From the terrorists' perspective, the attacks were successful in that they presaged the eventual withdrawal of the US and French military presence from Lebanon. The attacks are also often held up as the first examples of mass casualty bombing as a terrorist tactic. For the USA, the attacks led to the largest loss of military personnel in a single day since the assault on Iwo Jima in 1944. For the French, the loss of personnel was the largest since the Algerian war of independence.

Further reading
Quillen, C., 'A Historical Analysis of Mass Casualty Bombers' *Studies in Conflict and Terrorism* 25(5) 2002, pp. 279–92.

BIN LADEN, OSAMA

Born in Jeddah in Saudi Arabia on 10 March 1957, Osama bin Laden emerged throughout the 1990s as synonymous with what scholars such as Bruce Hoffman have called '**new terrorism**'. His status as perhaps the most wanted person in the Western world was cemented by the **9/11** attacks, which were perpetrated by **al Qaeda** – the group that he ostensibly heads. Despite his high profile and symbolic power as both hero and evil incarnate – depending on the audience – bin Laden himself has seen very little direct terrorist action. His status has been built instead on his organizational prowess in forging the al Qaeda network and turning it into a group with a global presence. For his role in planning and authorizing the 9/11 attacks, the US government placed a US$25 million bounty on bin Laden.

He was born the seventeenth child of fifty-four fathered by Mohammed bin Laden, a Yemeni migrant who, by the time of his death in 1967, had built the largest construction corporation in Saudi Arabia. Bin Laden's mother, Alia Ghanem, a Syrian, was Mohammed bin Laden's tenth wife although the couple divorced soon after bin Laden was born. Like all of Mohammed bin Laden's children, Osama enjoyed a privileged upbringing, attending elite private schools before studying economics and business management at university. There are conflicting accounts as to whether bin Laden completed his studies, although it is clear that in 1979 he postponed a position in the family business and travelled instead to Afghanistan to join the Mujahedeen resistance against the Soviets. While in Afghanistan he used money from his substantial inheritance to help fund the resistance. It was also here that he was introduced to the influential Palestinian Islamist ideologue **Abdullah Azzam** and decided to commit his life to the Islamist cause. By 1984 bin Laden and Azzam had established Maktab al-Khidamat – the MAK (Afghan Services Bureau) – to recruit foreign volunteers and raise funds.

Bin Laden's reputation in resistance circles grew significantly, as did his connections with members of Saudi and Pakistani intelligence – both of which played a key role in assisting the anti-Soviet resistance. On 24 November 1989, Azzam was killed when unknown assailants bombed a car in which he was travelling. After Azzam's death, bin Laden became the head of the MAK, staying on in Afghanistan until Iraq's invasion of Kuwait drew him back to Saudi Arabia. While there he used his connections to the ruling family to offer the Afghan resistance army as a force for driving Saddam Hussein's army from Kuwait. Riyadh's rejection of his offer and the subsequent stationing of thousands of US and other Western military personnel in the country infuriated him. Critical of the ruling family, he was placed under house arrest and, in 1991, forced to leave the country, finding sanctuary in Sudan. While in Sudan he began to rebuild contacts with the Afghanistan network, deciding that a coordinated international campaign targeting Saudi and US interests was required to end the subjugation of Muslims to Western and apostate forces. Although attacks such as the first World Trade Center bombing in 1993 have been linked to individuals such as **Khalid Sheikh Mohammed** and **Ramzi Yousef**, who would eventually gravitate towards bin Laden's group, the first large-scale attack that drew the attention of international experts was a 1995 truck bombing at a US military base in Riyadh which killed five Americans and two Indians. The attack led the US and Saudi governments to pressure the Sudanese administration to expel bin Laden, and in 1996 he returned to Afghanistan with his three wives and ten children.

On his arrival in Afghanistan, bin Laden worked to establish a rapport with the ruling **Taliban** government, and, in return for recognizing their sovereignty and providing volunteers to assist the Taliban in the war against the Northern Alliance, Taliban leader Mullah Omar allowed bin Laden to establish a series of training camps which he used to consolidate his network and plan attacks. Later that year, bin Laden declared a holy war against the USA and its allies. The year 1988 was pivotal as not only did bin Laden oversee a merger with other resistance groups, such as the **Egyptian Islamic Jihad** headed by **Ayman al-Zawahiri**, and the subsequent formation of the **World Islamic Front for Combat against Jews and Crusaders**, but also he oversaw the first major al Qaeda attacks overseas in the form of the **East Africa embassy bombings**. It was, however, the attacks of 9/11 that earned bin Laden and his organization its infamy. Seven years after the US-led coalition invaded Afghanistan and toppled the Taliban, bin Laden's whereabouts remained unknown. Most analysts surmised that he was hiding at various locations in the mountainous borders between Pakistan and Afghanistan where he is assisted in his efforts to avoid capture by sympathetic elements of the Pakistani intelligence services. In the years immediately after the US-led invasion of Afghanistan, bin Laden released a series of video and audiotape messages. However, between 2004 and September 2007, video messages vanished and were replaced by occasional audiotape messages. The 2007 video shows bin Laden looking gaunt and tired, feeding speculation that he was ill and suffering from a life on the run in the inhospitable terrain of southern Afghanistan.

Further reading
Bergen, P., *The Osama bin Laden I Know: An Oral History of al Qaeda's Leader*. New York: The Free Press 2006.
Bin Laden, O., *Messages to the World: The Statements of Osama bin Laden* (trans. James Howarth). London: Verso 2005.
Ranstorp, M., 'Interpreting the Broader Context and Meaning of Bin-Laden's *Fatwa*' *Studies in Conflict and Terrorism* 21(4) 1998, pp. 321–30.

BLACK SEPTEMBER
Black September was formed in September 1970 in response to the expulsion of the **Palestinian Liberation Organization (PLO)** and several smaller Palestinian groups from Jordan. Reluctant to give up their bases in Jordan because of their proximity to targets in Israel, the PLO and allies such as the **Popular Front for the Liberation of Palestine** fought a vigorous resistance against efforts by Jordanian authorities to remove them. Approximately 3,000 Palestinians died during the conflict. Operating under a collective leadership that included high-profile resistance figures such as Salah Khalef (Abu Iyad), Mohammed Youssef (Abu Youssef), Abu Doaud and Ali Hassan Salameh (Abu Hassan), the group shot to notoriety with the murder of the Jordanian Prime Minister Wasfi al-Tel on 28 November 1971. But Black September's most notorious attack was the 1972 **Munich Olympic attack**, an assault on the Israeli athletes' compound in which eight Black September cadres killed two Israeli athletes and took another nine hostage. A botched rescue effort led to a fatal shoot-out at a nearby military airbase, in which the remainder of the Israeli hostages and several of the terrorists were killed. Israeli intelligence services then set about tracking down and assassinating those Black September members who eluded arrest or detention, under **Operation Wrath of God**. Despite the harm done to the Palestinian cause by the events in Munich, less than one year later the **Fatah** leadership used Black September members to attack Saudi Arabia's embassy in Sudan in an attempt to dissuade Arab states from commencing peace talks with Israel without a Palestinian presence. However, by the end of 1974 most Black September members had been re-absorbed into older Palestinian resistance groups and given new tasks and functions.

Further reading
Reeve, S., *One Day in September: The Full Story of the 1972 Munich Olympics Massacre and the Israeli Revenge Operation 'Wrath of God'*. New York: Arcade Publishing 2006 [2000].
Sayigh, Y., *Armed Struggle and the Search for the State: The Palestinian National Movement 1949–1993*. Oxford: Oxford University Press, 1997.

BLACK WIDOWS (Also: Black Widows Brigade)
The term 'Black Widows' is a media-generated appellation applied to a group formed in 2000, consisting mainly of Chechen women whose husbands had been killed in the war against Russia. Critics of the group argue that many of these women have been coerced into suicide attacks through the use of narcotics or various forms of violent intimidation. The most notorious of actions involving these women included the 2002 siege of the Dubrovka Theatre in Moscow when 41 Chechen terrorists, including 19 women, took over 700 patrons hostage. The terrorists and more than 100 of the patrons were killed during the Russian government's rescue attempt. In June 2000 a Black Widow suicide bomber drove a car laden with explosives into a Russian Special Forces building killing 27 personnel; on 5 July 2003 two female Chechen suicide bombers attacked a rock concert just outside Moscow, killing around 20 and injuring 40 more.

Further reading
Abdullaev, N., 'Unravelling Chechen "Black Widows"' *Journal of Homeland Security* 5(5) 2007, pp. 18–21.
Nivat, A., 'The Black Widows: Chechen Women Join the Fight for Independence – and Allah' *Studies in Conflict and Terrorism* 28(5) 2005, pp. 413–19.

BOOTH, JOHN WILKES
John Wilkes Booth (1838–65) was an actor and Confederate spy who assassinated American President Abraham Lincoln on 14 April 1865 at Ford's Theatre in Washington DC. Booth's original plan had been to kidnap Lincoln in an attempt to force the release of Confederate prisoners of war, but he changed his plans after becoming infuriated at a speech given by Lincoln in which the President promised to give black Americans the vote. Immediately after delivering the single fatal shot, Booth leapt from the balcony onto the stage and, turning to the audience, repeated a phrase first attributed to Marcus Brutus

on his assassination of Julius Caesar in 44 BC – *Sic semper tyrannis!*
('Thus always to tyrants!'). Despite breaking his leg in the fall to the
stage, Booth managed to escape from the theatre. He remained on
the run for twelve days but was eventually captured in a barn in
nearby Virginia. A short time later, he died from gunshot wounds
inflicted during his capture.

Further reading

Booth, J. W., *Right or Wrong, God Judge Me: The Writings of John Wilkes Booth*
(ed. John Rhodehamel and Louise Taper). Chicago: The University of
Illinois Press 2001 [1997].

Kauffman, M. W., *American Brutus: John Wilkes Booth and the Lincoln Con-
spiracies*. New York: Random House 2004.

BOUYERI, MOHAMMED

Mohammed Bouyeri was born in the Netherlands to Moroccan immigrant parents in 1978, and achieved notoriety when he murdered
Dutch filmmaker Theo van Gogh on 2 November 2004. A member
of **The Hofstad Group**, an extremist Islamist cell based in Amsterdam
and constituted almost exclusively by second-generation European
Muslims, Bouyeri stalked van Gogh on a bicycle before shooting him
and stabbing him repeatedly. At his trial in July 2005, Bouyeri claimed
he was motivated to avenge Islam after van Gogh had directed a
documentary critical of the treatment of Muslim women in the
Middle East and Southeast Asia. He was sentenced to life in prison.
Before drifting into extremist circles, Bouyeri had performed well at
junior school and, after graduation, enrolled in advanced courses in
accounting and information technology, but he eventually left college
without completing his degree. According to friends he became
increasingly militant in his views after **9/11**. The US-led invasion of
Iraq in 2003, followed by the death of his mother, and his father's
remarriage, seems to have accelerated his progression towards violent
extremism. This militancy further intensified after he began attending a mosque frequented by other extremists later convicted on
terrorism-related charges.

Further reading

Vidino, L., 'The Hofstad Group: The New Face of Terrorist Networks in
Europe' *Studies in Conflict and Terrorism* 30(7) 2007, pp. 579–92.

BRAY, MICHAEL

A former midshipman at the US naval academy and a fundamentalist Christian who believes in the inerrancy of the Bible, Michael Bray is noted for his support of, and alleged involvement in, the murders of doctors involved in performing abortions. In 1985 he was arrested and convicted on two counts of conspiracy and one count of being in possession of explosives. It was believed that he planned to join with fellow Christian fundamentalists to bomb women's health clinics and women's welfare centres in Maryland, Virginia and Washington DC. He was given a four-year sentence, reduced from ten years, after a plea bargain. On his release from prison he remained a vocal supporter of extremist Christian positions, notably violent anti-abortion groups. He became a high-profile spokesman in support of Paul Hill, a pastor convicted of murdering doctors linked to abortion clinics who was executed in Florida in 2003. He also claims to be a minister in the shadowy **Army of God**. In a television interview in the late 1990s he stated that any person proven in a court of law to have committed adulterous or homosexual acts should be sentenced to death.

Further reading

Bray, M., *Time to Kill: A Study Concerning the Use of Force and Abortion.* Portland: Advocates for Life Publications.

Mason, C., 'From Protest to Retribution: The Guerrilla Politics of Pro-Life Violence' *New Political Science* 22(1) 2000, pp. 11–29.

CANADIAN SECURITY INTELLIGENCE SERVICE (CSIS)

Formerly a part of the Royal Canadian Mounted Police, the CSIS was established as a separate agency in June 1984. Barely a year later, it was pressed into action on the terrorism front when Canadian-based Sikh militants bombed an Air India flight soon after it had left Montreal, with the loss of 329 lives. The CSIS is responsible for protecting Canada's national security by countering threats both at home and abroad. Unlike many of its Western counterparts, Canada lacks a dedicated external foreign intelligence agency, hence the CSIS plays a key role in identifying threats and analysing threat trends. Reflecting the politically sensitive nature of domestic intelligence collection in Canada, particularly in light of historical tensions between the English and French portions of the community, the CSIS is subjected to high levels of review. The organization comes under the auspices of the Minister for Public Safety and is subject to review by the parliamentary Security Intelligence Review Committee and by the Federal Court of Canada, as well as several other bodies. On terrorism-related issues it cooperates closely with the counter-terrorism section of the Royal Canadian Mounted Police, focusing in particular on the activities of international terrorist groups seeking to use Canadian territory to launch attacks against the USA, but also on domestic terrorist groups involved in issues ranging from secessionism to anti-globalization, anti-abortion violence and animal rights.

Further reading
Chalk, P. and Rosenau, W., *Confronting 'the Enemy Within': Security Intelligence, the Police, and Counterterrorism in Four Democracies*. Santa Monica: Rand Corporation 2004.

CAR BOMB

Terrorism has always been a dynamic phenomenon in that, throughout history, terrorists have shown a remarkable ability to adapt their tactics to shifting technologies and social habits. This is especially evident in the evolution of the car bomb in the final decades of the twentieth century. By combining developments in explosives technology with modern society's dependence on the automobile, by the latter part of the century terrorist groups around the world had evolved a highly effective way of carrying out their attacks. The preferred method is to place the explosive device inside or under the car and detonate it via remote control or a timing device. Alternatively, the explosives can be wired to the automobile's electrical system so that the vehicle is detonated on ignition. This latter technique has been especially popular as a mode of targeted assassination. More recently, an extra dimension has been added through the use of suicide bombings whereby the terrorist(s) manoeuvre the vehicle into the preferred site, usually that calculated to cause maximum damage to property and/or lives.

Further reading
Davis, M., *Buda's Wagon: A Brief History of the Car Bomb*. London: Verso 2008.

CARLOS THE JACKAL
SEE: RAMÍREZ SÁNCHEZ, ILYICH

CELLS

Throughout history, most terrorist groups have organized their members into small self-contained units known as 'cells'. This practice serves several important functions. At an administrative level, the splitting of the group into cells allows the hierarchy to develop an effective division of labour whereby certain cells are tasked with specific functions such as assassinations, the procurement of weapons, or recruitment. This allows for the more efficient use of scarce resources and an effective use of the particular skills of different members. At an operational level the use of cells allows the hierarchy to expand operations across a wider geographic area. Finally, at the level of security, the existence of self-contained cells with members who do not know members of other cells reduces the risk that the capture of one cell will compromise the entire terrorist network. Cells can be structured through a number of networking configurations: a chain-based cell structure, for example, involves a hirerachy of cells stretching from the apex of the group down to functionaries whose role might be as simple as acting as look-outs for police. This kind of network is highly vulnerable to penetration and disruption because of the clear chain of command. Star or hub-based cell networks involve a series of autonomous cells that branch off the centre like the spokes on a wheel. While this structrure can protect the integrity of the terrorist network because one cell does not have contact with other members and therefore has no information that can be garnered through interrogation by counter-terrorism authorities, proximity to the centre raises the risk that penetration will lead quickly to those in command. Finally, all-channel networks involve a dispersal of the powers of the hierarchy across a network of disconnected cells united mainly by shared ideologies and coordinated by individuals whose links to the cell itself are kept at a distance. More recently, the significance of cell-based networks has diminished in the face of self-starter terrorist groups with no clear leadership or network base. These cells are constituted mainly by individuals who are radicalized through informal networks and who use skills culled from the accoutrements of late modernity – such as the Internet – to communicate with like-minded individuals in a relatively anonymous fashion.

Further reading

Sageman, M., *Leaderless Jihad: Terror Networks in the Twenty-First Century.* Philadelphia: University of Pennsylvania Press 2008.

Zanini, M. and Edwards, S. J. A., 'The Networking of Terror in the Information Age' in John Arquilla and David Ronfeldt (eds.) *Networks and Netwars: The Future of Terror, Crime, and Militancy.* Santa Monica: Rand 2002, pp. 29–60.

CENTRAL DIRECTORATE OF INTERIOR INTELLIGENCE (Direction centrale du renseignement intérieur (DCRI))

The DCRI is a French intelligence agency established by a July 2008 merger between the National Police's Direction de la surveillance du territoire and the Direction centrale des renseignements généraux. The DCRI's principal functions include counter-terrorism, counter-espionage and the protection of infrastructure from cybercrime. Comprised of both intelligence analysts and collectors, the DCRI undertakes surveillance of potentially dangerous individuals and groups within France. It falls under the ambit of the Ministry of the Interior.

Further reading

Bloch, L., 'Evaluating the Effectiveness of French Counter-Terrorism' *Jamestown Foundation Terrorism Analysis* 3(17) 2005. Available at www.jamestown.org/programs/gta/single/?tx_ttnews%5Btt_news%5D= S60&tx_ttnews%5BbackPid%5D=180&no_cache=1 (accessed 4 April 2007).

CENTRAL INTELLIGENCE AGENCY

Established initially in 1942 and called the Office of Strategic Services, the CIA is the USA's principal agency for the collection and analysis of intelligence relating to threats to American security from foreign sources. By definition, for it to carry out these functions, 'the Agency', as it is referred to colloquially, works in conjunction with other US institutions such as the **Federal Bureau of Investigation**

(FBI), the National Security Agency (NSA) and the US Department of Defense. However, relationships between the CIA and other organizations charged with intelligence tasks, such as the FBI and NSA, have not always been cooperative. This is especially so in the case of counter-terrorism where political interference, inter-service rivalries and demarcation disputes have sometimes undermined efficiency. The CIA also has a number of partner agreements with similar foreign organizations, sometimes engaging in joint intelligence collection and analytical operations but also sharing some of its intelligence with partner countries. A Director who is appointed by the President, but who also needs to be ratified by the Senate, heads the CIA. The organization is divided into four main departments: the Directorate of Operations (DO), which is responsible for the covert collection of intelligence on foreign targets; the Directorate of Intelligence, which is responsible for synthesizing the intelligence collected by the DO and other sources, and for the production of analytical reports which help shape US foreign and military policy; the Directorate of Science and Technology (DST), which carries out research into, and development of, technologies designed to help field officers; and, finally, the Directorate of Support. Smaller offices within the organization are charged with carrying out paramilitary operations, public affairs, human resources, the development of innovative ways of carrying out collection missions, relations with Congress and internal auditing. The events of 9/11 initiated a storm of criticism of US intelligence services and their failure to intercept the threat by the nineteen terrorists. Following an extensive inquiry, President George W. Bush signed the Intelligence Reform and Terrorism Prevention Act, which initiated the most significant shake-up of the US intelligence community since 1947. The positions of Director of Central Intelligence (DCI) and Deputy Director of Central Intelligence (DDCI) were scrapped and replaced by the position of Director of the Central Intelligence Agency (D/CIA), and an oversight position was created, in the form of the office of the Director of National Intelligence (DNI), which has a mandate to oversee the operations of the US intelligence community.

Further reading

Risen, J., *State of War: The Secret History of the CIA and the Bush Administration*. New York: The Free Press 2006.

Weiner, T., *Legacy of Ashes: The History of the CIA*. New York: Doubleday 2007.

CHRISTIAN IDENTITY MOVEMENT

A US-based network, the Christian Identity Movement (CIM) is a loose-knit collection of highly conservative Protestant groups and extreme right-wing political organizations united by several common themes: a belief in the innate supremacy of the white races (sometimes arguing that non-whites do not have souls and referring to them as 'the mud races'), anti-Semitism (in some cases anti-Catholicism), and a virulent hostility towards homosexuality. Among its more prominent groups is the Ku Klux Klan. According to some estimates, the movement includes around 50,000 active members. Most groups associated with the movement promote violent ideologies even though they are not actively involved in terrorist violence themselves, preferring instead to wait for Armageddon, when they believe that God will destroy impure groups. However, there are cases where individuals associated with the beliefs of the CIM have been involved in domestic terrorism within the USA. In 1984 a white nationalist group known as 'The Order', inspired by a novel written by the White Supremacist leader William Pierce, entitled *The Turner Diaries*, and believing that the US government was controlled by an anonymous group of Jewish financiers, drew up a hit list of prominent US Jews. On 18 June 1984, their first victim was Alan Berg, a prominent liberal radio talk-back host who was gunned down in the driveway of his home. The CIM was also implicated in the Ruby Ridge shoot-out between US federal agents and an ultra-right-wing Christian fundamentalist, former Green Beret Randy Weaver, and his family.

Further reading
Barkun, M., *Religion and the Racist Right: The Origins of the Christian Identity Movement*. Chapel Hill: The University of North Carolina Press, 1994.

COALITION OF THE WILLING

The term 'Coalition of the Willing' was popularized in the 1990s when it was usually appended to collections of states intervening militarily in other countries on humanitarian or strategic grounds. It achieved particular prominence in the case of the Australian-led UN peacekeeping action in East Timor in 1999–2000 and, more controversially, in reference to the small coalition of states that participated in the 2003 US-led invasion of Iraq. It was in this later case that the term first assumed its counter-terrorism connotations when the US Administration of President George W. Bush sought to justify the invasion, which was not sanctioned by the United Nations, on the grounds that it was necessary to prevent the Iraqi regime of Saddam Hussein passing weapons of mass destruction to terrorist groups. It was later proven that the Iraqi regime had disposed of such weapons in the mid-1990s.

Further reading
Newnham, R., 'Coalition of the Bribed and Bullied? U.S. Economic Linkage and the Iraq War Coalition' *International Studies Perspectives* 9(2) 2008, pp. 183–200.

COERCIVE INTERROGATION

A term that became synonymous with the counter-terrorism approach adopted by the Bush Administration in the years following the attacks of 9/11, the phrase 'coercive interrogation' was a rhetorical device used to refer to interrogation techniques that would have once been classified as approximating torture. Based on the premise that terrorists were motivated by a zealotry that could not be handled through conventional interrogative or legal means, and believing that another terrorist attack might be imminent, US authorities utilized a range of extra-judicial techniques designed to weaken a terrorist suspect's resolve and produce a willingness to cooperate. The main objectives were to force suspects to confess their status and reveal any knowledge about other terrorist activity. However, the Administration was aware of the dubious legality of such practices and ensured that coercive interrogation was not carried out within areas under US criminal or civil jurisdiction but was confined to special military prisons, such as Camp X-Ray at Guantánamo Bay on a US-controlled portion of the island of Cuba, at Abu Ghraib in Iraq, Bagram airbase in Afghanistan, or on the island of Diego Garcia in the Indian Ocean. Perhaps the most notorious of these practices was 'water boarding', whereby a prisoner was strapped to a board, his/her head lowered to below the level of their feet, cellophane wrapped over the face and then water poured over the head. The practice almost immediately induces the gag reflex, as the prisoner believes he/she is drowning. US media reports based on interviews with **Central Intelligence Agency** (CIA) officers suggested the average time a person took before offering to 'confess' was 14 seconds. Other coercive interrogation techniques included withholding of sleep and other forms of sensory deprivation, and mock executions. The ethical dimensions of these practices notwithstanding, there exists widespread doubt even in intelligence circles about their effectiveness. It is felt by many that they solicit false or misleading information as the accused will say anything to end the suffering. It is also counter-productive in terms of the large numbers of innocent people subjected to these practices (including reports of accidental deaths), a phenomenon used by terrorist recruiters as evidence of the malevolence of the USA and its allies towards ordinary people. In cases where US officials felt that coercive interrogation would be insufficient, suspects were transported to countries that practise more conventional forms of torture, in a practice known as 'rendering'. Officials from these countries would torture the suspects and pass on any information gathered to the US or allied authorities.

Further reading
Bellamy, A. J., 'Dirty Hands and Lesser Evils in the War on Terror' *The British Journal of Politics and International Relations* 9(3) 2007, pp. 509–26.
Saul, B., 'Torturing Terrorists after September 11' *International Journal of Law and Psychiatry* 27(6) 2004, pp. 645–70.

COMMUNIST PARTY OF NEPAL (MAOIST)

The Communist Party of Nepal (Maoist) (CPN-M) has moved from being a group designated by many countries as 'terrorist' in the 1990s to becoming the single largest group in the elected Constituent Assembly in Nepal. Its leader, Prachanda (born Pushpa Kumal Dahal), was sworn in as the country's first democratic Prime Minister in August 2008. The CPN-M's transition from a designated terrorist organization to an active participant in parliamentary democracy came after a decade-long insurgency in which more than 13,000 Nepalese were killed. Prachanda (which literally means 'the fierce one') launched the insurgency ('the Nepalese People's War') in 1996 following a split within the Communist Party of Nepal (Unity). From early on, the CPN-M built a formidable support base among rural folk, and from 1996 to 2005 it controlled large swathes of the countryside in the west and east of the country, focusing its attacks on soldiers, police, local officials and the rural elite. A large part of its support rested on the group's ability to tap into deep anger and growing resentment among the poor towards the established hierarchy headed by Nepal's royal family. Its key objectives were to end the privileges enjoyed by the country's hereditary elite and to establish a Maoist state model adapted for 'Nepalese conditions'. At its height in the early 2000s, the group boasted around 30,000 armed combatants. As well as having bases in Nepal itself, the CPN-M also operated several outposts in India. By the early 2000s the insurgency had reached a stalemate and the CPN-M changed tactics, seeking an alliance with mainstream parties opposed to the leadership of King Gyanendra. In the face of growing public unrest in 2006, the monarchy agreed to a timetable for its dismantling. At parliamentary elections in early 2008, the CPN-M won 229 seats in the 601-seat assembly. Prachanda was sworn in as Prime Minister on 18 August 2008.

Further reading
Deraniyagala, S., 'The Political Economy of Civil Conflict in Nepal' *Oxford Development Studies* 33(1) 2005, pp. 47–62.
Sharma, K., 'The Political Economy of Civil War in Nepal' *World Development* 34(7) 2006, pp. 1237–53.

COMMUNIST PARTY OF THE PHILIPPINES
SEE: NEW PEOPLE'S ARMY

COMMUNITY OF SUPPORT

An often-overlooked aspect of terrorism is that, underpinning the violence, is a core constituency that the terrorists consider their 'in-group'. More precisely, terrorists believe that their 'in-group', or 'their community', is on the defence and at risk of subjugation or annihilation by a larger and more powerful 'out-group'. Historically speaking, it has been rare that the terrorists' perception of oppression is as widely shared as they imagine. However, it is also the case that without a modicum of public support it is unlikely that the ideologies and socio-psychological drivers towards terrorism will occur. In this sense, the 'community of support' refers to that group of individuals who share the terrorists' worldview and who offer both the material and spiritual support required to sustain the struggle. Materially, this community supplies the recruits, money and other materials (such as safe-houses and street-level intelligence) required to sustain a sophisticated terrorist campaign. At the spiritual level, this community provides the emotional support that helps maintain the terrorists' belief that what they are doing is right. Maintaining the cohesion of the community of support can be one of the most difficult tasks confronting the terrorists. In particular, a miscalculated use of violence can alienate supporters and turn them against the group, robbing them of their moral authority. Conversely, poorly calibrated counter-terrorism tactics used by the state, especially when they have a brutalizing effect on that segment of the population that the terrorists seek to appeal to, can grow the community of support and thereby enhance the resilience of the terrorists.

Further reading
Horgan, J., *The Psychology of Terrorism*. London and New York: Routledge 2005.

CONTINUITY IRISH REPUBLICAN ARMY
Proscribed by: EU, Republic of Ireland, UK, USA
The Continuity IRA (CIRA) was formed in 1986 after a small hardline faction led by the Commandant General of the **Irish Republican Amy's** Western Command, Tom Maguire (d. 1993), broke away from the Provisional IRA (see **Irish Republican Amy (Provisional)**) after a debate over the policy of abstentionism, a practice whereby Sinn Fein members elected to the *Oireachtas* (Houses of Parliament of the Republic of Ireland) were prohibited from taking their seats. Members of the CIRA opposed the abolition of the policy of abstentionism and walked out in protest. Exact estimates of the size of the group proved difficult to establish, with UK authorities estimating up to 200 members, Republic of Ireland authorities suggesting no more than 150, and US authorities calculating it never had more than 50. The group's modus operandi consisted mainly of small-scale bombings and targeted assassinations of British and Unionist figures. The group remained anonymous and refused to acknowledge its existence openly until January 1994. The identity of the group's current chief of staff is not widely known. The CIRA publicly condemned the Provisional IRA's 2005 decision to decommission its weapons as an act of surrender.

Further reading
Bowyer Bell, J., *Secret Army: The IRA* (3rd edn). Edison NJ: Transaction Publishers 1997.
Tonge, J., ' "They Haven't Gone Away You Know". Irish Republican "Dissidents" and "Armed Struggle" ' *Terrorism and Political Violence* 16(3) 2004, pp. 671–93.

CONVENTION ON THE PREVENTION AND PUNISHMENT OF CRIMES AGAINST INTERNATIONALLY PROTECTED PERSONS, INCLUDING DIPLOMATIC AGENTS

Worried about a rise of terrorist violence against political and diplomatic targets in the early 1970s, the United Nations moved to establish an international convention that would oblige states to take all steps necessary to protect political and diplomatic officials from murder, kidnapping or any other forms of violence, regardless of the location in which such an act might occur. The Convention, which entered into force on 20 February 1977, defines 'internationally protected persons' as heads of states, ministers of foreign affairs and representatives or officials of a state or international organization, as well as the families of such people. The Convention criminalized acts against such individuals and obliged member states to impose penalties that 'take into account their grave nature'.

Further reading
Shamwell, H. F., 'Implementing the Convention on the Prevention and Punishment of Crimes against Internationally Protected Persons, Including Diplomatic Agents' *Studies in Conflict and Terrorism* 6(4) 1983, pp. 529–43.
Wood, M. C., 'The Convention on the Prevention and Punishment of Crimes against Internationally Protected Persons, Including Diplomatic Agents' *International and Comparative Law Quarterly* 23(4) 1974, pp. 791–817.

COUNCIL OF EUROPE CONVENTION ON THE PREVENTION OF TERRORISM

Declared in 2006, the Council of Europe Convention on the Prevention of Terrorism (CECPT) was a response to the changed social and political environment ushered in by the 9/11 attacks and, more importantly, the train bombings in Madrid on 11 March 2003 and the London bombings on 7 July 2005. Building on previous agreements, such as the European Convention on the Suppression of Terrorism (1977), the new document adds three new terrorism-related offences: Public Provocation to Commit a Terrorist Offence, Solicitation of Persons to Commit Terrorist Offences, and the Provision of Training for Terrorist Offences. Under the terms of the Convention, signatory states are obliged to encode these new offences within their national legal systems. In defining a 'terrorist offence', the Convention is ambiguous, referring instead to acts listed under existing international conventions on terrorism.

Further reading
Hunt, A., 'The Council of Europe Convention on the Prevention of Terrorism' *European Public Law* 12(4) 2006.

COUNTER-TERRORISM

The challenge posed by terrorism takes on many forms and, to meet these challenges, governments have developed an array of policies and strategies that are referred to collectively under the term 'counter-terrorism'. There is no accepted template for countering the threat posed by terrorism – a conundrum that is rooted deeply in the ambiguous and often invisible nature of the terrorist threat itself. Also, the social, political, historical and cultural circumstances that shape terrorist dynamics in one society are often different from those at work in another, even if, outwardly, two groups espouse similar goals and employ the same tactics. Finally, at the core of every counter-terrorism policy-making process, especially in democracies, is the degree to which the struggle against terrorism should be allowed to compromise human rights and political freedoms. At their best, counter-terrorism strategies have proven most effective when they address the underlying conditions conducive to the spread of the ideologies that sustain terrorism and which facilitate the growth of the **community of support** without which the terrorists would struggle to survive. At worst, counter-terrorism strategies can exacerbate the terrorist threat by deepening the socially and politically enabling conditions that encourage individuals' embrace of violence. This is true at both the domestic and international policy levels. At the domestic level, the deleterious consequences of poorly designed and implemented counter-terrorism policies were demonstrated by events in Northern Ireland at the outset of 'The Troubles' in the early 1970s, when new counter-terrorism measures conferred upon the Royal Ulster Constabulary and British army greater powers to arrest, detain and interrogate suspected supporters of the **Irish Republican Army (IRA)**. An injudicious use of these powers worked to alienate many in the nationalist (predominantly Catholic) community and to drive them closer towards the IRA. Similar criticisms have been made of the counter-terrorism policies of many Western governments in the wake of the **9/11** attacks, when a series of legislative initiatives, such as the **USA PATRIOT Act**, enhanced the capacity of the police and other security agencies to intrude into the lives of ordinary citizens in the cause of detecting terrorist activity at an early stage. Applied mainly against Muslim diasporas, many of these measures have had an alienating effect, driving a wedge between Muslim and non-Muslim communities and creating an environment more conducive to the spread of radical ideologies. Alternatively, counter-terrorism measures designed to address feelings of alienation and anger and build community resilience have generally proven to be more effective in shrinking the terrorists' community of support and rendering their operations more problematic. At the international level, counter-terrorism initiatives have often been transnational in nature, principally through a series of **multilateral counter-terrorism conventions**, but also through an expanding network of bilateral counter-terrorism agreements involving such initiatives as the sharing of intelligence and joint training and counter-terrorism operations.

Further reading
Donohue, L. K., *The Cost of Counterterrorism: Power, Politics, and Liberty.* Cambridge: Cambridge University Press 2008.
Duyvesteyn, I., 'Great Expectations: The Use of Armed Force to Combat Terrorism' *Small Wars and Insurgencies* 19(3) 2008, pp. 328–51.

CYBER-TERRORISM

Just as there is no universally agreed-upon definition of terrorism, so too there is a lack of consensus over the term 'cyber-terrorism'. Similarly, there is also a vibrant debate over the extent to which cyber-terrorism constitutes an extant risk, or whether under present conditions it is largely a figment of the imaginations of conspiracy theorists. Those who adhere to the latter view argue that there exist no concrete examples of cyber-attacks by terrorists, and that those that are often reported as such should more accurately be described as simply attacks by computer hackers. Those who adhere to this view tend to adopt a thin definition of cyber-terrorism, defining it as the use of technology by recognized terrorist groups to interrupt critical information systems (such as those regulating air traffic control, communication and energy supplies) with a view to causing mass disruption and public panic. A thicker definition of cyber-terrorism defines it as deliberate use of information technologies with a view to causing panic, disruption or even death, in the name of a political objective. According to this definition, even though terrorists might not have launched a successful cyber-attack to date, there is evidence that several groups, including those linked to **al Qaeda**, are attempting to develop the ability to do so, and therefore in the future cyber-terrorism could pose a major threat to societies.

Further reading

Goodman, S. E., Kirk, J. C. and Kirk, M. H., 'Cyberspace as a Medium for Terrorists' *Technological Forecasting and Social Change* 74(2) 2007, pp. 193–210.

Weimann, G., *Terror on the Internet: The New Arena, the New Challenges*. New York: United States Institute of Peace 2006.

CZOLGOSZ, LEON

The assassin of William McKinley, the twenty-fifth President of the USA, Leon Czolgosz (b. 1873) was one of seven children of Polish migrants. When he was five, the family moved to Detroit, and at sixteen he started working in a glass factory. After two years he returned to Michigan where he socialized very little and immersed himself in Anarchist literature. The Lithuanian-born radical Emma Goldman, who in 1901 introduced him to a wider circle of American Anarchists, had a particularly strong influence over the development of his politics. Czolgosz was convinced that the USA had become irreparably inequitable and that there was little option for the poor to improve themselves except by taking matters into their own hands. The assassination occurred on 26 September 1901 when Czolgosz secreted himself in a crowd of well-wishers waiting to shake the President's hand in Buffalo New York. As McKinley reached Czolgosz, the latter reached out and fired two shots. After a trial lasting less than a day, he was sentenced to die by the electric chair.

His final statement before his death was, 'I killed the President because he was the enemy of the good people – the good working people. I am not sorry for my crime.' An autopsy performed on Czolgosz's brain after his execution led to a series of articles, including by one of the lead psychiatrists, Dr Carlos F. MacDonald, who interviewed Czolgosz prior to his execution and was present at the autopsy after his death, which provided an early example of the debate over the alleged insanity of terrorists. From the point of view of MacDonald and others, Czolgosz demonstrated no signs of mental impairment.

Further reading

MacDonald, C. F., 'The Trial, Execution, Autopsy and Mental Status of Leon Czolgosz, Alias Fred Nieman, The Assassin of President McKinley' *The American Journal of Insanity* 58(3) 1902, pp. 369–86. (Journal subsequently renamed *American Journal of Psychiatry*.)

Vials, C., 'The Despotism of the Popular: Anarchy and Leon Czolgosz at the Turn of the Century' *Americana: The Journal of American Popular Culture 1990 to the Present* 3(2) 2004. Available at www.americanpopularculture.com/journal/articles/fall_2004/vials.htm (accessed 2 November 2006).

DECOLONIZATION

For most historians of international affairs, the decades immediately after the Second World War are defined in terms of the Cold War and the role played by US–Soviet rivalry in shaping anti-colonial movements. Proxy wars were fought between the USA, China and Russia in areas stretching from Africa through Southeast Asia to South America. The catalyst for most of these conflicts was the postwar rise of anti-colonial movements and the corresponding push for independence by countries that for several centuries had been dominated by Western powers. Less well studied is the role that terrorism played in shaping the directions and outcomes of these wars. Indeed, pitted against the technologically and financially superior Western militaries, terrorism loomed as a 'weapon of the weak', and was used by, among many others, independence movements such as Israel's **Stern Gang**, the **Palestinian Liberation Organization**, the **Irish Republican Army** (in its various manifestations), **Umkhonto we Sizwe** (the military wing of the **African National Congress**) and the **Moro National Liberation Front** in the Philippines. One of the most thoroughly documented terrorist campaigns in the name of national liberation was that conducted by Algeria's **National Liberation Front** (Front de Libération Nationale – FLN). An active supporter of the FLN cause was the psychiatrist Frantz Fanon, whose books *The Wretched of the Earth* and *A Dying Colonialism* valorized the use of terrorism as remasculating the colonized, as recovering their humanity after centuries of subjugation. Fanon's ideals became a leitmotif for the anti-colonial movement and also attracted support from prominent Western thinkers such as Jean-Paul Sartre. Importantly, most anti-colonial terrorism during this period, which lasted until the 1980s, was underpinned by secular ideals, particularly nationalism and socialism. The role of religion as a rallying point for anti-colonial terrorism, epitomized by groups such as **Hamas** and even **al Qaeda** (which grounds its anti-colonial credentials in its rhetorical opposition to neo-imperialism), grew in prominence following the 1979 revolution in Iran which toppled the secular US-backed regime and established an Islamic state that subsequently sponsored groups such as **Hezbollah**.

Further reading
Burleigh, M., *Blood and Rage: A Cultural History of Terrorism*. London: Harper Press, 2008.
Fanon, F., *The Wretched of the Earth*. New York: Grove Press, 2005 [1961].

DEFENCE INTELLIGENCE STAFF (DIS)
The Defence Intelligence Staff has two prime objectives; to provide intelligence assessments of issues that bear on UK security to senior members of the UK policy apparatus and other relevant government departments and, secondly, to provide analyses that support UK combat operations. Its work informs decisions on the generation and maintenance of operational military capability and it contributes to wider national intelligence collection and assessment efforts regarding conventional and non-conventional military threats (such as terrorism) to the UK. Like the **Defense Intelligence Agency** in the USA, the DIS also maintains a network of liaison officers in partner countries, but particularly those in NATO as well as Australia and Japan, and in countries of wider strategic interest to the UK. In terms of counter-terrorism, the DIS plays an important role in providing analyses of the threat posed to UK military personnel in combat zones,

but also in areas such as weapons procurement and shifts in the tactical profile of different terrorist groups.

Further reading
Andrew, C. M., *Secret Service: The Making of the British Intelligence Community*. London: Heinemann, 1985.
Richelson, J. T., *Foreign Intelligence Organizations*. Cambridge, Mass.: Ballinger Publishing Company, 1988.

DEFENSE INTELLIGENCE AGENCY (DIA)

As a part of the US Department of Defense, the Defense Intelligence Agency (DIA) is charged with providing support to combat units as well as other senior defence and national security officials. It has a particular focus on providing analysis of changes in the economic, political and social dynamics of different countries and how these factors might contribute to the military capabilities of potential adversaries. The DIA's 'product' therefore plays an important role in helping policy planners in developing new technologies to combat emerging threats. In the field of counter-terrorism, the DIA collects and analyses intelligence in areas such as the potential proliferation of high-tech weaponry to terrorist organizations, how emerging terrorist tactics might impact on the safety and capabilities of US combat forces in areas such as Iraq and Afghanistan, information warfare and the counter-terrorism utility of new technologies such as unmanned aerial drones.

Further reading
Odom, W. E., *Fixing Intelligence for a More Secure America*. New Haven: Yale University Press, 2003.
Richelson, J. T., *The US Intelligence Community*. Boulder: Westview Press, 2007.

DEMOCRACY

The subject of the relationship between terrorism and democracy remains one of the enduring debates within the field of terrorism studies. On one hand, quantitative research by respected scholars such as Eubank and Weinberg suggests that democratic societies tend to experience higher rates of terrorist violence, partly because the fluidity of government structures renders them, in the mind of the would-be terrorist, more responsive to violent intimidation. Importantly, Eubank and Weinberg do not argue that this positive causal relationship should provide the basis for a reduction in civil rights or a retreat towards a more authoritarian form of politics, which is a view put forward by some conservative voices. Rather, the argument is used to call for a set of counter-terrorism protocols calibrated to be consistent with core democratic values. An opposing point of view presents a nuanced version of this argument by suggesting that it is fragile democratic states, rather than robust democracies such as the United States, that are more vulnerable to terrorism. Against both these views is the argument that, because it offers multiple avenues for the peaceful expression of dissent, democracy is better able to dissipate feelings of political impotence that are an essential ingredient in the development of terrorist ideologies. Complicating the debate over the relationship between democracy and terrorism is the process of globalization, which has allowed terrorism to migrate beyond national borders, so that anger with repressive conditions in one country can erupt as terrorism in another democratic country.

Further reading

Art, R. J. and Richardson, L. (eds.), *Democracy and Counterterrorism: Lessons from the Past*. Washington, DC: United States Institute of Peace Press, 2007.

Weinberg, L. B., Eubank, W. L. and Francis, E. A., 'The Cost of Terrorism: The Relationship between International Terrorism and Democratic Governance' *Terrorism and Political Violence* 20(2) 2008, pp. 257–70.

Wilkinson, P., *Terrorism versus Democracy: The Liberal State Response*. Abingdon: Routledge, 2006.

DEPARTMENT OF HOMELAND SECURITY (US)

One of the most significant consequences for the US bureaucracy following from the 9/11 attacks was a June 2002 decision by the Administration of President George W. Bush to merge a number of hitherto independent government agencies into a single Department of Homeland Security. Congress approved the proposal in November 2002, formally combining over twenty bodies, such as the US Coast Guard, Border Patrol Service, the Transportation Security

Administration, the US Immigration and Naturalization Service, the Secret Service and the Federal Emergency Management Agency, into a single Cabinet-level department. The *raison d'état* behind the decision was a desire to coordinate better domestic defence against terrorist threats and natural disasters. The Department consists of four divisions: (1) border and transportation security; (2) emergency preparedness and response; (3) chemical, biological, radiological and nuclear countermeasures; (4) information analysis and infrastructure protection. It has over 200,000 staff, making it the third-largest department within the US bureaucracy, after the Department of Defense and Department of Veterans' Affairs. For critics, however, the scale and size of the Department militates against efficiency and, after the administrative debacle surrounding the Department's response to Hurricane Katrina in 2005, there have been growing calls for a re-disaggregation of its functions.

Further reading
Kettl, D. F., *System under Stress: Homeland Security and American Politics* (2nd edn). Washington, DC: CQ Press, 2007.
Studeman, M. W., 'Strengthening the Shield: U.S. Homeland Security Intelligence' *International Journal of Intelligence and Counterintelligence* 20(2) 2007, pp. 195–216.

DHANU
SEE: RAJARATNAM, THENMULI

DIRECTORATE-GENERAL FOR EXTERNAL SECURITY (Direction générale de la sécurité extérieure – DGSE)
The DGSE is France's major external intelligence agency. Falling under the aegis of the Ministry of Defence it has more than 4,000 staff made up of administrative and operational personnel deployed in France and around the world, and involved in the collection of both signals intelligence (the interception and decoding of transmissions sent by foreign governments or organizations of interest to France) and human intelligence (the collection of information from human agents). In the latter sense, the majority of DGSE officers work under diplomatic cover, although there are also an unknown number of individuals working under business and academic cover. In terms of monitoring the threat of terrorism to France, the DGSE plays an

important role in gathering information on a wide range of terrorist groups, but especially those in North Africa that have a history of violence in France and which, because of family connections, can often travel freely from the region to the EU. In this role the DGSE works closely with counterpart agencies in Europe and elsewhere.

Further reading
Oqueteau, F., 'National Security and Global Security: The Adaptation of French Intelligence Services' *Canadian Journal of Criminology and Criminal Justice / Revue canadienne de criminologie et de justice pénale* 48(3) 2006, pp. 435–52.
Porch, D., *The French Secret Services: A History of French Intelligence from the Dreyfus Affair to the Gulf War*. New York: Farrar, Straus and Giroux, 2003.

EARTH LIBERATION FRONT
Founded by radical members of the activist environmental group 'Earth First!' in 1992 in the UK town of Brighton, but spreading to almost twenty countries, the Earth Liberation Front is a militant organization committed to environmental causes through direct action and, where necessary, violence. Adopting a non-hierarchical 'leaderless resistance structure' – encouraging members to act according to their own conscience and under their own volition – actions have included arson attacks against luxury homes of individuals whose lifestyles are deemed detrimental to the environment, animal research laboratories, four-wheel-drive dealerships, and companies involved in the fur trade and timber industry. Members focus on attacking property rather than people with a view to inflicting maximum economic damage. A decentralized command-and-control structure makes infiltration by security agencies difficult and complicates legal proceedings against those arrested for violent activities. Inevitably, these individuals are tried for crimes that cannot be linked back to any tangible leadership group. The group has strong links with the **Animal Liberation Front**.

Further reading
Leader, S. H. and Probst, P., 'The Earth Liberation Front and Environmental Terrorism' *Terrorism and Political Violence* 15(4) 2003, pp. 37–58.
Rosebraugh, C., *Burning Rage of a Dying Planet: Speaking for the Earth Liberation Front*. Brooklyn, NY: Lantern Books, 2004.

EAST AFRICA EMBASSY BOMBINGS

On 7 August 1998 two near-simultaneous truck bombs exploded at around 10.45 a.m. outside the US embassies in the Kenyan capital of Nairobi and the Tanzanian capital, Dar-es-Salaam. The attack, which killed more than 220 people (mainly Kenyan and Tanzanian citizens – only 12 US nationals were killed) and wounded 5,000, was the first large-scale terrorist strike by **al Qaeda** and its most deadly strike until **9/11**. The largest attack occurred in Nairobi, where there were approximately 210 fatalities and 4,000 injuries. The exact number of dead eluded authorities because the size of the blast and the carnage it caused made precise identification impossible. Construction of the 900-kilogram (2000 lb) devices was supervised by al Qaeda bomb-maker Mohammed Odeh. Following the attacks, al Qaeda leader **Osama bin Laden** issued a confused series of justifications, including revenge for US actions in Somalia, an alleged plan by the Clinton Administration to partition Sudan, and punishment for the USA for allegedly planning the Rwandan genocide. Lawrence Wright, who speculates that the attacks might have been designed to draw the USA into a land war in Afghanistan, offers a more credible explanation. If Wright is correct, al Qaeda failed, with Washington responding in August 1998 not by deploying troops but by launching a series of retaliatory cruise missile attacks on Sudan and al Qaeda camps in Afghanistan under the code name '**Operation Infinite Reach**'. The US government eventually indicted twenty-one individuals for the planning of the attacks, many of whom were connected with **Egyptian Islamic Jihad**, a group headed by **Ayman al-Zawahiri** which had been folded into al Qaeda. By late 2008, at least twelve of these individuals had been captured or killed.

Further reading
Bergen, P., *Holy War, Inc.: Inside the Secret World of Osama bin Laden*. New York: The Free Press, 2002.
Lyman, P. N. and Morrison, J. S., 'The Terrorist Threat in Africa' *Foreign Affairs* 87(1) January/February 2004, pp. 75–86.

EAST TURKESTAN LIBERATION ORGANIZATION
SEE: **XINJIANG**

ECO-TERRORISM

The term 'eco-terrorism' is used mostly to refer to those individuals and groups prepared to use violence against targets deemed as causing irreparable damage to the global ecosystem. The term is used to describe groups such as the **Animal Liberation Front**, the **Earth Liberation Front** and other groups that have adopted measures such as the fire bombing of companies involved in animal experimentation or the genetic engineering of food crops. However, as with almost all uses of the term 'terrorism', this definition is not without its critics. Firstly, in rejecting the charge of terrorism, supporters of direct action claim they have a moral obligation to defend the right of current and future generations to a sustainable environment. Secondly, the term has been used injudiciously to delegitimize even peaceful pro-environmental activists.

Further reading
Best, S. and Nocella II, A. J. (eds.), *Igniting a Revolution: Voices in Defense of the Earth*. Oakland and Edinburgh: AK Press, 2006.
Vanderheiden, S., 'Radical Environmentalism in an Age of Anti-Terrorism' *Environmental Politics* 17(2) 2008, pp. 299–318.

EGYPTIAN ISLAMIC JIHAD (Also: al-Jihad)

Proscribed by: Australia, Canada, Israel, Russia, UK, USA
Established under the title 'al Jihad' in the late 1970s, the aim of Egyptian Islamic Jihad (EIJ) was to topple the secular government of Anwar Sadat and replace it with a regime based on Islamic law. To this end, al Jihad was involved in the 1981 assassination of Sadat. With this objective at the forefront of its activities, the EIJ attracted mainly individuals who had been persecuted by the state for their overt linking of religion with the call for political change, as well as unemployed graduates and other young people frustrated at a perceived lack of opportunity in a society overseen by a regime believed to be increasingly corrupt. Soon after Sadat's assassination the group split into two factions, with a group led by Abbud al-Zumarin becoming the EIJ and another faction headed by Karam Zuhdi forming al-Gama'a al-Islamiyah (see **Islamic Group**). In the late 1980s, leadership of the EIJ passed to **Ayman al-Zawahiri** and, under his directions, the group attempted unsuccessfully to assassinate the Egyptian Interior Minister Hassan Al-Alfi and Prime Minister Atef Sedky, both

in 1993. Barely two years later, the group carried out an assassination attempt against President Hosni Mubarak in Addis Ababa, but again it failed. However, it achieved more success elsewhere, for instance in November 1995 it bombed the Egyptian embassy in Islamabad. Around this time al-Zawahiri became increasingly committed to the idea of a global struggle and he was progressively attracted to the idea of folding the EIJ into the larger transnational terrorist network being forged by **Osama bin Laden**. An important step towards securing this merger occurred in 1998 when al-Zawahiri authored and bin Laden issued a fatwa announcing the formation of the World Islamic Front for Combat Against Jews and Crusaders, which called for the killing of US nationals as well as those of its allies. The alliance was formalized in 2001 when the two groups merged to form Jamaa'at Qa'idat al-Jihad. However, this shift caused significant rifts within the organization and soon after a schism developed. Even al-Zawahiri's brother Mohammed, hitherto the EIJ's military commander, split from the group. By the late 2000s most of the EIJ's Egyptian-based leaders had been captured or killed and the group had become a shadow of its former self.

Further reading

Blaydes, L. and Rubin, L., 'Ideological Reorientation and Counterterrorism: Confronting Militant Islam in Egypt' *Terrorism and Political Violence* 20(4) 2008, pp. 461–79.
Kepel, G., *The Trail of Political Islam*. London: I. B. Tauris, 2003.

EJERCITO DE LIBERACIÓN NACIONAL (ELN)
SEE: NATIONAL LIBERATION ARMY

EU FRAMEWORK DECISION ON COUNTERING TERRORISM
The EU Framework Decision on Countering Terrorism is an agreement that came into effect on 31 December 2002 and which is designed to harmonize the prosecution of terrorism-related offences. Prior to the Framework, only seven member countries had promulgated laws specifically designed to use the legal system to combat the threat of terrorism. Among the remaining members, terrorism was prosecuted through a combination of criminal and civil laws. Drawing on Article 29 of the Treaty of the European Union, which defines

terrorism as a crime that needs to be prevented through common action, in 2002 EU members agreed to introduce and harmonize (as far as possible) counter-terrorism laws. The Framework Agreement was designed to facilitate this process and to ensure that all EU members introduced policies to enhance police and judicial cooperation so that similar terrorism-related crimes would not be prosecuted differently in different states. The Framework provides a list of specific offences that are regarded as essential for an act to be considered terrorist in nature, but it also contains a subjective dimension in that there needs to be proof that the intended act was motivated by political rather than purely criminal objectives. The Framework was amended in 2007 to cover the public advocacy of violent acts as well as recruitment and training for terrorist actions. Against the objections of some civil rights groups, the changes also boosted the ability of member countries' police and security agencies to solicit cooperation from Internet service providers. Even though the Framework contains provisions designed to guarantee core civil rights, many have argued that it provides the basis for an erosion of fundamental political liberties within the EU.

Further reading

Dumitriu, E., 'The E.U.'s Definition of Terrorism: The Council Framework Decision on Combating Terrorism' *German Law Journal* 5(5) 2004, pp. 585–602.

Peers, S., 'EU Responses to Terrorism' *International and Comparative Law Quarterly* 52(1) 2003, pp. 227–43.

EUSKADI TA ASKATASUNA (ETA) (Basque Fatherland and Liberty)

Proscribed by: Canada, EU, UK, USA

Founded in the early 1950s as a discussion group at the University of Duesto in the Spanish city of Bilbao, ETA soon evolved into an underground group committed to the use of violence to secure an independent homeland for the Basque people indigenous to parts of northern Spain and southern France. The centres of its activities, both political and military, have been in the northern Spanish provinces of Vizcaya, Guipuzcoa, Alava and Navarra and the southwestern French departments of Labourd, Basse-Navarra and Soule. There are approximately 2.5 million Basques living in these areas and, even though many are proud of their heritage and resentful of the dominant cultures of the majorities, ETA's brand of violent resistance has turned many against the group. ETA's ideological orientation was heavily influenced by the post-colonial ferment of the 1950s and 1960s (especially within the context of Cuban revolutionary socialism and the struggle of nationalists in Northern Ireland), but also by wider intellectual trends popular at that time (such as existentialism). Hence the group's ideology has traditionally been nationalist (emphasizing the unique nature of Basque language and culture) and socialist (shaped in part by its experiences under the Franco regime). At an operational level ETA's violence has focused on Spanish infrastructure and the targeted assassinations of local political figures and policemen. On 20 December 1973, it achieved its largest coup when it assassinated the Spanish Prime Minister and heir apparent to General Franco, Admiral Luis Carrero Blanco, in retaliation for the execution of several convicted ETA members. Offers of amnesty and a place in the mainstream political process caused a split in the organization in the late 1970s, with the outcome being that hardliners opposed to any compromise with Madrid gained control of the organization. In the 1980s the newly democratic Spanish government launched a 'dirty war' against the group, using paramilitary groups named Grupos Antiterroristas de Liberación ('Antiterrorist Liberation Groups') to carry out extra-judicial assassinations and torture against known and suspected ETA members and sympathizers. Media revelations of the campaign caused a political outcry and many of those involved were charged and sentenced to jail. However, their actions also had the effect of boosting ETA's appeal among Basque communities. In the 1990s and 2000s the scope of ETA's attacks increased to encompass larger bombings, including a strike against Madrid's main airport in 2006 and car bombings at major Spanish holiday resorts. In March 2006 ETA declared a 'permanent ceasefire' and entered into peace talks with the Spanish government. However, by late 2007 the ceasefire had collapsed and ETA had recommenced its attacks. Even so, by 2008 more rigorous anti-terrorism powers and closer cooperation between French and Spanish authorities had degraded ETA's operational flexibility and led to the arrests of senior ETA figures.

Further reading
Reinares, F., 'Who Are the Terrorists? Analysing Changes in Sociological Profile among Members of ETA' *Studies in Conflict and Terrorism* 27(6) 2004, pp. 465–88.

Shabad, G. and Ramo, F. J. L., 'Political Violence in a Democratic State: Basque Terrorism in Spain' in M. Crenshaw (ed.) *Terrorism in Context.* Philadelphia: Pennsylvania University Press, 1995, pp. 410–71.

Watson, C. J., *Basque Nationalism and Political Violence: The Ideological and Intellectual Origins of ETA.* Reno: Center for Basque Studies, University of Nevada, 2008.

Fatah

The Fatah movement (also known as Fatah Revolutionary Council) emerged in the late 1950s as a secular Palestinian resistance movement formed by Palestinian graduates **Yasser Arafat**, Khalil Wazir and Salah Khalaf, while in exile in Kuwait. It soon extended its bases to include Palestinian refugee camps in Lebanon and Jordan and commenced cross-border raids into Israel in 1965. Shortly after the Arab defeat in the Six Day War in 1967, Fatah relocated its headquarters to Jordan from where it continued to mount attacks on Israel. On 18 March 1968, a school bus in southern Israel struck a mine that had been set by Palestinian fighters, killing and wounding several adults and children. Israel retaliated by targeting the Fatah headquarters outside the Jordanian town of Karameh. During the battle, Fatah guerrillas inflicted heavy casualties on Israeli forces and Arafat became a heroic figure throughout the Middle East for his role in overseeing the battle. Fatah built on this momentum by expanding its power base in Jordan, drawing support from both Muslim and Christian Palestinian refugees. Soon after, Fatah merged with the **Palestinian Liberation Organization (PLO)**, and in 1969 Arafat became chairman of the PLO executive committee. However, the actions of the PLO and other Palestinian groups during this period led to the 'Black September' crack-down by King Hussein of Jordan and the forced relocation of Fatah to Lebanon. Arafat subsequently embroiled the movement within the Lebanese Civil War and began to attack rival groups such as the **Abu Nidal Organization** as well as the regimes that sheltered them. The movement was weakened by the 1982 Israeli invasion of Lebanon and was again forced to relocate, this time to Tunisia. Arafat eventually accepted the need for a political solution to the Israeli–Palestinian conflict, which culminated in the Oslo Accords of 1993. Under the terms of the Accord, Arafat renounced terrorism in exchange for the right to form a Palestinian-led administration in Gaza and the West Bank (the 'Palestinian Authority'). For many Palestinians, Fatah's more accommodating approach to Israel was a sell-out and in 1995 Arafat formed a new militia, called Tanzim, in an attempt to stymie growing support for more hard-line Islamist alternatives to Fatah, in the form of **Hamas** and Islamic Jihad (see **Palestinian Islamic Jihad**). Mounting allegations of corruption and maladministration against Fatah and Arafat aided the growth of the Islamist alternative. With the outbreak of the second Intifada in 2000, Tanzim stood accused of being embroiled in the violence, especially through its links to a new terrorist group, the **al Aqsa Martyrs Brigades**, that was responsible for a series of suicide bombings, mainly against Israeli civilian targets. In 2006, Fatah lost to Hamas in an election in the Gaza Strip, although Israel, the United States and many EU countries refused to acknowledge Hamas' authority. The loss widened schisms within Fatah that the group's new head, Mahmoud Abbas, who took over leadership of the organization on the death of Arafat in 2005, has struggled to reconcile.

Further reading
Baumgarten, H., 'The Three Faces/Phases of Palestinian Nationalism 1918–2005' *Journal of Palestine Studies* 34(4) 2005, pp. 25–48.
Sayigh, Y. *Armed Struggle and the Search for State: The Palestinian National Movement, 1949–93.* New York: Oxford University Press, 2000.

FATWA
A ruling or religious edict passed by an Islamic religious authority (Imam) and based on an understanding of passages from the Qur'an or the Hadiths (sayings of the Prophet Mohammed). They are not necessarily binding. Within the Sunni Islamic tradition the lack of a religious hierarchy often leads to a proliferation of contradictory fatwas, with individuals choosing those they consider most convenient. There has even emerged the habit of 'shopping for fatwas', a phrase that refers to the use of modern communications technology such as the Internet to seek out those Imams most likely to provide fatwas that coincide with a predetermined preferential course of action. This habit has become increasingly prevalent among extremist groups searching for religious sanction to commit acts of violence. It occurs less often within Shi'a Islam which has a clearer religious hierarchy and which therefore can call on senior Imams to resolve disputes over interpretation. Yet, even within Shi'a Islam, competing fatwas issued by different Imams are not uncommon. **Osama bin Laden**'s 1998 fatwa ('A Declaration of the World Islamic Front for

Combat against Jews and Crusaders' (see **al Qaeda**)), stating that it was a moral obligation for all Muslims to kill Jews, Americans and their allies, was treated by many Muslims on the path to radicalization as a religious sanction to engage in terrorism. However, many Islamic scholars have pointed out that bin Laden lacks the religious training and credentials required to issue fatwas and the 1998 statement was therefore not only presumptuous but had no basis in Islamic law. Bin Laden stopped issuing fatwas soon after and has henceforth relied on a small band of extremist Imams spread in numerous countries to issue them on his behalf.

Further reading

Esposito, J. (ed.), *The Oxford Encyclopedia of the Modern Islamic World*. Vol. II. Oxford and New York: Oxford University Press, 2001.

Ranstorp, M., 'Interpreting the Broader Context and Meaning of Bin-Laden's Fatwa' *Terrorism and Political Violence* 21(4) 1998, pp. 321–30.

FAWKES, GUY

Guy Fawkes (1570–1606) was an English Catholic who, in May 1604, joined with four others to plot the overthrow of the government of King James I and bring about a Catholic restoration. Their plan, known as 'the Gunpowder Plot', involved secreting a number of barrels of gunpowder under the Houses of Parliament and detonating them at the opening ceremony, killing a large number of parliamentarians, and possibly the King and his two sons, and thereby creating an opening for the restoration of Catholicism as the official religion of England. The plotters were eventually arrested after one of their number revealed the plot to the authorities. Although history has emphasized Fawkes' role in the plot, it was Robert Gatesby who acted as ring-leader. Fawkes' notoriety stems from his role as the person in charge of manufacturing the bomb.

Further reading

Fraser, A., *Faith and Treason: The Story of the Gunpowder Plot*. New York: Anchor, 1997.

Kyle, C. R., 'Early Modern Terrorism: The Gunpowder Plot of 1605 and its Aftermath' in B. Bowden and M. T. Davis (eds.) *Terror: From Tyrannicide to Terrorism*. St Lucia: The University of Queensland Press, 2008, pp. 42–55.

FAZUL, ABDULLAH MOHAMMED

Listed on the **Federal Bureau of Investigation**'s Most Wanted Terrorists list, Abdullah Mohammed Fazul is a senior member of **al Qaeda**'s African operations. He first came to notice following his involvement in the 1998 **East Africa embassy bombings**, although since then he has been active in a number of mainly East African states, including Somalia, Kenya and Madagascar. Born in the Comoros Islands on either 25 August 1972, 25 February 1974 or 25 December 1974 (he has used all three dates), he and several other al Qaeda operatives were targeted in a US helicopter gun-ship strike along the Somali–Kenya border area in January 2007. The Somali government claimed he had been killed in the operation, but this was disputed by the USA, which, ten years after the attacks against its embassies in East Africa was continuing to search for him. Fazul has dual Comoros Island and Kenyan nationalities, has more than twenty known aliases, and is proficient in five languages.

Further reading
Rosenau, W., 'Al Qaida Recruitment Trends in Kenya and Tanzania' *Studies in Conflict and Terrorism* 28(1) 2005, pp. 1–10.

FEDERAL BUREAU OF INVESTIGATION (FBI)

The FBI was founded in 1908 during the presidency of Theodore Roosevelt. However, it was under the directorship of J. Edgar Hoover, who led the Bureau from 1924 until his death in 1972, that the organization flourished to become the most important law enforcement agency in the United States. The Bureau's mandate is largely domestic, focusing on the investigation of federal crimes such as kidnapping and money laundering, although it also plays a key role in counter-espionage and counter-terrorism. In the years since **9/11** a series of major reforms have been implemented to address perceived weaknesses in its operations; these include demarcation disputes with other agencies, especially the **Central Intelligence Agency**, and a tendency to slide into axiomatic thinking which in the past has allowed criminals, including terrorists, to adapt their operational protocols to wrong-foot the Bureau. In the years since 9/11, the FBI has dramatically expanded its counter-terrorism capabilities, placing more covert agents in the field and boosting its analytical department. There has also been an overhaul of the way it interacts with other agencies, especially in the area of information sharing, and a significant investment in new technologies. December 2005 saw the establishment of the National Security Branch (NSB), which emerged out of a presidential directive to establish a dedicated 'National Security Service', which includes a 'Terrorist Screening Center', designed to provide real-time intelligence to state and local police forces. This was followed in July 2006 by the establishment of a 'Weapons of Mass Destruction Directorate' that, as part of its mandate, monitors attempts by terrorists to secure access to chemical, biological or radiological weapons.

Further reading
Gentry, C., J. *Edgar Hoover: The Man and his Secrets*. New York: W.W. Norton and Co., 2001.
Zegart, A., *Spying Blind: The CIA, the FBI, and the Origins of 9/11*. Princeton, NJ: Princeton University Press, 2009.

FENIANS
The term 'Fenian' emerged in the late nineteenth century to refer to Irish nationalist groups such as the Fenian Brotherhood, founded in 1858 by the Irish American scholar John O'Mahoney, and the Irish Republican Brotherhood. O'Mahoney borrowed the name from 'Fianna', a mythical group of Irish warriors. The term was eventually applied to supporters of Irish nationalism in general, assuming a derogatory anti-Irish-Catholic undertone in England and Scotland. Despite the term entering into popular usage in the late nineteenth century, the roots of the Fenian movement can be traced back to the late eighteenth century and groups such as the Society of United Irishmen which, in 1798, launched an ill-fated rebellion against British rule.

Further reading
Kelly, M. J., *The Fenian Ideal and Irish Nationalism, 1882–1916*. Woodbridge: Boydell and Brewer, 2006.
Ramon, M., *Provisional Dictator: James Stephens and the Fenian Movement*. Dublin: University College Dublin Press, 2008.

FIGNER, VERA
Born on 7 July 1852 in Kazan in Russia, by her early thirties Vera Figner had become one of the most wanted terrorists in Tsarist Russia for her involvement in planning the assassination of Tsar Alexander

II on 11 March 1881. After abandoning a marriage and medical studies in Austria, Figner returned to Russia in 1875 and almost immediately joined the Narodnaya Volya ('The People's Will'), or Narodniks, an underground group dedicated to toppling the Tsarist state through a combination of violence against its upper echelons and education of the masses about the nature and extent of their exploitation. By 1879 Figner had become a key figure within the terrorist faction of the Narodniks, and it was within this group that she helped to plan the Tsar's assassination. After the murder, Figner escaped to St Petersburg where she linked up with that city's Narodnik network; however, she was captured on 10 February 1883 after information from an informer alerted police to the whereabouts of Figner and several other high-profile Narodnik leaders. In September 1884 she was sentenced to death, but this was commuted to twenty years' hard labour. On her release in 1904 she was exiled to several remote Russian cities, but in 1906 was permitted to travel abroad and toured Europe where she spoke to meetings in an attempt to raise awareness of the plight of political prisoners in Russia. On returning to Russia she joined the Russian Socialist Revolutionary Party, which was formed by former colleagues and which also replicated the revolutionary violence of the Narodniks. Figner died in Moscow on 15 June 1942.

Further reading

Figner, V. N., *Memoirs of a Revolutionist*. DeKalb: Northern Illinois University Press, 1991.

Hartnett, L., 'The Making of a Revolutionary Icon: Vera Nikolaevna Figner and the People's Will in the Wake of the Assassination of Tsar Aleksandr II' *Canadian Slavonic Papers* 43(2–3) 2001, pp. 249–70.

FIRST OF OCTOBER ANTI-FASCIST RESISTANCE GROUP (Grupo de Resistencia Anti-Fascista Primero de Octubre – GRAPO)
Proscribed by: EU
GRAPO was formed in Spain in 1975 following the death of the fascist dictator General Franco, and was the military wing of the then outlawed Reconstituted Communist Party of Spain (Partido Comunista de España – Reconstitutido – PCE-R). At its foundation the group was headed by Juan Carlos Delgado de Codex, who was killed in a police shoot-out in 1979. From 1979 until 2003 Manuel Perez Martinez ('Comrade Arenas') led the group, and during this time it used violence to oppose post-Franco reforms that were designed to

establish Spain's credentials as an open capitalist state and a member of NATO, and to bolster the bilateral relationship between Madrid and Washington. The group took its name from the first major violent act of resistance by the PCE-R, the assassination of four Spanish police officers on 1 October 1975 in retaliation for the execution of five anti-fascist activists (including two members of ETA – see **Euskadi Ta Askatasuna**) several days earlier. In subsequent years GRAPO used a combination of shootings and bomb attacks to target police, members of the judiciary, politicians and high-profile business people. GRAPO never managed to attract widespread support, and counter-terrorism raids by the Spanish police regularly resulted in the capture or death of members. GRAPO did, however, establish contact with fellow West European revolutionary terrorist groups such as the **Italian Red Brigades** and the German **Baader-Meinhof Gang**. Struggling to attract fresh members, the group's activities and significance declined through the 1980s, and, although an attempt to reorganize the group and reassert itself in 1987 led to a brief revival of its fortunes, these proved unsustainable. In 2000 Martinez was arrested in France and charged with activities relating to the preparation of terrorist action. In 2003 he was extradited to Spain and, in July of that year, sentenced to ten years in prison. Following **9/11**, a statement issued by GRAPO praised the attacks as striking a blow against 'the symbols of imperialist power'.

Further reading
Jiménez, F., 'Spain: The Terrorist Challenge and the Government's Response' *Terrorism and Political Violence* 4(4) 1992, pp. 110–30.

FRONT DE LIBÉRATION NATIONALE – FLN
SEE: NATIONAL LIBERATION FRONT

FRONT DE LIBÉRATION DU QUÉBEC (Quebec Liberation Front)
The Front de Libération du Québec (FLQ) was formed in February 1963 with a view to securing an independent French-speaking state within Canada. Overlaid with socialist themes, the FLQ used violence in an effort to improve the living standards of working-class Québecois (native French speakers). The apex of its activities occurred between 1963 and 1970, during which time the group set

off more than ninety bombs, the most powerful of which went off in February 1969, causing over two dozen injuries at the Montreal stock exchange. This was followed in the late 1970s by the kidnapping of two senior government officials by the group's 'Liberation cell' and 'Chenier cell' in an attempt to force the release of FLQ prisoners. Confronted with signs of growing support for the group's actions among some Québecois personalities, labour leaders, academics and students, the governor of the province asked Prime Minister Pierre Trudeau to deploy the military and grant the provincial government emergency powers. The Chenier cell, which was holding the Minister for Labour hostage, responded by strangling their captive to death, dumping his body in the boot of a car, and issuing a public statement that it had killed the 'Minister of Unemployment and Assimilation'. The subsequent crack-down led to the arrest of more than 500 suspected FLQ members, including key leaders. Some were granted free passage to Cuba where they were granted exile status by the Castro administration, while others received lengthy jail sentences. The violence used by the group, especially the execution of one of the hostages, resulted in a loss of moral authority for many Québecois separatists and, despite isolated small-scale acts of violence against fast food chains and iconic images of a united Canada – such as the vandalization of a statue of Canada's first Prime Minister John Macdonald – the movement has ceased to pose a serious challenge to national security.

Further reading

Charters, D. A., 'The Amateur Revolutionaries: A Reassessment of the FLQ' *Terrorism and Political Violence* 9(1) 1997, pp. 133–69.

Tetley, W., *October Crisis, 1970: An Insider's View*. Montreal and Kingston: McGill-Queens University Press, 2006.

FRONTE DI LIBERAZIONE NAZIUNALE DI A CORSICA (FLNC)
SEE: NATIONAL LIBERATION FRONT OF CORSICA

FUERZAS ARMADAS REVOLUCIONARIAS DE COLOMBIA – EJÉRCITO DEL PUEBLO (FARC-EP)
SEE: REVOLUTIONARY ARMED FORCES OF COLOMBIA – PEOPLE'S ARMY

GADAHN, ADAM YAHIYE

The only US-born **al Qaeda** member on the **Federal Bureau of Investigation**'s Most Wanted Terrorists list, Adam Yahiye Gadahn (b. 1978), also known as Azzam the American, Azzam Al-Amriki Abu Suhayb Al-Amriki, Abu Suhail Al-Amriki, Abu Suhayb, Yihya Majadin Adams, Adam Pearlman and Yayah, was indicted in the Central District Court of California on 11 October 2006 for treason and for providing material support to al Qaeda. Of mixed Jewish and Catholic heritage, he was born in Oregon but raised in California from a young age after his parents purchased a small farm. After flirting briefly with fundamentalist Christianity, he converted to Islam in 1995 after a self-confessed spiritual void led him to seek out a deeper sense of existential meaning. His early introduction to Islam occurred at a southern California mosque being used for prayer meetings and discussion groups by a number of hard-line Islamists. In 1998 he moved to Pakistan, married an Afghan woman, and began to mix in extremist circles that included a number of al Qaeda members, among them the principal architect of the **9/11** attacks, **Khalid Sheikh Mohammed**. As a native English speaker, and with a clear American accent, Gadahn has proved a useful propaganda tool for al Qaeda through its media production unit **as-Sahab**, and in 2004 he appeared in his first video for the group – a 75-minute monologue threatening further attacks against the USA. On the fifth anniversary of the 9/11 attacks, in 2005, he appeared in his second video, an 11-minute monologue warning of al Qaeda attacks in Los Angeles and Melbourne. Gadahn is the first US citizen since the Second World War to be indicted for treason.

Further reading
Khatchadourian, R., 'Azzam the American. The Making of an al-Qaeda Homegrown' *New Yorker* 82(46) 22 January 2007, pp. 50–63.

GADDAFI, MUAMMAR

Despite formally resigning from all public offices in 1979, Colonel Muammar Abu Minyar Gaddafi (b. 1942) has been leader of Libya since heading a military coup in 1969. Bestowed with the grandiose title 'Guide of the First of September Great Revolution of the Socialist People's Libyan Arab Jamahiriya', Gaddafi long proved a thorn in the side for Western governments through his support for liberation movements and terrorist groups in different parts of the world. Groups that have benefited from his support over the years include the Provisional IRA (see **Irish Republican Army (Provisional)**) as well as **Black September** and other Palestinian groups. It is also alleged that Gaddafi was behind the 1988 bombing of a PanAm Flight 103 that crashed in the Scottish town of **Lockerbie**, killing 270 passengers and townspeople. Gaddafi's refusal to hand over the two men for trial in either the USA or Britain resulted in widespread sanctions against Libya. In 1999 a compromise was negotiated by Nelson Mandela that led to the curious decision to transfer the two men to the Netherlands, where they were tried under Scottish law. The imposition of multilateral sanctions against Libya in 1992 played an important part in Gaddafi's decision to end support for terrorist groups. In an attempt to improve his international image, in 2003 Gaddafi accepted full responsibility for the Lockerbie bombing and offered compensation to the families of the victims. Gaddafi also offered himself as a mediator for a number of secessionist conflicts in places such as the Southern Philippines. After the events of **9/11**, Gaddafi's conciliatory overtures intensified, undertaking to support the USA and other Western nations in their attempts to combat terrorism in the Middle East. This led to a relaxation of economic sanctions against Libya.

Further reading
Collins, S. D., 'Dissuading State Support of Terrorism: Strikes or Sanctions? (An Analysis of Dissuasion Measures Employed against Libya)' *Studies in Conflict and Terrorism* 27(1) 2004, pp. 1–18.
Romen, Y., *Quaddafi's Libya in World Politics*. Boulder: Lynne Rienner, 2008.

AL-GAMA'A AL-ISLAMIYAH
SEE: ISLAMIC GROUP

GODSE, NATHURAM VINAYAK
Mahatma Gandhi's assassin, Nathuram Godse, was born in India's Pune District on 19 May 1910. While at school he was an admirer of Gandhi, but in his mid-teens he was introduced to the teachings of Veer Savarkar, an Indian politician and early architect of the militant form of Hindu nationalism known as Hinduvta. With its emphasis on the sanctity of the caste system and its notion of a unified India

(including Pakistan) as an innately Hindu state, Hinduvta was (and remains) an ideology at odds with the egalitarian humanism propounded by Gandhi. For Savarkar and others committed to Hinduvta, Gandhi's vision constituted an inexcusable sacrifice of India's Hindu traditions for the sake of the country's minorities, particularly its Muslims. Godse's rapid embrace of this ideology saw him drop out of school and dedicate himself to grassroots activism within the main political organization representing the Hinduvta movement, the Rashtriya Swayamsevak Sangh (RSS – National Volunteers Organization). On 30 January 1948, he approached Gandhi while the latter was taking his nightly walk at Birla House in New Delhi, shooting him three times. It was the second assassination plot against Gandhi that Godse had been involved in – the first, several weeks earlier, was abandoned after a guard became suspicious. Ten others were arrested and charged along with Godse for being involved in the assassination. Apart from Godse, one other conspirator was found guilty and sentenced to death (against the wishes of Gandhi's family). The rest were sentenced to lengthy prison sentences or acquitted.

Further reading

Godse, N. V., *Why I Assassinated Mahatma Gandhi*. New Delhi: Surya Bharti Parkashan, 1993 [1949].

Malgonkar, M., *The Men Who Killed Gandhi (On the Assassination of Mohandas Karamchand Gandhi, 1869–1948)*. Delhi: Macmillan Company of India, 1978.

GOLDSTEIN, BARUCH

Baruch Goldstein (1956–94) was an Orthodox Jewish doctor, born in New York, who immigrated to Israel where he took up residence in the settlement of Kiryat Arba near Hebron, working as a physician and serving in the Israeli army reserve. On 25 February 1994, the Jewish holiday of Purim, he entered a mosque at the Cave of the Patriarchs and shot dead 29 Muslim worshippers, and wounded another 150. Like many others in the Jewish settlements, Goldstein was angered by the stoning of their vehicles and by other violence coming from the Palestinian side, and he was also frustrated at what he perceived to be the weak response of the Israeli authorities to these provocations. The night before the Purim holiday, he attended a traditional prayer reading at a Jewish site near the Cave of the Patriarchs and was infuriated when Israeli guards refused to stop catcalling by

Palestinian youths. The following day, he returned to the site and wearing his reservist uniform and carrying a semi-automatic weapon, walked into the Ibrahimi mosque and opened fire. The assault stopped only when Goldstein was overwhelmed by a crowd of worshippers who then beat him to death. Goldstein is regarded as a hero and a martyr among ultra-conservative Jewish groups in Israel.

Further reading
Juergensmeyer, M., *Terror in The Mind of God: The Global Rise of Religious Violence* (3rd edn). Berkeley: University of California Press, 2003.

GOOD FRIDAY AGREEMENT

Also known as the Belfast Agreement, the Good Friday Agreement was signed on 10 April 1998. The document provides the basis for a ceasefire between nationalist and unionist forces in Northern Ireland, including the mutual disarmament of terrorist groups on both sides of the sectarian and political divide. It is the issue of the decommissioning of weapons that has generated most of the obstacles to the full implementation of the Agreement. However, a statement by the Provisional IRA (see **Irish Republican Army (Provisional)**) – the largest of the republican terrorist groups and the military wing of Sinn Fein – in September 2005, claiming that it had decommissioned all of its weapons, allowed the peace process as outlined by the Agreement to move forward. A key element of the Agreement concerns the devolution of political power from Westminster to the Northern Irish Assembly. Associated provisions facilitate the establishment of a government and other political and social institutions that are more inclusive of Northern Ireland's Catholic minority. Parallel initiatives include a renunciation by the Republic of Ireland of its territorial claim over the north and the establishment of a North–South Ministerial Council to promote cross-border cooperation. The Agreement also provides for the establishment of an Equal Rights and Equality Commission, the early release of terrorist prisoners, reforms to criminal justice and policing practices, and the decommissioning of paramilitary weapons.

Further reading
Morrissey, M. and Smythe, M., *Northern Ireland after the Good Friday Agreement: Victims, Grievance and Blame*. London: Pluto Press, 2002.

Ruane, J. and Todd, J., 'The Politics of Transition? Explaining Political Crises in the Implementation of the Belfast Good Friday Agreement' *Political Studies* 49(5) 2002, pp. 923–40.

GROUPE ISLAMIQUE COMBATTANT MORROCAIN (GICM)
SEE: MOROCCAN ISLAMIC COMBATANT GROUP

GRUPO DE RESISTENCIA ANTI-FASCISTA PRIMERO DE OCTUBRE (GRAPO)
SEE: FIRST OF OCTOBER ANTI-FASCIST RESISTANCE GROUP

GUEVARA, ERNESTO ('CHE')
Born in Argentina in 1928, Che Guevara studied medicine before joining Marxist rebels and participating in the Cuban revolution led by Fidel Castro. Guevara's embrace of revolutionary Marxism was inspired by poverty he witnessed during a journey made with his cousin from Argentina to Guatemala. Popularized through his published diary of the trip, *The Motorcycle Diaries*, Guevara emerged as an iconic figure for left-wing revolutionary movements around the world. After the success of the Cuban revolution, Guevara was charged with chairing tribunals established to try to review sentences handed out to supporters of the ousted Batista regime. In this capacity he condemned to death some of those charged. Soon after, Guevara was appointed President of the national bank, and he also served for a brief period as the Minister for Industry. After a falling-out with the Castro regime over Guevara's growing support for China and criticism of the Soviet Union, he left Cuba in 1965, travelling to the Congo and Bolivia where he joined Marxist guerrilla groups attempting to foment revolution. He was captured and executed in Bolivia in 1967.

Further reading
Castaneda, J. G., *Compañero: The Life and Death of Che Guevara*. New York: Vintage Books, 1998.
Guevara, E., *The Motorcycle Diaries: Notes on a Latin American Journey*. New York: Ocean Press, 2003.

GUZMÁN, ABIMAEL

Manuel Rubén Abimael Guzmán Reynoso was born in Peru on 3 December 1934 and progressed from being the son of a wealthy businessman's mistress to become a professor of philosophy, and finally the founder and leader of one of South America's most powerful and feared terrorist groups, **Sendero Luminoso**. He was known also by the alias Presidente Gonzalo Guzman. He and his mainly student followers (the *senderistas*) announced their armed struggle on 17 May 1980 by snatching and burning ballot boxes in an attempt to sabotage national elections. Inspired by Maoist notions of revolutionary insurgency, Guzman's strategy was to focus on the peasantry as a source of political upheaval. This did not stop Guzman, however, from ordering mass killings of rural folk suspected of collaborating with the government in Lima. At a more general level, Guzman's appeal to the *senderistas* rested in his promulgation of an explanatory model that provided a simplistic and easily understood framework for overcoming the deeply embedded discrepancies of wealth and power that defined Peruvian society. In an effort to undermine these structural inequities, the *senderistas* focused their violence on state targets, wealthy landowners and foreign multinationals, as well as peasants and trade unionists suspected of working with the government. However, Guzman was also partly motivated by delusions of ideological and philosophical grandeur and a strong sense of self-importance. In fact, despite his revolutionary rhetoric, when he was arrested he was found to be living in a comfortable residence in an up-market Lima suburb. Guzman was captured on 12 September 1992 and charged with terrorism and treason offences, for which he was given a life sentence. During a second trial in 2004, which was preceded by a successful challenge to the constitutionality of the anti-terrorism laws under which he was initially tried, Guzman evinced little remorse and shouted revolutionary slogans until the presiding judges shut down proceedings and excluded outside observers. In 2006 he was again found guilty and sentenced to life in prison.

Further reading
Palmer, D. S. (ed.) *The Shining Path of Peru*. New York: St Martin's Press, 1994.

HAGANAH

Formed in the British Mandate of Palestine in 1920, Haganah was a Zionist paramilitary group set up to protect Palestinian Jews from attacks by Arabs. The British authorities found it near impossible to stop tit-for-tat violence between the two groups, which were inspired mainly by disputes over land. An escalation in this violence in the late 1920s boosted Haganah's membership and prompted the group to source weapons from overseas. From 1936 to 1939 Haganah cooperated with the British in suppressing a mass uprising by Palestinian Arabs, and although the British never formally recognized Haganah, goodwill built through cooperation would eventually lead to London supporting an independent Jewish state. Over the years the Haganah leadership's policy of restraint angered more militant elements within the organization and provided a catalyst for a number of schisms. The first occurred in 1931 when a group split to form Irgun (Irgun Zwei Leumi, or 'National Military Organization'). In 1940 Irgun also split over its leadership's policy of following Haganah and not attacking British forces in Palestine for the duration of the Second World War. The new group was headed by Avraham Stern and was known by the acronym Lehi (Lohamei Herut Yisrael, or 'Fighters for the Freedom of Israel'), although it is often referred to as 'the **Stern Gang**'. Soon after the conclusion of the Second World War, it became clear that Britain had no intention of surrendering its mandate over Palestine, in response to which Haganah launched a fresh campaign of bombings against British military targets and infrastructure.

Further reading
Bregman, A., *Israel's Wars: A History Since 1947*. London: Routledge, 2002.
Morris, B., *Righteous Victims: A History of the Zionist–Arab Conflict, 1881–2001*. New York: Vintage Books, 2001.
Wagner, S., 'British Intelligence and the Jewish Resistance Movement in the Palestine Mandate, 1945–46' *Intelligence and National Security* 23(5) 2008, pp. 629–57.

HAGUE CONVENTION (Convention for the Suppression of Unlawful Seizure of Aircraft)
The Hague Convention is one of a series of inter-connected conventions formulated under the auspices of the United Nations to combat the threat of terrorist hijackings. Crafted in 1970 in response to a surge in hijackings and the practice of third countries offering asylum to hijackers, the Convention makes it an offence to use, or threaten to use, force to board an aircraft in contravention of the laws of the

state in which the aircraft is at that time grounded, or to seize or attempt to seize control of that aircraft. It also makes it illegal to act as an accomplice to any of these activities. Signatories of the Hague Convention are required to impose 'severe penalties' on those found guilty of acting in contravention of these laws and to extradite offenders suspected of such offences for prosecution in the country in which the aircraft is registered. They are also obliged to assist with the prosecution of such individuals wherever possible, for example through the provision of evidentiary materials.

Further reading
Abramovsky, A., 'Multilateral Conventions for the Suppression of Unlawful Seizure and Interference with Aircraft: I. The Hague Convention' *The Columbia Journal of Transnational Law* 13(3) 1974, pp. 381–405.
United Nations Office on Drugs and Crime, *Legislative Guide to the Universal Anti-Terrorism Conventions and Protocols*. New York: United Nations Publications, 2004.

HAMAS (Harakat al-Muqāwama al-Islāmiyya (Islamic Resistance Group))
Proscribed by: Canada, EU, Israel, Japan, USA
Hamas was founded in February 1988 when Sheikh **Ahmed Yassin**, Dr Abdul Aziz Rantisi and Mohammed Taha split from the **Muslim Brotherhood**. For the first few years of its existence, its activities were concentrated in Gaza, but it soon spread to the West Bank. It formed a military wing, the Izz ad-Din al-Qassam Brigades, in 1992. Believing that the Muslim Brotherhood's Pan-Islamic focus offered little specifically for the Palestinian people, and that its emphasis on *da'wa* (preaching) rather than direct action robbed the Palestinians of their only avenue for resistance, Hamas was unique in the Palestinian context because of its hardline rejection of the secular ideologies of the **Palestinian Liberation Organization (PLO)** and other Palestinian resistance groups. Hamas used Islamic scripture to cast Palestine, including the state of Israel, as land bestowed from God. As such, it was a religious obligation on all Muslims to fight to maintain that which had been gifted by Allah. Not to do so was regarded as a sin. Hamas therefore viewed its fighters in religious terms, portraying them as soldiers for Allah and depicting those

killed in action as martyrs. These themes are encapsulated in the Hamas Charter, issued in 1988. However, in 2008 a spokesperson for the group implied it would accept a separate state, provided that Israel retreated from land seized during the Six Day War in 1967 and granted the right of return to Palestinian refugees in neighbouring countries. Hamas' principal modes of attack include shootings, car bombings, grenade and mortar attacks and homemade missiles (**Qassam rockets**). But Hamas also played a pioneering role in using suicide bombers. The first attack of this type occurred on 6 April 1994 when a member of the Izz ad-Din al-Qassam Brigades detonated a bomb on a bus in northern Israel, killing 9 people (including himself). In a statement issued soon after, Hamas claimed the attack was in retaliation for **Baruch Goldstein**'s massacre of worshippers at the Cave of the Patriarchs two months earlier. Between 1994 and 2005, Hamas launched more than fifty such attacks, the largest being on 27 March 2002 when a suicide bomber killed 29, mainly elderly, Israelis enjoying a Passover meal at a hotel in Netanya. Retaliation by Israel was conducted under the aegis of Operation Defensive Shield involving military incursions into major Palestinian towns, resulting in over 500 deaths, 1,500 injuries and more than 4,000 arrests, and costing the Palestinians over US$300 million in damage to their infrastructure. The operation led to a drop in the number of suicide bombings, but it also increased Palestinian reliance upon welfare services, the most efficient of which were, ironically, provided by Hamas. In March 2004 a missile fired by an Israeli helicopter gun-ship killed Sheikh Yassin as he was being wheeled out of morning prayers, and in April his successor Abdel Aziz Rantisi was killed when his car was also hit by an Israeli missile. But the targeted assassinations of Hamas' leaders did little to undermine its public support. Indeed, the organization's ability to capitalize upon the practice of collective punishment meted out against Palestinians was a major reason for its success in the 2006 Palestinian elections, when it defeated Fatah. Subsequent intramural fighting between Hamas and Fatah led to Hamas officials being dislodged from their positions in the West Bank, although they continued to control Gaza. It is alleged that Hamas receives covert funding from Saudi Arabia and Iran and private donations from Palestinian expatriates and private citizens in the Middle East. While Canada, the EU, Israel and the USA proscribe the entire Hamas organization, Australia and the UK have only proscribed its military wing, the Izz ad-Din al-Qassam Brigades.

Further reading
Robinson, E. G., 'The Fragmentation of Palestine' *Current History* 106(704)
2007, pp. 421–7.
Tamimi, A., *Hamas: Unwritten Chapters*. London: C. Hurst & Co. Publishers
Ltd, 2006.

HAMBALI (Also: Riduan Isamuddin)
Until his capture in a joint Thai intelligence / **Central Intelligence
Agency** operation in Thailand on 11 August 2003, Hambali (b. 1966)
was the operations chief for the Indonesian-based **Jemaah Islamiyah**.
Born Encep Nurjaman in West Java, he changed his name to Riduan
Isamuddin after travelling to Afghanistan in the 1980s to join the
anti-Soviet resistance. It was in Afghanistan that he was introduced
to individuals who would later go on to form **al Qaeda**, including
Osama bin Laden. After leaving Afghanistan in 1990 he returned
briefly to Indonesia before travelling to Malaysia in 1991, where he
mixed in circles coordinated by two militant Islamist Indonesian
exiles, Abdullah Sungkar and Abu Bakar Ba'asyir, who would later
found Jemaah Islamiyah. Throughout this period he also had contact
with individuals later connected to al Qaeda, including bin Laden's
brother-in-law Mohammed Jamal Khalifa – then head of the Manila
office of the NGO the International Islamic Relief Organization – and
Ramzi Yousef, the nephew of **Khalid Sheikh Mohammed** and implicated in the 1993 attack on the World Trade Center and, two years
later, a plot (**Operation Bojinka**) to blow up aircraft flying across the
Pacific to the USA and also to assassinate Pope John Paul II. In 2000
he attended a meeting in Kuala Lumpur at which several of the **9/11**
attackers were also present, and later that year he helped to organize
and finance a series of bombings against Christian churches across
Indonesia. Soon after his capture he was transferred to a secret location, where he was interrogated. According to a 2003 media report,
allegedly based on leaked interrogation records, Hambali confessed
to receiving large amounts of funds from al Qaeda. Hambali was then
transferred to Guantánamo Bay. Hambali's status as one of the most
senior terrorists captured in Southeast Asia post-9/11 led Washington to rebuff informal requests from Indonesia for his extradition.

Further reading
Singh, B., 'The Challenge of Militant Islam and Terrorism in Indonesia'
Australian Journal of International Affairs 58(1) 2004, pp. 47–68.

International Crisis Group, *Jemaah Islamiyah: Damaged but Still Dangerous* Asia Report No. 63. Brussels: International Crisis Group, 26 August 2003.

HARAKAT UL-MUJAHEDEEN (HuM)
SEE: MOVEMENT OF HOLY WARRIORS

HARKAT-UL-JIHAD-AL-ISLAMI – BANGLADESH
SEE: ISLAMIC STRUGGLE MOVEMENT

HEARST, PATTY

The kidnapping of the nineteen-year-old Patty Hearst (b. 1954) – publishing heiress, part-time actress, and granddaughter of US media baron Randolph Hearst – by a self-styled left-wing urban guerrilla group, the **Symbionese Liberation Army** (SLA), in February 1974, attracted enormous interest in the USA and in much of the Western world. Initially the SLA attempted to use Hearst as ransom to secure the release from prison of several of its members, but after this failed they demanded that the Hearst family provide $70 of food to each underprivileged Californian, a demand which officials calculated would have cost several hundred million dollars. Hearst's family responded by providing $6 m in food to underprivileged people in San Francisco, but the SLA rejected the gesture. Matters took a bizarre turn when Hearst released an audiotape saying she had voluntarily joined the SLA and, two months after her disappearance, Hearst was filmed by a security camera as an apparently willing accomplice in an SLA bank robbery. After being captured in September 1975, her defence team argued in court that she had been brainwashed. Hearst was found guilty and sentenced to thirty-five years in prison, although this was later reduced to seven. She served two years before President Jimmy Carter commuted her sentence and, in January 2001, was granted a full pardon by President Bill Clinton.

Further reading
Graebner, W., *Patty's Got a Gun: Patricia Hearst in 1970s America*. Chicago: University of Chicago Press, 2008.
Hearst, P. C. and Moscow, A., *Patty Hearst: Her Story*. Avon: Mti Rei Edition, 1988.

HEZB-E-ISLAMI GULBUDDIN
Proscribed by: UK
Headed by Gulbuddin Hekmatyar, a former Prime Minister of Afghanistan, Hezb-e-Islami Gulbuddin (HIG) is a terrorist group operating mainly in the Jalalabad area east of Kabul. Fanatically anti-American, Hekmatyar is seen as something of a renegade insurgency leader. He became acquainted with **Osama bin Laden** during the anti-Soviet war in the 1980s but, even though he shares many of **al Qaeda**'s aims, he has denied claims that the two groups are formally linked. HIG has been responsible for a series of attacks on coalition forces in Afghanistan, although, unlike other insurgency groups linked to the **Taliban** and al Qaeda, HIG has stated that it is not necessarily opposed to the US-backed government led by Hamid Karzai. In a letter addressed to the Karzai regime in 2008, Hekmatyar held out the possibility of talks with the government, an initiative that some observers consider could be used to draw HIG away from other anti-coalition insurgent groups. Others have pointed to Hekmatyar's history of erratic behaviour and ambitions to lead Afghanistan again and are therefore sceptical about the value of accommodation with HIG.

Further reading
Jones, S. G., 'Averting Failure in Afghanistan' *Survival* 48(1) 2006, pp. 111–28.

HEZBOLLAH (Also: Hizbollah – Party of God)
Proscribed by: Canada, Israel, USA
Hezbollah is a radical Shi'ite organization based in Lebanon but with agents scattered across the world. Its main goal is to establish a Shi'ite theocracy in Lebanon. The group emerged out of the Lebanon's Bekaa Valley following Israel's 1982 invasion of Southern Lebanon. As such, Hezbollah acted as a lightning rod for those frustrated at the long-running political impotence of traditional Shi'ite leaders. During this formative stage, Hezbollah received logistic, material and diplomatic support from the government of Iran, who saw the organization as a vehicle for expanding Tehran's influence within the broader Middle East. Indeed, early Hezbollah leaders such as Muhammad Husayn Fadlallah had studied in Iran where they forged relationships with fellow clergy who would rise to senior

leadership positions following that country's 1979 revolution. Although the group's ties to Iran have been significantly reduced in recent years, Hezbollah is still the recipient of financial, diplomatic and military assistance from both Iran and Shi'ite groups in Syria. This support has allowed Hezbollah to wage a campaign based on car bombings, shootings, grenade and mortar attacks, as well as kidnapping. Its principal targets have been Israeli and the group's manifesto commits it to working for the destruction of the Jewish state. To this end, Hezbollah has claimed much of the credit for forcing Israel's decision in 2000 to withdraw all of its forces to the Israeli side of the border. Support for Hezbollah in Lebanon has also been enhanced by its provision of a wide range of social services, including orphanages, schools and hospitals, to the Shi'ite community – traditionally the poorest group within that country. In 1996 Hezbollah won positions in Lebanon's coalition government, holding two Cabinet posts. The party also performed well in Lebanon's 2009 general election. Hezbollah's involvement in mainstream Lebanese politics, its welfare role, and comments in the late 2000s by its leader, **Hassan Nasrallah**, that it would not interfere in peace talks between Israel and the Palestinians, despite remaining implacably opposed to the very existence of Israel, has led to debate over whether Hezbollah should still be classified as a terrorist entity. On the one hand, the USA, Canada and Israel proscribe the whole organization while, on the other, Australia and the UK have only proscribed Hezbollah's military wing.

Further reading

AbuKhalil, A., 'Ideology and Practice of Hizbollah in Lebanon: Islamization of Leninist Organisational Principles' *Middle Eastern Studies* 27(3) 1991, pp. 390–403.

Qassem, N., *Hizbullah: The Story from Within*. London: Saqi Books, 2005.

Saad-Ghorayeb, A., *Hizbu'llah: Politics and Religion*. London: Pluto Press, 2002.

THE HOFSTAD GROUP

The Hofstad Group is thought to be a cabal of Muslim extremists based in the Netherlands and made up mainly of second-generation Dutch of North African heritage. Although several members of the group were found guilty in 2006 of being involved in terrorist activities, in January 2008 a higher Dutch court overturned these verdicts, partly on the grounds that there was insufficient evidence to support the claim that the Hofstad Group even existed. Two of the alleged group remained in jail; **Mohammed Bouyeri**, imprisoned for life in 2005 for the murder of the Dutch film maker Theo van Gogh, and Samir Azzouz, initially suspected but acquitted by a Dutch court of plotting to attack the Dutch parliament, Amsterdam's Schiphol airport and a nuclear power station. Azzouz was rearrested in 2005 on suspicion of planning attacks against Dutch politicians and the headquarters of the Dutch intelligence service.

Further reading
De Wijk, R., 'The Multiple Crises in Dutch Parallel Societies' in François Heisbourg and Michael Emerson (eds.) *Readings in European Security*. Brussels: Centre for European Policy Studies, 2007, pp. 51–64.
Vidino, L., 'The Hofstad Group: The New Face of Terrorist Networks in Europe' *Studies in Conflict and Terrorism* 30(7) 2007, pp. 572–92.

HOSTAGE TAKING
Hostage taking is a tactic with a long pedigree. In a strictly political sense, the practice was documented as long ago as in ancient Rome when members of the social elite, or their progeny, were held as bargaining chips within the context of larger political machinations. Until the nineteenth century, hostage taking was widely considered to be a legitimate military tactic; however, there emerged throughout the twentieth century a body of domestic and international laws that proscribed the practice as a criminal act. As a tactic employed by terrorists, hostage taking has typically been used as a means for soliciting concessions from adversaries. In contemporary times terrorists have used hostages seized through initiatives such as airline hijackings or embassy sieges as a way to force governments to release colleagues from prisons or, as in the case of the **Munich Olympic attack**, to generate publicity for their cause.

Further reading
Dolnik, A., and Fitzgerald, K. M., *Negotiating Hostage Crises with New Terrorists*. New York: Praeger, 2007.

INTERNATIONAL CONVENTION AGAINST THE TAKING OF HOSTAGES

The International Convention against the Taking of Hostages emerged out of an initiative taken by the Federal Republic of Germany in the United Nations General Assembly in September 1976. Still dealing with the aftermath of the **Munich Olympic attack** just four years earlier and against the background of a rise of terrorist kidnappings in other parts of the world, such as the 1975 abduction of 11 OPEC Ministers from a conference in Vienna by a group led by **Ilyich Ramírez Sánchez ('Carlos the Jackal')**, the West German government wrote to the General Assembly requesting that it consider drafting and adopting a convention on the taking of hostages. The proposal was accepted in December 1979 and the Convention entered into force on 3 June 1983. Signatories to the Convention are obliged to apply severe penalties against any person who is directly or indirectly involved in the illegal detention of an individual as well as any threats to harm that person made with a view to compelling a state, intergovernmental organization or even a person or group of persons to behave in a certain way. The Convention also requires signatories to take all necessary steps to secure the release of the hostages. More controversially, it explicitly precludes the defence of hostage taking in the name of 'national liberation', with Article 12 requiring signatory states to do all they can to facilitate the extradition of individuals found guilty of crimes defined under this Convention to those countries in which they occurred. Many post-colonial countries objected to the implication that only non-state groups could be guilty of hostage taking and wanted the definition expanded to include hostage taking as a form of state-sponsored terrorism.

Further reading

Verwey, W. D., 'The International Hostages Convention and National Liberation Movements' *The American Journal of International Law* 75(1) 1981, pp. 69–92.

INTERNATIONAL CONVENTION FOR THE SUPPRESSION OF TERRORIST BOMBINGS

An important part of a series of UN conventions designed to equip the international community to deal better with the threat of terrorism, this was adopted by the United Nations on 15 December 1997 and entered into force on 23 May 2001. The Convention commits signatories to criminalizing any acts that involve any person intentionally placing, assisting in placing or directing others to place or detonate an explosive device (or any other potentially lethal mechanism) either at a state facility, against national or local infrastructure, or in a public space, with the intention of causing death, serious injury or economic loss. Signatories to the Convention are also required to assist other states in the investigation of such acts and facilitate extradition when legally appropriate. If extradition is not approved, signatories are obliged to prosecute the offence under domestic laws. The Convention specifically excludes acts undertaken by the military during war and acts undertaken by the military in the course of its normal duties outside of war.

Further reading
Greenwood, C., 'International Law and the War against Terrorism' *International Affairs* 78(2) 2002, pp. 301–17.

INTERNATIONAL CONVENTION FOR THE SUPPRESSION OF THE FINANCING OF TERRORISM

The International Convention for the Suppression of the Financing of Terrorism grew out of an initiative by France in the UN General Assembly, was adopted by the UN on 9 December 1999, and entered into force on 10 April 2002. As such it was one of the first UN responses to terrorism post-9/11. The Convention prohibits any person(s) or organizations 'from directly or indirectly, unlawfully, and wilfully providing or collecting funds with the intention that they should be used, or in the knowledge that they are to be used, to carry out an act that constitutes an offence under one of the nine treaties', regardless of the political, philosophical, cultural or religious considerations. Signatories to the Convention are required to take the necessary legislative measures to establish full jurisdiction over any financing of terrorism offences that might be committed within their state, including on-board foreign or national air or sea vessels passing through the territory of that state, and also including the activities of non-citizens or stateless persons who might be residing within that state. Signatories are also required to pass domestic legislation compelling banking and other financial institutions to introduce new financial monitoring mechanisms. However, there remains some debate about the overall efficacy of the obligations under this Convention, with some critics pointing out that very little terrorist funding is transferred internationally through formal banking institutions. Rather, informal money transfers occur through networks of money-lenders or, more commonly, terrorists raise their own funds through donations from members or through engaging in low-level crime such as the sale of drugs, car theft or credit card fraud.

Further reading
Bantekas, I., 'International Law of Terrorist Financing' *American Journal of International Law* 97(2) 2003, pp. 315–33.

INTERNATIONAL SIKH YOUTH FEDERATION (ISYF)

Proscribed by: Canada, EU, India, UK, USA

The International Sikh Youth Federation was founded in Britain in 1984 as an expression of Sikh anger at the Indian army's storming of the Golden Temple in Amritsar (the holiest shrine in Sikhdom) to end a siege by Sikh separatists led by **Jarnail Singh Bhindranwale**. Raising money mainly through the Sikh diaspora in North America and Western Europe, the ISYF is committed to supporting the establishment of an independent Sikh homeland, Khalistan, in India's Punjab region. In 1991 a Canadian court convicted an ISYF member, Inderjit Singh Reyat, of making the bomb that destroyed an Air India flight from Canada to Mumbai in 1985 and the attempted bombing of another Air India flight later that same year. Since then the group has been implicated in the financing and planning of several terrorist attacks, mainly within the Punjab – most of which have been stopped by Indian security forces. In December 2006 three ISYF members were arrested in the town of Jalandhar in possession of 12 kilograms of the explosive RDX, detonators and hand grenades. Soon after its founding, the ISYF split into two factions, and in the years since then has experienced several more schisms. The group is also thought to have connections with other extremist Sikh organizations, such as **Babbar Khalsa** International and the Khalistan Liberation Army. According to Indian intelligence sources, all three organizations receive covert support from the **Pakistan Directorate for Inter-Services Intelligence.**

Further reading
Oberoi, H., 'Sikh Fundamentalism: Translating History into Theory' in M. E. Marty and R. Scott Appleby (eds.) *Fundamentalisms and the State: Remaking Polities, Economies, and Militance.* Chicago: University of Chicago Press, 1993, pp. 256–87.

IRISH NATIONAL LIBERATION ARMY (INLA)

Proscribed by: Republic of Ireland, UK

The Irish National Liberation Army was formed in December 1974 as a neo-Marxist organization led by former members of the **Irish Republican Army (IRA)**, and was the paramilitary wing of the Northern Ireland-based Irish Republican Socialist Party. The main focus of its violence, predominantly shootings and bombings, has been British forces stationed in Northern Ireland, other Northern Irish security forces, Protestant paramilitary groups and occasionally rival republican groups. Among the most noteworthy of its attacks were the May 1979 assassination of Airey Neave, a Conservative member of the British parliament and friend of Prime Minister Margaret Thatcher; the December 1982 bombing of a bar frequented by British soldiers, which killed seventeen people; and the 1997 killing of Billy 'King Rat' Wright, leader of the **Loyalist Volunteer Force**, inside Long Kesh prison. The INLA strongly opposes the 1998 **Good Friday Agreement**, but, realizing that public support for it among the nationalist/Catholic population was high, the INLA leadership declared a ceasefire that was followed by a period of relative inactivity. Although the group last claimed responsibility for a terrorist attack in 1998, it remains active in some parts of Northern Ireland, where it serves as a self-appointed police force, dispensing punishment to petty criminals and others considered as anti-social nuisances. Reports also suggest some INLA members have become involved in cross-border narcotics trafficking. Members of the INLA sometimes used alternative organizational names, including 'The Catholic Reaction Force (CRF)' and 'The Peoples' Liberation Army (PLA)'.

Further reading
Coogan, T. P., *The IRA* (revised edn). New York: Palgrave, 2002.
Moloney, E., *A Secret History of the IRA.* New York: W.W. Norton and Company, 2002.

IRISH REPUBLICAN ARMY (IRA)

The Irish Republican Army (IRA) grew out of a series of earlier independence movements, most notably the Irish Volunteers whose members were involved in the 1916 Easter Rising when republican volunteers attempted a coup in Dublin. The contemporary roots of the IRA lay in a convention convened in 1917 to reorganize the Irish Volunteers in the wake of the failure of the Rising. In 1919 the Dáil Éireann (the de facto Irish parliament formed in 1919 by 73 Sinn Fein MPs who had been elected to Westminster but refused to take an oath to the Crown or take their seats in the British parliament) upheld the declaration of a free Irish state made at the Easter Rising, with the Irish Volunteers regarded as its army. The Irish Volunteers then embarked on a two-year guerrilla campaign designed to drive the British from Ireland. In 1921 the British government offered concessions and, under the terms of the Anglo-Irish Treaty, an Irish Free State (Republic of Ireland) was declared and made up of those 26 of Ireland's 33 counties with a majority Catholic population. But the Treaty caused a split within the IRA. Some members, mainly those who coalesced around Michael Collins, the leader of the IRA and therefore the founder of the Irish National Army, supported the partition of Ireland as a reasonable compromise for both getting most of what they had fought for and ending the conflict. On the other side were IRA members who viewed the Treaty as an unacceptable capitulation. Tensions erupted into civil war between the two IRA factions that lasted throughout 1922–3, with the pro-Treaty faction prevailing. However, despite being on the losing side during the civil war, hardcore opponents of the Treaty continued to view it as an illegitimate compromise. This group continued to exist as the IRA until further ructions led to yet more schisms in the 1960s and 1970s.

Further reading

Cottrell, P., *The Irish Civil War: 1922–1923.* Oxford: Osprey Publishing, 2008.

Kautt, W. H., *The Anglo-Irish War, 1916–1921: A People's War.* Westport, Conn.: Praeger Publishers, 1999.

IRISH REPUBLICAN ARMY (OFFICIAL)

Proscribed by: Republic of Ireland, UK

It is popularly believed that a single group constitutes the **Irish Republican Army (IRA)**, but, as with most things relating to terrorism, reality is more complex. There are in fact several groups that have used the 'IRA' label in modern times, the largest and most significant of which are the Official Irish Republican Army (OIRA) and the Provisional Irish Republican Army (PIRA – see **Irish Republican Army (Provisional)**). The existence of these two organizations can be traced to a split in the republican movement in 1969. The OIRA was the original carrier of the name through the 1950s and 1960s and was linked to the Official Sinn Fein, which passed through a number of evolutionary stages and is now called the Workers' Party of Ireland. Like its political counterpart in Official Sinn Fein, throughout the 1960s the OIRA was increasingly influenced by Marxism and began to conceive of the conflict in Northern Ireland as a 'bourgeois war' in which the ruling Catholic and Protestant elites were conspiring to maintain their privileged positions by promoting conflict between their respective working classes. Under the influence of this ideology, the OIRA was reluctant to engage in offensive violence against Unionist or British military forces or even to provide protection for Catholic areas against Protestant attacks. Rather, it increasingly saw its roles as trying to awaken the Catholic and Protestant proletariats to their status as an oppressed workforce and to encourage them to unite to establish a unified Ireland based on socialist principles. The shift towards Marxist analysis frustrated traditional nationalists and opened a divide within the republican movement. A key turning point was the outbreak of communal violence in August 1969 when Unionists, assisted by members of the Royal Ulster Constabulary (RUC), attacked several nationalist areas and burned down Catholic houses in several streets. The failure to do more to defend the Catholic areas prompted high-profile IRA figures to break ranks from the Marxist leadership headed by Cathal Goulding in 1969 and form the Provisional IRA. Anger generated by Bloody Sunday in 1972, when British paratroopers fired on unarmed nationalists taking part in a civil rights march, prompted the OIRA to declare an offensive campaign against Unionist and British military targets, but it suspended this one year later. Thereafter, the group confined most of its activities to proselytizing for a class-based solution to the problems in Northern Ireland, initiating only a small number of 'reprisal attacks', mainly against British targets. This left breakaway factions such as the Provisional IRA and the **Irish National Liberation Army** to take the lead in offensive attacks against British and Unionist targets.

Further reading
Coogan, T. P., *The IRA* (revised edn). New York: Palgrave, 2002.
Townshend, C., 'The Culture of Paramilitarism in Ireland' in M. Crenshaw (ed.) *Terrorism in Context*. Philadelphia: Pennsylvania State University Press, 1995, pp. 311–51.

IRISH REPUBLICAN ARMY (PROVISIONAL) (PIRA)

Proscribed by: Republic of Ireland, UK

The PIRA emerged out of a tempestuous intramural conflict sparked by disagreements at the 1969 Special Army Convention when the IRA split into two factions, the PIRA and the Official Irish Republican Army (see **Irish Republican Army (Official)**). There were two catalysts for the split: the first was growing dissatisfaction among traditional IRA members with the increasingly Marxist approach of the organization's hierarchy and its reluctance to engage in direct violence against the Royal Ulster Constabulary, British military forces, and Protestant paramilitary groups, and its focus instead on building a cross-denominational proletarian movement that would rise up and overthrow both the Catholic and Protestant elites. The second was the issue of abstentionism, the policy of elected Sinn Fein members not sitting in the Dáil, the Republic of Ireland parliament, or Westminster. By the early 1970s the PIRA (or 'Provos') had emerged as the most powerful of the nationalist Irish groups, and for the next two and a half decades it carried out a deadly campaign of shootings, bombings and kidnappings against British military, Royal Ulster Constabulary (RUC), Unionist paramilitary and Protestant targets in Northern Ireland, in Britain and, on rare occasions, in Western Europe. Its objectives were to end British rule in Ireland and to establish a united socialist Irish Republic, goals inherited from the IRA's 1916 constitution. Funded by kidnapping-for-ransom operations, robberies and donations from the Republic of Ireland and the Irish diaspora in countries such as the USA, it amassed a large cache of weapons that allowed it to maintain a sustained and sophisticated level of violence. In the 1970s and 1980s it also received training and weapons from Libya. The PIRA also evinced a remarkable ability to replenish its ranks by capitalizing on mis-steps by the British military and RUC, especially their use of the practice of collective punishment against nationalist neighbourhoods following attacks by the PIRA and other groups such as the **Irish National Liberation Army**. The PIRA also developed an extensive intelligence network with spies inside the RUC and other Northern Ireland institutions that not only allowed better-planned attacks but minimized the impact of counter-terrorism operations deployed against them. Under the leadership that emerged in 1969, the PIRA launched a violent insurgency that lasted until 1975 when it declared a ceasefire after receiving assur-ances of negotiation on key issues from the UK government. One of the most spectacular of attacks during this period was in July 1972 when 22 PIRA bombs exploded within 70 minutes of each other, killing 9 and injuring another 120. The collapse of the ceasefire in 1976 ushered in a new leadership, headed by the Military Council, made up of a new generation of leaders, which oversaw a substantial escalation in PIRA violence but which would also steer the organiza-tion towards the **Good Friday Agreement** in 1998. Key among these individuals were **Gerry Adams** and **Martin McGuinness**, under whose leadership the PIRA launched some of its most audacious attacks, including the 1979 assassination of Queen Elizabeth's uncle Lord Mountbatten, the 1984 bombing of a Conservative Party conference at a hotel in the British resort town of Brighton which killed 4 as well as a range of other assassinations and bombings in Northern Ireland and Britain. During this time the PIRA also established links with external terrorist groups, including ETA (see **Euskadi Ta Askatasuna**) in Spain. In July 2005, seven years after the Good Friday Agreement, the PIRA Army Council announced a formal end to armed struggle and ordered members to focus on change through 'exclusively peace-ful means'. Even so, the PIRA remains a proscribed terrorist organi-zation in the UK and an illegal organization in the Republic of Ireland, although it is not listed in the USA.

Further reading
Coogan, T. P., *The IRA* (revised edn). New York: Palgrave, 2002.
Provisional Irish Republican Army, *Handbook for Volunteers of the Irish Republican Army: Notes on Guerrilla Warfare* ('The Green Book'). Boulder: Paladin Press, 1996.
Toolis, K., *Rebel Hearts: Journeys within the IRA's Soul*. New York: Thomas Dunne, 1995.

ISLAMIC ARMY OF ADEN (Also: Aden Abyan Islamic Army *and* Islamic Army of Aden Abyan *and* Aden Islamic Army)
Proscribed by: Australia, Canada, EU, UK, UN
Founded in 1996 by Zain al-Abidin al-Mihdar and other former members of Yemeni Islamic Jihad, the Islamic Army of Aden (IAA)

is a fundamentalist Sunni organization dedicated to establishing Yemen as an Islamic state. The group has links to **al Qaeda** that have been forged partly through shared experiences fighting the Soviets in Afghanistan. After al-Mihdar was executed in 1999 for orchestrating the kidnapping of sixteen Australian, British and US tourists, leadership passed to Khalid Abd al-Nabi, who surrendered to authorities in 2003. He was replaced by Abdul al-Nabi. The group is active mostly around the Yemeni capital Aden and the southern region of Abyan. Major strikes include bombings and hand grenade attacks against military targets, as well as planned strikes against Western embassies that have been interrupted by Yemeni authorities. An offensive against the IAA launched in 2003 is thought to have reduced its numbers to less than 100, although members still at large continued to pose a threat to local and foreign targets in Yemen.

Further reading
Schanzer, J., 'Yemen's War on Terror' *Orbis* 48(3) 2004, pp. 517–31.

ISLAMIC GROUP (al-Gama'a al-Islamiyah)
Proscribed by: Canada, EU, UK, USA
Active since the early 1970s, al-Gama'a al-Islamiyah had, by the 1990s, become Egypt's largest and most active terrorist group. However, by the late 2000s, its membership had shrunk from several thousand to less than 500 members, with a corresponding reduction in its ability to damage the secular regime of President Hosni Mubarak. Between 1998 and 2008 it carried out no terrorist attacks. Prior to 1998, the group's main targets were high officials – for example it orchestrated a 1995 assassination attempt against President Mubarak, members of the Egyptian security forces and Coptic Christians. In 1997 a faction led by Rifa'l Ahmad carried out an attack against Western tourists at the archaeological site at Luxor. The decline in the group's potency as a terrorist organization is due to several factors, including the 1996 arrest of, and life sentence imposed on, Sheikh Umar Abd al-Rahman, al-Gama'a al-Islamiyah's spiritual leader, for his role in planning the 1993 attacks against New York's World Trade Center. Public outrage at the Luxor attacks and an extensive crackdown against Islamist militants created a split in the group. In 2002 a moderate faction denounced the use of violence. However, a more extreme faction signed **Osama bin Laden**'s 1998 fatwa sanctioning violence

against Israel and the USA and its allies. This hard-core faction continues to operate at the fringes of Egyptian society, although many members are thought to have fled to join the insurgencies in Iraq and Afghanistan.

Further reading
Kepel, G., *The Trail of Political Islam*. London: I. B. Tauris, 2003.
Nedoroscik, J. A., 'Extremist Groups in Egypt' *Terrorism and Political Violence* 14(2) 2002, pp. 47–76.

ISLAMIC JIHAD
SEE: EGYPTIAN ISLAMIC JIHAD OR PALESTINIAN ISLAMIC JIHAD

ISLAMIC MOVEMENT OF UZBEKISTAN (IMU)
Proscribed by: Australia, Canada, Russia, UK, UN, USA
Founded in 1998 by former members of the Islamic Resistance Party, which was banned by the Uzbek regime in 1992, the IMU is opposed to the secular Uzbek government of Islam Karimov and dedicated to establishing an Islamic state. In the past it has had bases in Afghanistan, Kazakhstan, Tajikistan and Uzbekistan itself. A former Soviet paratrooper, Tohir Abdouhalilovitch Yuldeshev, and Mullah Jumaboi Ahmadzhanovitch Khojaev, who later changed his name to Juma Namangani, founded the group. Namangani was reportedly killed in a US airstrike in November 2001. At its formation the IMU received seed money from **al Qaeda** but also from Saudi and Turkish charities. Since then it has received funds through its involvement in opium trafficking from Afghanistan. The IMU also has links to the Eastern Turkistan Islamic movement, a loose network of Uyghur separatist groups based in the western Chinese province of **Xinjiang**. The IMU's ideology is a combination of militant Sunni Islam and nationalism. Although it has less than 1,000 members, between 1998 and 2004 it caused significant disruption and damage in Uzbekistan, Tajikistan and Kyrgyzstan through a combination of car bombings, kidnappings and shootings. In March 2002 many IMU members fought alongside **Taliban** and al Qaeda members in the battle for Shah-I-Kot in southeast Afghanistan, losing a large number of personnel in the process. Since then a determined counter-terrorism effort by the Karimov

regime, supported by intelligence from China, Russia and the USA, has diminished the group's capabilities. However, links between Namangani and **Osama bin Laden** and former Afghanistan Taliban leader Mullah Omar have not always worked to the IMU's advantage. Both Bin Laden's extremist brand of Wahabbi Islam and the radical Deobandi Islam of the Taliban are considered alien by many Uzbeks and, as a result, many see the IMU as controlled by foreign interests. By the late 2000s, most IMU members were fighting in Afghanistan or had allied themselves with anti-government Islamist militants in Pakistan's Northwest Frontier.

Further reading
Cornell, S. E., 'Narcotics, Radicalism, and Armed Conflict in Central Asia: The Islamic Movement of Uzbekistan' *Terrorism and Political Violence* 17(4) 2005, pp. 619–39.
Sanchez, A. W., 'A Central Asian Security Paradigm: Russia and Uzbekistan' *Small Wars and Insurgencies* 18(1) 2007, pp. 113–33.

ISLAMIC STRUGGLE MOVEMENT (Harakat-ul-Jihad-al-Islami)
Proscribed by: Bangladesh, UK, USA
Formed initially in Pakistan as a group committed to fighting the Soviet forces in Afghanistan, Harakat-ul-Jihad-al-Islami (HUJI) later turned its attention to the disputed territory of Kashmir, where it was involved in dozens of terrorist attacks against Indian military and police targets. Unlike other Pakistan-based terrorist groups such as **Lashkar-e-Tayyiba** and **Jaish-e-Mohammed**, both of which have strong links to the Afghan **Taliban**, HUJI's focus has been almost exclusively on Kashmir. The Bangladeshi branch of HUJI, usually denoted as HUJI-B, was formed in the mid-1990s and is committed to establishing Bangladesh as an Islamic state. To this end, HUJI-B has been implicated in assassination attempts against figures from the liberal arts as well as a plot to kill former Prime Minister Sheikh Hassina. In 2005 it was also responsible for a series of bombings at several locations around Bangladesh.

Further reading
Datta, S., 'Islamic Militancy in Bangladesh: The Threat from Within' *South Asia: Journal of South Asian Studies* 30(1) 2007, pp. 145–70.

ISRAEL INSTITUTE FOR INTELLIGENCE AND SPECIAL TASKS – MOSSAD

At the forefront of Israel's struggle against terrorism is the Israel Institute for Intelligence and Special Tasks, better known by the name 'Mossad' (Hebrew for 'Institute'). The bulk of its activities centre on threats to Israel itself and, more broadly, to Israeli interests overseas. Formed in April 1949, when it was known as the Central Institute for Coordination, Mossad's primary directive was to provide intelligence that constituted 'the first line of defence' against Israel's enemies. The organization is divided into several departments, the largest of which is the Collections Division that oversees human intelligence collection via a network of spies based around the world. These spies operate under diplomatic, cultural, corporate, media-based and student covers. The Special Operations Division conducts sabotage, paramilitary and assassination operations, while the Political Action and Liaison Department coordinates relationships with Israel's allies and friends. Mossad's Psychological Warfare Department designs and implements propaganda and deception activities, while the Technology Department manages the development of new technologies to assist other departments in their work, and the Research Department oversees intelligence analysis.

Further reading
Thomas, G., *Gideon's Spies: The Secret History of the Mossad* (3rd edn). London: St Martins Griffin, 2007.

ISRAEL SECURITY AGENCY – The Shabak (Shin Bet)

The Israel Security Agency is a counterpart to Mossad (see **Israel Institute for Intelligence and Special Tasks**) and Aman (military intelligence), with all three constituting the main components of the Israeli intelligence community. Unlike Mossad, which has a mandate to protect Israel's interests from external threats, and Aman, which focuses on military developments mainly in the Middle East and surrounding areas, the Shabak has an internal focus and monitors threats, particularly from terrorist groups, from within Israel and the Occupied Territories. To this end it relies heavily on human intelligence collected from an extensive network of informers within Israel, the Gaza Strip and the West Bank, although it also accesses electronic intercepts of telephone communications and e-mails. The Shabak has managed to penetrate all of the Palestinian resistance groups, sometimes to the upper echelons. For example, it was information passed from informers that allowed the organization to cooperate with the Israeli military to assassinate **Hamas** leaders Sheikh **Ahmed Yassin** and Abdad Aziz Rantisi through missiles fired from helicopter gunships. An acronym for 'Sherut Bitahon Klali' ('General Security Service'), the Shabak was established with Israel's declaration of independence in 1948, when it was a part of the Israeli Defence Forces; however, after a series of scandals, the Israeli parliament passed a new law in 2002 that placed it under the aegis of the Prime Minister's office. Most of these scandals relate to human-rights-related concerns about the manner in which the Shabak treats detainees, especially during interrogation. It was complaints about such measures that led to the 1987 Landau Commission (headed by a former Justice of the Supreme Court of Israel, Moshe Landau). The Commission found that the Shabak's methods often transgressed Israeli law and that the culture of the organization encouraged agents to lie in court when such allegations were raised. The report also set out guidelines for the use of 'moderate physical pressure' during interrogation, but in a 1994 report it was revealed that the Shabak was still employing methods that violated the Laundau Commission's guidelines.

Further reading
Kahana, E., 'Reorganizing Israel's Intelligence Community' *International Journal of Intelligence and Counterintelligence* 15(3) 2002, pp. 415–28.

ITALIAN RED BRIGADES

The Italian Red Brigade was founded by Renato Curcio, a student at the University of Trento, his girlfriend Margherita Cagol (Mara Cagol) and Alberto Franceschini. Based on Marxist–Leninist principles, the Red Brigade embraced violence as a way to force the Italian government to abrogate the country's role in NATO and to usher in a socialist state. In the service of these goals it was involved in assassinations, kidnappings and sabotage. Soon after its foundation the group underwent an informal split between the Trento faction headed by Curcio and the Reggio Emilia group made up mostly of former members of the Communist Youth movement who grouped around Franceschini. In 1975 Curcio was captured and imprisoned, but several weeks later was freed from prison by fellow Red Brigade members led by Cagol (by this time his wife). Cagol was killed in a shoot-out with police soon after, and Curcio was recaptured and resentenced. This gave the ascendancy to the Franceschini faction. As pointed out by the Italian scholar Della-Porta, the Red Brigade's embrace of terrorist violence was gradual, passing through a series of incremental steps that began with members engaging in low-level acts of civil disobedience before graduating to bombings, kidnapping and assassinations. In 1978 a cell linked to Franceschini and led by Mario Moretti kidnapped former Prime Minister Aldo Moro and held him hostage to secure for the release from prison of Red Brigade members. The government refused to negotiate and, after being held hostage for fifty-four days, Moro was executed. Several years later, in 1981, four Red Brigade members posing as workers gained access to the Verona residence of the NATO Deputy Chief of Staff for Southern Europe, the US Army Brigadier General James L. Dozier, kidnapped him and his wife and held them hostage for forty-two days. Public support (mainly among trade unions) and in-group cohesion disintegrated rapidly after the Moro execution, and a major split in 1984 led many of the group's more moderate members to provide information to the Italian police that allowed investigators to arrest some of their more militant counterparts. In the 1990s a new group called the Red Brigade – PCC (Red Brigade – Communist Combatant Party) emerged, and in 1999 it executed an advisor to Prime Minister Massimo D'Alema. Three years later, it killed an advisor to Italian Prime Minister Silvio Berlusconi. This new group is not thought to have any formal links to the Red Brigade of the 1970s and 1980s.

Further reading
Della Porta, D., 'Left-Wing Terrorism in Italy' in M. Crenshaw (ed.) *Terrorism in Context*. Philadelphia: Pennsylvania State University Press, 1995, pp. 105–59.
Social Movements, Political Violence, and the State: A Comparative Analysis of Italy and Germany. Cambridge: Cambridge University Press, 2008.
Moss, D., 'The Kidnapping and Murder of Aldo Moro' *Archive Européenne de Sociologie* 20 1981, pp. 265–95.

IZZ AD-DIN AL-QASSAM BRIGADES
SEE: HAMAS

JAISH-E-MOHAMMED
Proscribed by: Australia, Canada, India, UK, UN, USA
Jaish-e-Mohammed (JeM – 'Army of Mohammed') is a Pakistan-based group that operates mainly in the disputed province of

Kashmir. Its principal goals are to force India to relinquish its claim to the Muslim-majority province of Kashmir and to incorporate it into Pakistan. More generally, Jaish-e-Mohammed is also committed to the establishment of Pakistan as a fundamentalist Sunni state. At a meeting of extremist Pakistani and Afghan groups in mid-2008, leaders of the group agreed to refocus some of their energies on attacking US and coalition forces in Afghanistan. Its modus operandi includes shootings, bomb and hand grenade attacks against Indian police and military targets in Kashmir. According to intelligence services, Jaish-e-Mohammed members joined with counterparts from another Kashmiri militant group based in Pakistan, **Lashkar-e-Tayyiba**, to carry out the December 2001 attack on the Indian parliament in New Delhi. The group was founded by Maulana Masood Azhar, a former member of the **Harakat ul-Mujahidin** (HuM), in early 2000, soon after HuM members forced his release from an Indian jail by hijacking an Indian Airlines jet carrying 155 passengers. Among the three other HuM members released as part of the ransom agreement was the British-born terrorist **Sheikh Omar Saeed**, charged with helping to organize the kidnapping and execution of the *Wall Street Journal* correspondent Daniel Pearl. But this is not the only connection Jaish-e-Mohammed has to the UK. A British citizen implicated in the 2006 **Trans-Atlantic Airline Plot**, Rashid Rauf, is the brother-in-law of JeM founder Azhar, while Rauf's father-in-law is head of the radical Darul Uloom Madina madrassa in Azhar's hometown in Pakistan. Soon after forming Jaish-e-Mohammed, Azhar was joined by more than half of the HuM membership base, after which he travelled to Afghanistan to meet **Osama bin Laden**, who provided material and logistical assistance to help consolidate the new group. JeM has around 700 members, made up of Kashmiri Muslims and Pakistanis, as well as Afghan and Arab volunteers. The group receives its funds from other extremist groups in Pakistan and Kashmir, but also from donations solicited through extremist magazines, as well as mosques and madrassas sympathetic to their cause. In 2002 JeM formed an informal coalition, called Lashkar-e-Omar, with Harkat-ul-Jihad-al-Islami (HUJI) and **Lashkar-i-Jhangvi**.

Further reading
Bajpai, K. S., 'Untangling India and Pakistan' *Foreign Affairs* 82(3) May–June 2003, pp. 112–26.

Sondhi, S., 'Terrorism and Governance in Kashmir' *Journal of Conflict Studies* 24(2) 2004. At http://journals.hil.unb.ca/index.php/JCS/article/viewArticle/202/359.

JAMAAT UL MUJAHEDEEN BANGLADESH (JMB)

Proscribed by: UK

Jamaat ul Mujahedeen Bangladesh (lit: 'Party of the Mujahedeen') was founded in 1998 in Dhaka by Sabir Quazi, and from the outset has been dedicated to toppling secular government in Bangladesh and creating an Islamic state modelled on that implemented in Afghanistan under the **Taliban**. For its first few years the JMB operated without attracting much government or public attention, but this altered in 2001 when authorities discovered a cache of explosives and documents outlining plans to commit acts of terrorism. Despite this discovery, Dakha was reluctant to move against the group, mainly out of a fear of investing it with more credibility among disenchanted Bangladeshis. Timidity on the part of the state allowed the JMB to grow significantly, and by 2005 it had built an extensive network that stretched across the country and was supported by a complex series of overt and covert links to other militant groups such as the shadowy Al Mujahideen, Jama'atul Jihad, Jagrata Muslim Janata Bangladesh, Harkat-ul-Jihad-al-Islami – Bangladesh (see **Islamic Struggle Movement**), Hizbut Tawhid, Tawhidi Janata and Shahadat-e al Hiqma. Through this network the JMB is estimated to have built a base of around 10,000 active members and at least 100,000 supporters. Claims that it has a several-thousand-man-strong suicide squad have appeared in some media outlets, but these have not been verified. Moreover, the JMB's preferred mode of attack has been through small pre-set explosive devices (sometimes containing sawdust rather than the more common practice of inserting metal shrapnel) instead of suicide missions. But even outwardly benign bombings can have a powerful demonstrative effect. For example, in August 2005 the JMB detonated around 500 such devices, targeting mainly government buildings at more than 300 locations in almost every province of Bangladesh, all of which exploded within ninety minutes of each other. Despite the extent of the bombings only a few people were killed, with several dozen more injured. The killing of two judges several months later prompted the government to finally outlaw the organization and, soon after, Bangladeshi security forces arrested six key leaders. All were executed by hanging in March 2007. Along with a smaller but similarly extremist group, Jagrata Muslim Janata Bangladesh (JMJB), the JMB receives significant political support from Bangladesh's ultra-conservative Islamic political party, Jamaat-e-Islami. The JMB and JMJB share some common leadership personnel, although the consensus is that they remain different organizations.

Further reading

Hussain, I., 'Fundamentalism and Bangladesh: No Error, No Terror' *South Asian Survey* 14(2) 2007, pp. 207–29.

Riaz, A., 'Bangladesh in 2005: Standing at a Crossroads' *Asian Survey* 46(1) 2006, pp. 107–13.

JAMIAT UL-ANSAR
see: **Movement of Holy Warriors**

JAPANESE RED ARMY

Although it never numbered more than around forty members, the Japanese Red Army (JRA) earned a reputation in the 1970s as one of the world's most notorious terrorist groups. Founded in February 1971 by **Fusako Shigenobu** and Tsuyoshi Okudaira after a split from the Japanese Communist League – Red Army Faction, the group carried out several attacks in Japan before Shigenobu and several of her comrades escaped to Western Europe. The group's aims at its inception were to end the Japanese monarchy, topple the government and help bring about world revolution. However, these aims shifted after the move to Europe and then to Lebanon, where the group developed close links with the **Popular Front for the Liberation of Palestine (PFLP)**. In 1972, several JRA members joined with counterparts from the PFLP in an assault on Tel Aviv's Lod airport that killed twenty-six and injured amore than eighty others. In 1974, several JRA members took over the French embassy at The Hague, where staff were held captive until Paris released one of their comrades from a French prison. In the 1980s the group launched a series of mortar attacks against Western embassies in places as diverse as Jakarta, Kuala Lumpur and Rome. During these years the JRA adopted a variety of different names, including the Anti-Imperialist International Brigade (AIIB), Holy War Brigade, and the Anti-War

Democratic Front. In November 2000, Shigenobu was arrested in Japan and sentenced to a twenty-year jail sentence. In 2001 she issued a statement from prison formally declaring that the JRA had been disbanded. Another leftist Japanese revolutionary group active at this time was the United Red Army, which, although it was also an off-shoot of the Japanese Communist League – Red Army Faction, was not connected to the JRA.

Further reading
Gallagher, A., *The Japanese Red Army*. New York: Rosen Publishing Group, 2003.
Steinhoff, P. G., 'Hijackers, Bombers, and Bank Robbers: Managerial Style in the Japanese Red Army' *The Journal of Asian Studies* 48(4) 1989, pp. 724–40.

JEMAAH ISLAMIYAH
Proscribed by: Australia, Canada, Russia, UK, UN, USA
Founded in January 1993 by two Indonesian clerics, Abdullah Sungkar and Abu Bakar Bashir, Jemaah Islamiyah's initial goal was to establish an Islamic state in Indonesia. However, by the late 1990s the group's longer-term goals had grown on the back of links with other Southeast Asian groups to include the establishment of a Southeast Asian Caliphate incorporating Indonesia, Malaysia, Brunei, southern Thailand and the southern Philippines. Although Jemaah Islamiyah has links to **al Qaeda**, the group is not, as some have claimed, the latter's 'Southeast Asian wing'. These links with al Qaeda and other groups and individuals in the region reflected personal relationships forged in the 1980s between Southeast Asian volunteers in the struggle against the Soviet occupation of Afghanistan. Throughout the 1990s, Sungkar and Bashir focused their energies on recruiting members through a series of religious schools (madrassas) located mainly in East Java. Jemaah Islamiyah's embrace of the tactic of terrorism first manifested itself in 2000 with an attack against the residence of the Philippine Ambassador in Jakarta, which was followed later that year by coordinated attacks against Christian churches celebrating Christmas services. However, it was a series of attacks against tourist spots in Bali on 12 October 2002 that earned the group its international status. The suicide attacks killed over 200 people, including 88 Australians. In 2003 Jemaah Islamiyah bombers attacked the Marriott hotel in Jakarta; in 2004 a suicide bomber attacked the

Australian embassy, also in Jakarta; while, later that same year, the group launched another suicide attack in Bali that killed over 20 people. Since then, Jemaah Islamiyah has suffered a number of major setbacks, including the arrest and death of senior leaders such as the head of operations and main conduit to al Qaeda, **Hambali**, and, in June 2007, Ainul Bahri Abu Dujana and Zarkasih (also known as Abu Irsyad). Coupled with declining support among the wider population (partly because the group's attacks have killed more Muslims than non-Muslims), these arrests have led to a significant diminution of the group's capabilities. By the late 2000s, it had split into several factions, of which only one, headed by the late Noordin bin Top, was assessed as still adhering to a violent agenda. Other factions have turned to preaching and opened publishing houses to spread their militant Sunni ideology through more peaceful means.

Further reading
Barton, G., *Indonesia's Struggle: Jemaah Islamiyah and the Soul of Islam.* Kensington: University of New South Wales Press, 2005.
Jones, S., 'The Changing Nature of Jemaah Islamiyah' *Australian Journal of International Affairs* 59(2) 2005, pp. 169–78.

JIBRIL, AHMED

Ahmed Jibril was born in the Palestinian town of Jaffna in 1938, although his family moved to Syria while he was still young. In 1956 Jibril enlisted in the Syrian army but was discharged in 1958 for being a communist. The following year, Jibril founded the Palestinian Liberation Front, which in 1967 merged with the Arab Nationalist Movement headed by George Habash to form the **Popular Front for the Liberation of Palestine (PFLP)**. Less than a year later, disagreements between Jibril and Habash saw the former walk away from the union to found the pro-Syrian **Popular Front for the Liberation of Palestine – General Command (PFLP-GC)**, which remains headquartered in Damascus. Jibril's ideology centres on the belief that, if guerrilla attacks against Jewish targets are maintained, Tel Aviv's willingness to fight will eventually wane. To this end, Jibril has been responsible for launching a series of highly inventive strikes, including a 1987 attack on an Israeli military outpost by a PFLP-GC member attached to a hang-glider. During the 1990s, support for the organization began to dissolve as supporters of the **Oslo Peace Accords** shifted to **Fatah**, while more militant members of the Palestinian community gravitated towards **Hamas** and other Islamist groups.

Further reading
Alexander, Y., *Palestinian Secular Terrorism: Profiles of Fatah, Popular Front for the Liberation of Palestine, Popular Front for the Liberation of Palestine – General Command and the Democratic Front for the Liberation of Palestine.* Leiden: Hotei Publishing, 2003.

JIHAD

An Arabic word which means 'to exert one's best efforts', or 'struggle' or 'resist' in the pursuit of a particular goal. Contrary to the manner in which many terrorist groups have misappropriated the word, jihad does not necessarily involve violent struggle. Indeed, a more common use of the term refers to the inner struggle against a person's 'nafs', an Arabic term meaning 'the lower self'. In short, the concept of 'greater jihad' refers mostly to the internally generated behaviour required to avoid the temptations of sin so that one can live as a good person. Used in its limited military context, 'lesser jihad' is used to refer to the struggle against armed aggression, which is necessarily a limited and temporary act. It is important to note, however, that not all scholars of Islam share this view. For instance, Bernard Lewis has argued that, in both a historical and contemporary sense, most Muslims perceive jihad as involving some degree of military aggression. For some terrorism watchers, this explains why terrorist organizations such as **al Qaeda** place jihad at the centre of their ideologies. The prioritization of the violent dimensions of jihad by some terrorist groups reflects a belief that Islam is under attack from a coalition of non-Islamic forces in the West and apostates within Muslim societies themselves.

Further reading
Bernard, L., *The Political Language of Islam.* Chicago: University of Chicago Press, 1988.
Esposito, J., *Unholy War: Terror in the Name of Islam.* Oxford: Oxford University Press, 2002.

JOINT INTELLIGENCE COMMITTEE – UK (JIC)

A part of the UK Cabinet Office, the Joint Intelligence Committee is Britain's main intelligence analysis forum, producing short- and long-term assessments for the Prime Minister, senior Cabinet members and other high-level officials. It also oversees and assesses the performance of the UK's intelligence collection agencies, which is measured against collection targets set by the JIC itself. It is constituted by a team of assessment staff made up of experts seconded from a range of ministries and reflecting a variety of expertise. Their reports are submitted and vetted by a senior committee made up of high-level representatives from all UK agencies with a national security focus – including the Foreign and Commonwealth Office, Ministry of Defence (including the Chief of Defence Intelligence), Home Office, Department of Trade and Industry, Department for International Development, Treasury and Cabinet Office – the heads of the three intelligence agencies (MI5 (see **Security Service – UK**), MI6 (see **Secret Intelligence Service –UK**), and the **Defence Intelligence Staff**) and the Chief of the Assessments Staff. Senior representatives from other ministries attend when issues fall within their administrative bailiwick. Intelligence representatives from Britain's allies can also attend these meetings when appropriate. The Chairman of the Joint Intelligence Committee, who reports directly to the Prime Minister, oversees the Committee's work and is charged with ensuring that the Committee's warning and monitoring role is discharged effectively. On terrorism-related matters, the JIC works closely with the Joint Terrorism Analysis Centre (JTAC) in assessing the threat posed by trends in international terrorism. The difference between the JIC and the JTAC is that, while the latter assesses current intelligence to help set current threat levels, the former crafts more in-depth analyses that focus on the longer-term processes that are shaping terrorist patterns around the world.

Further reading

Andrew, C. M., *Secret Service: The Making of the British Intelligence Community*. London: Heinemann, 1985.

Richelson, J. T., *Foreign Intelligence Organizations*. Cambridge, Mass.: Ballinger Publishing Company, 1988.

KACH

Proscribed by: Canada, EU, USA

Kach is a small extremist Jewish group formed in 1972 in Israel that advocates the use of violence to expand that country's borders so that they replicate the Jewish lands of biblical times and to expel all Arabs from this expanded Jewish state. At its peak it has never had more than around 100 members, although it does have a much larger informal body of support in Israel, especially in the Jewish Settlements. Its philosophy is heavily influenced by the teachings of the group's founder, a New-York-born Orthodox Rabbi named Meir Kahane. After migrating to Israel in 1971 Kahane tried several times to gain election to the Knesset, Israel's parliament. He was finally successful at the 1984 elections, although the party was banned from participating in subsequent polls. During the 1980s Kahanists were involved in a series of knife and grenade attacks against Palestinian targets, and even though the party defended this violence it was never clear that the assailants had been acting on specific instructions from the party hierarchy. Kahane was assassinated in New York on 5 November 1990. After Kahane's death, Kach split into two factions, with Kahane's son Binyamin forming a break-away faction called **Kahane Chai** (lit. 'Kahane lives'). The remainder of Kach stayed under the brief leadership of Rabbi Avraham Toledano, who was replaced soon after by Baruch Marzel. Despite the split, both groups continued to share many ideological and political objectives. In 2004 Marzel founded a new organization called the Jewish National Front, which participated in the 2006 elections but failed to win a seat. Marzel has become known not only for his virulent anti-Arab statements, but also for similarly intense anti-leftist and homophobic comments. Sceptics argue that Marzel's efforts are an attempt to put some distance between his group and the violence of Kach's past to reduce harassment by Israeli authorities and end the ban on the organization. Regardless, Tel Aviv continues to assess the ideals espoused by Kach as a potential terrorism risk and, as such, it remains an illegal organization.

Further reading
Cohen-Almagor, R., 'Vigilant Jewish Fundamentalism – from the JDL to Kach' *Terrorism and Political Violence* 4(1) 1992, pp. 44–66.
Pedahzur, A., 'The Transformation of Israel's Extreme Right' *Studies in Conflict and Terrorism* 24(1) 2001, pp. 25–42.

KACZYNSKI, THEODORE
SEE: UNABOMBER

KAHANE CHAI

Proscribed by: Canada, EU, USA

Kahane Chai is a small Jewish extremist group founded by Binyamin Ze'ev Kahane, the son of Rabbi Meir Kahane after the latter's assassination in 1990. On its foundation it inherited almost all of the ideological and political ambitions of the political party **Kach** established in the 1970s by the elder Kahane. Kahane Chai is based mainly in the West Bank settlements of Kfar Tapuach and Kiryat Arba. Binyamin Kahane and his wife were assassinated on 31 December 2000 although the **Palestinian Liberation Organization**'s paramilitary wing Force 17, the group responsible, described the killings as 'luck', saying that they were targeting random Jewish settlers. Despite his death, the politics of Kahane Chai continues to influence some extremist Israelis. For example, **Baruch Goldstein**, who was responsible for the massacre of twenty-nine worshippers at the Al Aqsa Mosque, was a supporter of the group. And in 2005 a nineteen-year-old Israeli soldier with links to the organization opened fire on a bus, killing four Arab passengers. Like Kach, with which the group shares some members, Kahane Chai receives funding from extremist Jewish groups in Israel and the United States. In 1994 the Israeli government banned the group.

Further reading

Lustick, I., *For The Land and The Lord* (2nd edn). Washington, DC: Council on Foreign Relations 1994 [1988].

Sprinzak, E., 'Extremism and Violence in Israeli Democracy' *Terrorism and Political Violence* 12(3&4) 2000, pp. 209–36.

KHALED, LEILA

Born in Haifa in 1944, Leila Khaled's introduction to Palestinian militancy was grounded in the experiences of her family, who were part of the mass exodus of Palestinians after the establishment of the Israeli state in 1948. She joined George Habash's Arab Nationalist Movement (ANM) in 1959 when she was just fifteen. Her approach to the Palestinian question in the years following her commitment to the ANM was influenced by the revolutionary philosophies of individuals such as **Ernesto ('Che') Guevara**. In 1966 the ANM joined with the **Palestinian Liberation Front** to form the **Popular Front for the Liberation of Palestine**, in whose name Khaled committed most of her acts of terrorism. In 1969 she was involved in the hijacking of a TWA flight from Rome to Athens. The aircraft was diverted to Damascus where Khaled and her co-conspirators evacuated all the passengers before blowing up the plane. The following year Khaled was involved in another hijacking when she and a Nicaraguan colleague attempted to seize an El Al flight from Amsterdam to New York. However, Israeli Special Forces disguised as passengers subdued Khaled and diverted the plane to London where she was arrested. Soon after, British authorities released her as part of a prisoner exchange agreement. Although never explicitly disavowing violence, in the mid-1970s Khaled disengaged from overt participation in terrorist activities. Now a member of the Palestinian National Council, she has been a prominent critic of the **Oslo Peace Accords**.

Further reading
Khaled, L., *My People Shall Live: Autobiography of a Revolutionary*. London: Hodder and Stoughton, 1973.
Viner, K., 'I Made the Ring from a Bullet and the Pin of a Hand Grenade' *The Guardian Supplement* 26 January 2001, pp. 2–3.

KHALID SHEIKH MOHAMMED
At the time of his arrest by Pakistani authorities (supported by **Federal Bureau of Investigation (FBI)** agents) in Rawalpindi on 1 March 2003, Khalid Sheikh Mohammed (b. 1964 or 1965) had become one of **al Qaeda**'s most important operational and planning officers. He first came to the attention of US authorities after playing a role in the 1993 World Trade Center bombing, which also involved his nephew **Ramzi Yousef**. But after a decade of steadily more audacious acts of violence, including being a main organizer of the foiled 1995 Manila-based plot **Operation Bojinka**, his career as a terrorist culminated with his role as the main planning and logistical person in the **9/11** attacks. Khalid was born in Kuwait but is of Pakistani heritage. After leaving school, he travelled to the USA where he graduated in 1986 with a degree in mechanical engineering. Soon after, he travelled to Afghanistan where he was introduced to several Mujahedeen groups engaged in combat against the Soviet forces there. After the Soviet departure from Afghanistan, he secured a job in Qatar, but remained involved in extremist groups. Encouraged by the accolades received by his cousin Yousef following the 1993 attack against the World Trade Center, he decided to become more deeply involved in terrorist activi-

ties. His next major contribution was to develop the timing devices that were to be used for Operation Bojinka, which he tested success- fully by bombing a movie theatre in Manila and a Japan Airlines flight from Manila to Tokyo. By the time the plot was discovered by Philip- pines police, he was back in Qatar, but after Yousef's capture in Pakistan he moved to Afghanistan to avoid efforts by US authorities to track him down. It was here that he was introduced to **Osama bin Laden** and presented him with a list of possible strikes against the USA. Khalid only joined al Qaeda in the late 1990s after bin Laden accepted his plans for large-scale strikes against the USA. But rela- tions between the two men were never close. Once the al Qaeda hierarchy had accepted the 9/11 plan, Khalid played the main role in liaising with the hijackers, finetuning the operation and arranging for the transfer of money. Following his capture, he was transferred to the US detention camp at Guantánamo Bay.

Further reading
Fouda, Y. and Fielding, N., *Masterminds of Terror: The Truth behind the Most Devastating Attack the World Has Ever Seen*. New York: Arcade Publishing, 2003.

National Commission on Terrorist Attacks, *The 9/11 Commission Report: Final Report of the National Commission on Terrorist Attacks upon the United States (Indexed Hardcover, Authorized Edition)*. New York: W. W. Norton and Company, 2004.

KING DAVID HOTEL BOMBING

On 22 July 1946, the right-wing Zionist group Irgun attacked the King David Hotel in Jerusalem, which housed the administration of the British Mandate of Palestine. The bombing killed ninety-one people and injured almost fifty more. Thirty minutes before the explosion, eight Irgun members dressed as Arabs forced their way into the hotel service bay, killing a British army officer in the process, and placed seven milk containers containing more than 350 kilo- grams of TNT and gelignite in a room directly beneath the civilian and military offices. Shortly after, the French consulate and the *Pal- estine Post* newspaper received telephone tip-offs, but it was too late to evacuate the premises. The attack was part of a systematic cam- paign waged against the British Mandate with a view to establishing an independent Jewish homeland. More immediately, the attack was designed to force the British to overturn a ban on Jewish immigration to Palestine, an agenda that took on a special urgency in the wake of the Holocaust and the displacement of large numbers of Jews from Western and Eastern Europe.

Further reading
Barker, J., 'The Bombing of the King David Hotel' *History Today* 56(7) 2006, pp. 50–6.
Clarke, T., *By Blood and Fire: The Attack on the King David Hotel*. St Albans: Hutchinson, 1981.

KONGRA-GELE (Formerly PKK)
Proscribed by: Australia, Canada, EU, UK, USA
The 'Peoples Congress of Kurdistan' (KGK – formerly the Kurdistan Workers' Party (PKK)) was founded by Kurdish students in 1972 and is a Turkish-based group dedicated to the establishment of an independent Kurdish homeland. Their embrace of terrorism is reflected in attacks mainly against members of the Turkish military, police, local government officials and civilians thought to be collaborating with the authorities. In the 1990s it also began to use suicide bombers. The change in name, which occurred in 2005, reflects an attempt to overcome the setback caused by the 1999 capture of its charismatic leader Abdullah Ocalan, and a decision by his successors to broaden their appeal among the Kurdish population by adopting a less overtly Marxist orientation and infusing their ideology with more of an Islamist flavour. Ocalan was eventually sentenced to life in prison, saved from execution only by Turkey's attempt to join the European Union by abolishing the death penalty in 2002. The KGK obtains most of its finances in the form of donations from wealthy Kurdish businesspeople and from the wider Kurdish diaspora. According to Ankara, the KGK receives funds and training from Syria. From the mid-1990s the KGK attempted to avoid strikes by the Turkish military by shifting bases from Turkish territory to the Kurdish areas of northern Iraq.

Further reading
Giraldi, P., 'Turkey and the Threat of Kurdish Nationalism' *Mediterranean Quarterly* 19(1) 2008, pp. 33–41.
Marcus, A., 'Turkey's PKK: Rise, Fall, Rise Again?' *World Policy Journal* 24(1) 2007, pp. 75–84.

LASHKAR-E-TAYYIBA (LET) (Army of the Righteous)
Proscribed by: Australia, Canada, EU, India, Russia, UK, UN, USA
Lashkar-e-Tayyiba (lit. 'Army of the Righteous' or 'Army of the Pure')
is a Pakistan-based terrorist organization founded in 1990 by veterans
of the anti-Soviet war in Afghanistan. These links to Afghanistan have
meant that LeT has always enjoyed connections with **al Qaeda**,
although the degree of influence that the latter exercises over the LeT
is open to debate. The LeT is the armed wing of the religious organization Markaz-ud-Dawa-wal-Irshad and has two major goals: to
separate the Muslim-majority provinces of Jammu and Kashmir from
India and incorporate them into Pakistan, and, secondly, to contribute to Pakistan's establishment as an Islamic state founded on
Wahabbi Islamist principles. It has also professed the grandiose long-
term goal of destroying Hinduism and establishing the entire sub-
continent as an Islamic state. Indian intelligence claims that the LeT
is supported by Pakistani intelligence (see **Pakistan Directorate for
Inter-Services Intelligence (ISI)**) are supported by many Western
intelligence sources. These links are based on personal contacts
forged between the ISI and senior members of the Pakistani jihadist
movement during the 1980s. During the 1990s, the LeT was involved
in a series of strikes against Indian police, military and political
targets in Jammu and Kashmir, but as the decade progressed the
group began to target civilians and push deeper into India, where it
was implicated in bomb attacks on commuter trains in Mumbai in
1994. In the mid- to late 2000s it was implicated in a series of attacks,
including: bombings at market and temple areas in Jaipur in May
2008; coordinated bomb attacks against law courts across Uttar
Pradesh state in November 2007; two explosions at a park and res-
taurant in Hyderabad in August 2007; the bombing of a commuter
train near Delhi in February 2007; coordinated attacks on Mumbai
commuter trains in July 2006; attacks at a railway station and Hindu
holy sites in Varanasi in March 2006; and the bombing of markets
in New Delhi in October 2005. The LeT is also suspected of being
involved in the December 2001 attack on the Indian parliament
in New Delhi, where it is thought to have cooperated with other
Pakistan-based groups fighting in Kashmir, particularly **Jaish-e-
Mohammed**. To avoid a government crackdown in the wake of the
9/11 attacks, the LeT adopted several alternative names, such as
Jamaat-ud-Dawa (JUD), and established a new welfare organization
called Idara Khidmat-e-Khalq (IKK) to raise the funds necessary to
continue recruitment and paramilitary activities. By far the largest

and most audacious attack involving the LeT occurred in late November 2008 when ten individuals linked to the group landed by boat in Mumbai and, with military precision, fanned out across the tourist sections of the city. Supplied with thousands of rounds of ammunition, grenades and laptop computers, they split into groups and assaulted Mumbai's main railway station, the exclusive Taj Mahal and Oberoi Trident hotels and a Jewish drop-in centre. The attack, which killed almost 200 people, demonstrated an extraordinary degree of pre-planning and knowledge of weak points in the Indian counter-terrorism apparatus. This was followed in March 2009 by an attack on the Sri Lankan cricket team while it was on a tour of Pakistan.

Further reading
Gregory, S., 'The ISI and the War on Terrorism' *Studies in Conflict and Terrorism* 30(12) 2007, pp. 1013–31.
Reidel, B., 'Pakistan: The Critical Battlefield' *Current History* 107(712) 2008, pp. 355–61.

LASHKAR-I-JHANGVI
Proscribed by: Australia, Canada, India, UK, UN, USA
Lashkar-i-Jhangvi (LiJ) is a Sunni extremist group based in Pakistan. Formed in 1996, it operated initially under the name of Sipah-e-Sahaba Pakistan (SeSP), which was founded by Maulana Haq Nawaz Jhangvi with the prime objective of establishing Pakistan as a fundamentalist Islamic state based on Deobandi Sunni lines. SeSP's first targets were Pakistan's minority Shi'a community, and it was in retaliation for a series of bombing and gun attacks that a Shi'a group assassinated Jhangvi in the late 1990s. Soon after, the SeSP changed its name to LiJ and began to diversify its activities, especially in, but not confined to, the Indian territory of Kashmir. In 2002 the LiJ launched a series of suicide attacks against Pakistani military and Western targets inside Pakistan. This included a suicide bombing against a Pakistani navy bus carrying eleven French engineers, all of whom were killed, and another suicide attack several months later when a car bomb exploded outside the US consulate in Karachi, killing twelve Pakistanis. The LiJ has also been implicated in cooperating with **Jaish-e-Mohammed** and Harkat-ul-Jihad-al-Islami (HUJI) in the kidnapping and murder of the US journalist Daniel Pearl. On 14 August 2001, the Pakistani government formally banned LiJ, and

many of its key leaders were arrested. Citing intelligence sources, some media reports indicate that, in 2002, the LiJ formed an informal coalition called Lashkar-e-Omar that includes Harkat-ul-Jihad-al-Islami (HUJI) and Jaish-e-Mohammed.

Further reading
Haqqani, H., 'Pakistan and the Islamists' *Current History* 106(699) 2007, pp. 147–52.
Reidel, B., 'Pakistan and Terror: The Eye of the Storm' *The Anals of the American Academy of Political and Social Science* 618(1) 2008, pp. 31–45.

LEHI
SEE: STERN GANG

LIBERATION TIGERS OF TAMIL EELAM (LTTE)
Proscribed by: Australia, Canada, EU, India, UK, USA
The Liberation Tigers of Tamil Eelam (LTTE) emerged in the late 1970s as the most deadly and effective of a series of pro-independence Tamil organizations in Sri Lanka. These groups sprang up in the 1950s in response to a series of post-independence policies introduced by governments dominated by the ethnically and religiously different, but more populous, Sinhalese community. For many Tamils, who constitute around 10 per cent of Sri Lanka's population, these policies constituted a form of ethnic and cultural discrimination and even threatened the eradication of their unique Hindu culture and language. On the other hand, for many Sinhalese the Tamils had benefited unfairly under British colonial rule and the policies of affirmative action were required to rectify historical injustices. When the ethnic and religious battle lines were drawn, the LTTE, led by the charismatic but reclusive **Velupillai Prabhakaran**, systematically eliminated most of its rivals through a campaign that included intimidation and assassination, so that, by the late 1980s, it had emerged as the principal vehicle for many of the political and cultural aspirations of Sri Lanka's Tamils. While it is impossible to state exactly the level of support enjoyed by the LTTE among Sri Lankan Tamils – especially in light of its history of forced recruitment and the use of conscripted child soldiers – the longevity of its operations in the face of sustained Sri Lankan military pressure, the ease with which it operated across large swathes of majority Tamil

territory, and the extensive financial assistance received from the Tamil community in India and diasporas in the USA, UK, Canada and Australia suggest that it enjoyed widespread support. The LTTE's resilience was aided by the heavy-handed manner in which Colombo responded to LTTE actions – in particular, the Sri Lankan military's systematic disregard for human rights in prosecuting the counter-terrorism effort. But it is in the area of tactics that the LTTE proved especially innovative. Its use of suicide bombers (male and female), first deployed in 1987 by a special unit known as 'the Black Tigers', was replicated by terrorist groups in other parts of the world. It successfully carried out more than a dozen high-level assassinations – including those of Indian Prime Minister Rajiv Gandhi in May 1991 and Sri Lankan President Ranasinghe Premadasa in May 1993 – as well as a long list of attacks on other high-level Sri Lankan ministers, public officials and military and police personnel. From the late 1980s until its military defeat in 2009, the LTTE is thought to have killed over 5,000 individuals through a combination of suicide bombings, grenade and mortar attacks, shootings and other forms of violence. At its peak, the LTTE had between 10,000 and 15,000 combatants, who were inducted with an intensive training programme that included inculcation of a near God-like status for Prabhakaran. Cadres were also known for wearing small cyanide capsules that were used to commit suicide if they were ever confronted with capture. A ceasefire negotiated by 2001 broke down in 2002, while a military offensive launched in 2009 led to the recapture of all territory formerly controlled by the LTTE and the killing of Prabhakaran, who died on 18 May when the LTTE's final stronghold was overrun by Sri Lankan forces.

Further reading
Tambiah, S. J., *Sri Lanka: Ethnic Fratricide and the Dismantling of Democracy*. Chicago: University of Chicago Press, 1991.
Winslow, D. and Woost, M. D., *Economy, Culture and Civil War in Sri Lanka*. Bloomington: Indiana University Press, 2004.

LIBYAN ISLAMIC FIGHTING GROUP (al Jamaa al Islamiyah al Muqatilah bi Libya)
Proscribed by: UK, UN, USA
Libyan veterans of the anti-Soviet war in Afghanistan founded the Libyan Islamic Fighting Group (LIFG) in 1995 with the principal

aims of toppling the regime of Colonel **Muammar Gaddafi** and establishing an Islamic state. Even though, for much of his tenure, Gaddafi has been a trenchant critic of the West, especially the USA, his hard-nosed secularism and intolerance of opposition voices earned him many enemies among a burgeoning grass-roots Islamist movement. The LIFG has emerged as the most potent symbol of this movement, launching several successful attacks against key Libyan infrastructure and other targets. In 1996 the group attempted to assassinate Gaddafi himself, an operation that some observers inside and outside Libya claim was funded partly by MI6 (see **Secret Intelligence Service – UK**). This allegation has never been substantiated. Shortly after **9/11**, the **United Nations Security Council Committee 1267** designated the LIFG as an **al Qaeda** affiliate. The claim, which has been denied by the LIFG, rested on growing evidence that it was linked to al Qaeda through a combination of individuals with shared membership in both organizations (such as the Libyan citizen and senior al Qaeda operative Atiyah Abdul-Rahman), and an interconnected network of charitable and business fronts that have funded terrorist acts in Morocco, Algeria and other parts of North Africa.

Further reading

Gambill, G., 'The Libyan Islamic Fighting Group' *Jamestown Global Terrorism Analysis* 3(6) 2005. Available at www.jameshown.org/programs/gta/single/tx-ttnews%5Btt_news%5D=305&tx_ttnews%5BbackPid%5D=180&no_cache=1 (accessed 30 April 2006).

LOCKERBIE

On 21 December 1988, PanAm Flight 103 from London to New York exploded above the Scottish town of Lockerbie killing 259 passengers and 11 residents on the ground. Initial suspicions focused on Iran; however, attention then turned to two Libyan men, Abdel Basset Ali Al Megrahi and Lamen Khalifah Fhimah, both of whom were charged. Libya initially refused to hand the two men over to British authorities, arguing that they would not receive a fair trial. A compromise was eventually struck whereby the men would be tried in the Netherlands under Scottish law, with a Scottish judge presiding. In 1999 the Libyan leader **Muammar Gaddafi** ordered the two men to be handed over to Western authorities. During the trial the prosecution alleged that, instructed by Libyan intelligence, the suspects had planted a bomb aboard the flight while working at London's Heathrow airport. It was further alleged that the attack was revenge for a series of skirmishes between Libyan and US military forces in the 1980s, including an attack on Libya by the US air force in April 1986, which was in response to the bombing of a West Berlin nightclub frequented by US military personnel. In 2001 Megrahi was found guilty and given a life sentence, while Fhimah was acquitted. In September 2009, a Scottish court commuted Megrahi's sentence on compassionate grounds after it was revealed he was suffering from terminal prostate cancer. The court's decision generated significant criticism, particularly in the United States. On returning to Libya, Megrahi intensified his efforts to clear his name. Although Libya has never admitted responsibility for the attacks, Gaddafi eventually agreed to pay $2.7 billion to compensate the families of the victims. Tripoli's gesture reflected a change in Libyan foreign policy throughout the 1990s, in which it abandoned its support for various terrorist groups in an attempt to end UN sanctions and improve its international image.

Further reading
Grant, J. P., *Lockerbie Trial: A Documentary History*. New York: Oceana Publications Inc., 2004.
Marquise, R. A., *Scotbom: Evidence and the Lockerbie Investigation*. New York: Algora Publishing, 2006.

LONDON BOMBINGS
SEE: 7/7

LOYALIST VOLUNTEER FORCE
Proscribed by: Republic of Ireland, UK
The Loyalist Volunteer Force (LVF) is a Protestant paramilitary group based in Northern Ireland, opposed to the republicanism of groups such as the Provisional Irish Republican Army (see **Irish Republican Army (Provisional)**). The LVF can therefore be alternatively defined as a group dedicated to ensuring that the six counties of Ulster remain a part of the United Kingdom. Billy Wright ('King Rat', see **Loyalist Volunteer Force**), formerly a local leader of the **Ulster Volunteer Force**

(UVF), established the group in 1996 after a falling out with the UVF hierarchy over the involvement of Wright's unit in the murder of a Catholic taxi driver. The murder occurred at a sensitive time, during a ceasefire declared by both sides during the negotiations that eventually led to the **Good Friday Agreement**. In an attempt to avoid retaliatory violence by nationalists and to quarantine the peace talks, the UVF leadership ordered Wright to disengage. Wright responded by breaking from the UVF and establishing the LVF as an independent entity. Wright was murdered in prison on 27 December 1997 by **Irish National Liberation Army** members who scaled a wall from an adjacent wing and targeted the LVF leader in retaliation for his role in earlier attacks on Catholic civilians. By the early 2000s the LVF had lost its political focus and degenerated into an organized crime gang with extensive links to drug cartels (some run by Irish republican groups). In 2005 the long-running feud with fellow Protestant paramilitary group the UVF erupted again, and several months later the LVF announced it was standing down its armed units.

Further reading

Bruce, S., 'Terrorism and Politics: The Case of Northern Ireland's Loyalist Paramilitaries' *Terrorism and Political Violence* 13(2) 2001, pp. 27–48.

Silke, A., 'Drink, Drugs and Rock'in'Roll: Financing Loyalist Terrorism in Northern Ireland, Part Two' *Studies in Conflict and Terrorism* 23(2) 2000, pp. 107–27.

MADRID BOMBINGS

On 11 March 2004, a series of ten coordinated explosions occurred between 7.37 a.m. and 7.40 a.m. on four separate commuter trains at the height of Madrid's morning rush hour. The attacks, which killed 191 people and injured more than 1,700 others, occurred against the backdrop of a close national election campaign, and the conservative Partido Popular (PP) government of Prime Minister José María Aznar initially claimed to have evidence that the attacks were the work of the Basque separatist group ETA (see **Euskadi Ta Askatasuna**). However, attention shifted quickly to extremist Islamist groups among Spain's North African diasporas. Public perceptions that the PP government had deliberately misled Spanish voters over the culprits of the attacks for political reasons, coupled with a sense that Spain might have been targeted because of its participation in the US-led invasion of Iraq, contributed to a backlash against the PP, which lost the election to the socialist Partido Socialista Obrero Español, headed by José Luis Rodríguez Zapatero. Despite lengthy investigations by the Spanish judiciary and security services that point to a deliberate plot involving local Muslims inspired by **al Qaeda**, who might have received training in Afghanistan, and with links to extremist Islamist groups in the Maghreb, there remain a number of conservative Spanish politicians and journalists who continue to insist the attacks were part of a deliberate conspiracy involving the Socialist Party, ETA and others to topple the Aznar government. Although subsequent inquiries were unable to identify a single leader or strategic planner, they did identify some key players including Jamal Zougam, Serhane Abdelmaji and Jamal Ahmidan. However, on 3 April 2004, as police began to storm the premises where Zougam, Abdelmaji and Ahmidan were holed-up, the occupants committed suicide by detonating explosives made of the same materials as those used to construct the devices used on the trains. Even so, twenty-eight individuals were eventually committed to stand trial for their involvement in the plot. On 31 October 2007, the national court of Spain found twenty-one of the defendants guilty of a range of crimes. The remaining seven defendants were acquitted.

Further reading
Nesser, P., 'Jihadism in Western Europe after the Invasion of Iraq: Tracing Motivational Influences from the Iraq War on Jihadist Terrorism in Western Europe' *Studies in Conflict and Terrorism* 29(4) 2006, pp. 323–42.
Reinares, F., 'After the Madrid Bombings: Internal Security Reforms and Prevention of Global Terrorism in Spain' *Studies in Conflict and Terrorism* 32(5) 2009, pp. 367–88.

MARIGHELLA, CARLOS
Carlos Marighella (1911–69) was a leader in the Brazilian Communist Party and member of the national legislature who was eventually expelled from the Party after he criticized its embrace of a reformist agenda which moved it away from Fidel Castro's version of revolutionary Marxism. Marighella went on to found and lead the radical revolutionary group Action for National Liberation (ALN). It was while leading this group that Marighella developed the idea of a 'scorched earth policy' – attacking the very foundations of the

Brazilian system, at that time led by a military junta, through robberies, kidnappings and more overt acts of terrorism such as assassinations. This strategy is laid out in a pamphlet he wrote entitled *The Mini-Manual of the Urban Guerrilla* – a treatise on how to challenge authority and foment revolution. The book had limited influence within Brazil, but it had a more significant impact on the development of the ideologies of many leftist terrorist groups in Western Europe, where Marighella's emphasis upon the urban poor had a greater resonance than the traditional revolutionary Marxist focus on peasants. Marighella was killed in a police ambush in Säo Paulo on 4 November 1969.

Further reading
Marighella, C., *Mini-Manual of the Urban Guerrilla*. St Petersburg, Fla.: Red and Black Publishers, 2008 [1969].

McGuinness, Martin

Martin McGuinness (b. 1950) is the Sinn Fein Member of Parliament for the constituency of Mid-Ulster, although, like fellow members, he refuses to take his seat in Westminster. He is also a member of the Northern Ireland Assembly. Before dedicating himself to mainstream political activities, McGuinness was a senior official in the Provisional Irish Republican Army (PIRA – see **Irish Republican Army (Provisional)**). After joining the PIRA at the age of twenty, he rose quickly to become second-in-command of the group's Derry cell. In 1972, McGuinness was convicted and sentenced to six months in prison after being found travelling in a car carrying ammunition and explosives. However, during the 1980s, McGuinesss lessened his involvement in the IRA and redirected his energies towards the group's political wing, Sinn Fein. In the mid-1990s he played a key role alongside Sinn Fein's leader, **Gerry Adams**, in negotiating the **Good Friday Agreement**. He subsequently served as Minister for Education from 1998 until 2002 and, following the Northern Ireland Assembly elections in 2007, as First Minister of Northern Ireland, a position shared with the Unionist leader Peter Robinson.

Further reading
Clarke, L. and Johnston, K., *Martin McGuinness: From Guns to Government*. Edinburgh: Mainstream Publishing, 2003.

MCVEIGH, TIMOTHY

Timothy McVeigh (1968–2001) was convicted of playing the leading role in the bombing that destroyed the Alfred P. Murrah Federal Building in Oklahoma City on 19 April 1995. The attack killed 168 people, including 19 infants at a day-care centre, and injured more than 450 others. McVeigh was born in New York State, where he was bullied at school and developed a reputation for being a solitary person. In 1988 he joined the US army, going on to serve in Operation Desert Storm in Iraq and Kuwait. For McVeigh, these collective experiences fostered a deep suspicion of, and eventually an outright hostility to, perceived bullying by authority, especially the US government. His anger was intensified even further after he was discharged from the army in 1992. Leading an increasingly ephemeral life, he travelled the USA seeking out former war buddies. Alone and unable to establish any long-term romantic relationship, he became progressively more alienated from mainstream American society. The siege at Ruby Ridge in 1992, where federal agents killed three members of a reclusive right-wing group, and then at Waco in 1993, where a 51-day standoff between US officials and the Branch Davidian sect culminated in a conflagration that killed almost eighty, intensified his anger. After considering a campaign of targeted assassinations against people such as the Federal Attorney General Janet Reno and senior US jurists, he decided that a retaliatory strike against a federal US building would be a more effective statement. Working with a friend from his days in the army, Terry Nichols, McVeigh decided to target the Murrah Building. He was arrested on traffic and weapons violations less than an hour after the attack, and charged two days later after forensic examinations linked him to the rental truck used in the explosion. In 1999 McVeigh was moved to the US Federal Penitentiary in Indiana, where he was executed by lethal injection on 11 June 2001.

Further reading
Crothers, L., 'The Cultural Foundations of the Modern Militia Movement' *New Political Science* 24(2) 2002, pp. 221–34.
Michel, L. and Herbeck, D., *American Terrorist: Timothy McVeigh and the Oklahoma City Bombing*. New York: Harper, 2001.

MEDIA AND PUBLICITY

An enduring myth about terrorism is that the violence perpetrated is an end in itself. However, terrorist violence should more accurately be understood as a means to an end, as a way of intimidating, punishing, humiliating or destroying those who are perceived by the terrorists to be the source of their own disempowerment or to be standing in the way of their own political aspirations. In short, terrorist violence might be perceived as a form of political theatre whereby the violent act, and the carnage it causes, is a carefully scripted event designed to send a particular message. For this strategy to succeed, it is obviously essential that the terrorists have an audience, and it is against this background that the media have emerged as a critical tool in the terrorists' arsenal. As a device for publishing the terrorists' actions, the media is used by the perpetrators of the violence to target two distinct audiences: the 'out-group' whom the terrorists want to terrify and intimidate through their actions, and the 'in-group' whom the terrorists seek to inspire. To this end, terrorists are becoming increasingly adept at manipulating different forms of media and new media technologies – such as the Internet – to spread their message. It is for this reason that **al Qaeda** has established its own media production company, **as-Sahab**.

Further reading
Cram, I., 'Regulating the Media: Some Neglected Freedom of Expression Issues in the United Kingdom's Counter-Terrorism Strategy' *Terrorism and Political Violence* 18(2) 2006, pp. 335–55.
Jenkins, P., *Images of Terror: What We Can and Can't Know about Terrorism*. Piscataway: Aldine Transaction, 2003.
Nacos, B. L., 'The Terrorist Calculus behind 9-11: A Model for Future Terrorism?' *Studies in Conflict and Terrorism* 26(1) 2003, pp. 1–16.

MEINHOF, ULRIKE
Ulrike Meinhof (1934–76) emerged in the 1970s as one of the most recognizable names in modern terrorism. Her notoriety was sealed when she made the transition from being a journalist at a left-wing news journal to joining a band of Marxist revolutionaries led by **Andreas Baader**. Indeed, it was Meinhof's part in helping Baader to escape from prison in 1970 that played a key role in building the mystique that surrounded her in subsequent years. In reality, however, despite the epithet **Baader-Meinhoff Gang**, she was never a leader of the group, which throughout its existence remained under the influence of Baader and his girlfriend Gudrun Ensslin. In fact, throughout her period with the group, Meinhof was a member of the

organization's second tier, enjoying influence similar to that of others such as Jan-Carl Raspe. Meinhof's transition to terrorism was also gradual and progressed from an early interest in left-wing causes through to her final embrace of revolutionary violence. In 1957 she joined the Socialist German Student Union, and the outlawed German Communist Party in 1959, before securing a job at the left-wing news magazine *konkret*. Between 1962 and 1964, Meinhof was the magazine's Editor-in-Chief. The disintegration of her marriage to *konkret*'s Editor in 1967 coincided with her increasing involvement with the extremist fringes of the leftist student movement. It was in these circles that she was introduced to individuals who would go on to form the Baader-Meinhof Gang. Before her capture on 15 June 1972, Meinhof spent two years on the run, during which time she was involved in a series of robberies and fatal bombings. In prison she grew progressively more depressed and eventually hanged herself in her cell in May 1976.

Further reading
Aust, S. and Bell, A., *Baader-Meinhof: The Inside Story of the R.A.F.* New York: Oxford University Press, 2009.
Meinhof, U., *Everybody Talks about the Weather . . . We Don't: The Writings of Ulrike Meinhof.* New York: Seven Stories Press, 2008.

MI5
SEE: SECURITY SERVICE – UK

MI6
SEE: SECRET INTELLIGENCE SERVICE – UK

MONTREAL CONVENTION (Convention for the Suppression of Unlawful Acts against the Safety of Civil Aviation)
The Convention for the Suppression of Unlawful Acts against the Safety of Civil Aviation (Montreal Convention) entered into force on 26 January 1973 and is a key plank in a network of multilateral counter-terrorism conventions that are collectively designed to facilitate international cooperation in the fight against terrorism. The timing of the Convention reflected growing anxiety among states in the late 1960s and early 1970s about the increasing number of hijack-

ings of civilian aircraft by a range of different terrorist groups. Among other things, the Convention encompasses the following offences: carrying out a violent act against another passenger while an aircraft is in flight if such behaviour is likely to threaten the safety of the aircraft; destroying or damaging an aircraft in such a way that it is unable to fly or that it cannot fly safely; placing or helping to place devices or substances that could destroy or damage the aircraft in such a way that it is unsafe in flight; deliberately communicating any incorrect information that could undermine the safety of an aircraft in flight or destroying or damaging air navigation facilities (if these facilities are used for international air navigation). The Convention also renders it an offence to be an accomplice of a person involved in any of these acts. States that are signatories to the Convention are obliged to bring such offences within the realm of their criminal law and prosecute severely those found guilty of engaging in such acts.

Further reading
Guillaume, G., 'Terrorism and International Law' *International and Comparative Law Quarterly* 53(3) 2004, pp. 537–48.

MORETTI, MARIO

Mario Moretti (b. 1946) was a founding member of the second **Italian Red Brigades** in early 1978 (most of the members of the first Red Brigades were incarcerated at this time). Moretti was also the key architect of the kidnapping of former Prime Minister of Italy Aldo Moro on 16 March 1978. Moro was held for fifty-four days before he was told by his kidnappers to cover himself in the trunk of a car. After he had done so Moretti shot him ten times. Despite being sentenced to six life sentences, Moretti was released after serving only fifteen years. His early release fuelled conspiracy theories claiming that, throughout his time with the Red Brigades, he was in fact an *agent provocateur* abetted by the Italian Gladio (anti-communist paramilitaries established in the wake of the Second World War with links to Christian Democrat politicians and security and intelligence services) to foment discord between Italy's various leftist groups.

Further reading
Moss, D., 'The Kidnapping and Murder of Aldo Moro' *Archives Européennes de Sociologie* 22(2) 1981, pp. 265–95.

Sciascia, L., *The Moro Affair*. New York: New York Review of Books Classics, 2004.

Moro Islamic Liberation Front

The Moro Islamic Liberation Front (MILF) is a separatist guerrilla organization active in the southern reaches of the Philippines archipelago. Founded by Hashim Salamat in 1981 as a break-away group from the **Moro National Liberation Front** (MNLF), its original goal was the establishment of an independent nation state for the indigenous Muslim peoples of the Southern Philippines. Although the schism within the secessionist movement was ostensibly over the MNLF leadership's reluctance to engage in a more assertive insurgency and its consideration of a peace agreement with Manila, the split was also underpinned by ethno-linguistic differences. Unlike the MNLF and the **Abu Sayyaf Group** (ASG), which draw their members mainly from Tausig-speaking peoples of the Sulu archipelago, the MILF's support base is made up mainly of Magindanoan-speakers from southern parts of the island of Mindanao. The MILF reached its military apex in the late 1990s when it had around 15,000 personnel under arms, including around 600 who had received training at **al Qaeda** camps in Afghanistan. It was during this period that the MILF also established links, with **Jemaah Islamiyah**, allowing the latter to use an area of its main camp to conduct their own training. Despite these links, the MILF hierarchy has always tried to keep at arms' length from al Qaeda and has refused to subsume its parochial ambitions to al Qaeda's global agenda. Large-scale MILF attacks against civilians have been rare. Throughout the 1990s, it gradually attenuated its demands from complete independence to an insistence on greater autonomy. In January 1997, the administration of President Fidel Ramos built on this and negotiated a delicate cessation of hostilities, during which time negotiators searched for some common ground upon which to build a more lasting compromise. The death of Hashim Salamat in 2003 and the passing of the leadership to Haj Murad Ebrahim exacerbated disciplinary problems, with some commanders now waging their own private wars against local authorities in contravention of orders from the MILF hierarchy. In 2007, the administration of President Gloria Macapagal Arroyo announced it had struck an agreement whereby the MILF would declare a ceasefire in return for greater Muslim autonomy over key ancestral lands.

However, in October 2008, the Philippine High Court declared the agreement unconstitutional.

Further reading
McKenna, T. M., *Muslim Rulers and Rebels: Everyday Politics and Armed Separatism in the Southern Philippines.* Berkeley: University of California Press, 1998.
Ringuet, D. J., 'The Continuation of Civil Unrest and Poverty in Mindanao' *Contemporary Southeast Asia* 24(1) 2002, pp. 33–50.

MORO NATIONAL LIBERATION FRONT

The Moro National Liberation Front (MNLF) is active in the Philippines provinces of Mindanao and the Sulu archipelago. The indigenous peoples of these areas are traditionally Muslim and, since the Spanish conquest of the region and the introduction of Christianity, the region has proved highly troublesome. Tensions persisted during the period of US colonialism, which lasted from 1898 to 1946, but escalated on independence when successive governments in Manila attempted to pacify the region through a combination of military force and large-scale migration from the Christian north. Indeed, so intense were these migratory patterns that, by the 1960s, southern Muslims, known colloquially as the indigenous Moro people, had become a minority in many areas of the south. However, the catalyst for the formation of the MNLF was the 1968 massacre of twenty-eight Muslim army recruits by their Christian superiors on the island of Corregidor. Established by Abul Khayr Alonto and Jallaludin Santos, the chairmanship of the group was awarded to an academic at the University of the Philippines, Nur Misuari. Under Misuari's leadership, the MNLF embarked on a paramilitary campaign that included terrorist strikes against military, police and local government officials. At its peak between 1973 and 1975, the MNLF boasted a membership of around 30,000. Peace talks in 1976 which led to an offer of partial autonomy for the Muslim populations led to a diminution of the MNLF's power and a reduction in the level of violence. A breakdown in the peace process in 1977 saw the MNLF struggle to regain momentum. A significant contributing factor in this regard was the foundation in 1981 of a break-away group, the **Moro Islamic Liberation Front** (MILF). Following the fall of the Marcos regime in

1986, the new administration of President Cory Aquino amended Article 10 of the 1987 Constitution to establish an Autonomous Region in Muslim Mindanao. However, a November 1989 plebiscite resulted in only four provinces voting to accept the government's autonomy measure. In 2001, Misuari, who had developed a reputation as a corrupt, nepotistic and generally incompetent leader, was deposed as governor of the Autonomous Region of Muslim Mindanao and as head of the MNLF, before being arrested. This led to a schism within the group, with a significant minority of his followers either defecting to the MILF or establishing new insurgent groups.

Further reading
McKenna, T. M., *Muslim Rulers and Rebels: Everyday Politics and Armed Separatism in the Southern Philippines*. Berkeley: University of California Press, 1998.
Vitug, M. and Gloria, G., *Under the Crescent Moon: Rebellion in Mindanao*. Quezon City: Institute for Popular Democracy, 2000.

MOROCCAN ISLAMIC COMBATANT GROUP (Groupe Islamique Combattant Morrocain (GICM))
Proscribed by: UK, UN, USA
The GCIM is a small Moroccan group dedicated to establishing Morocco as an Islamic state based on strict Sunni Islamic principles. It enjoys close links with senior **al Qaeda** figures, the origins of which stretch back to the anti-Soviet war in Afghanistan in the 1980s. The group has also made good use of the Moroccan diaspora in Western Europe and is thought to have cells in Belgium, Denmark, Egypt, France, Morocco, Spain, Turkey and the UK. The group has been implicated in a number of major attacks, including the 2004 **Madrid bombings** and an attack on a Casablanca market involving a dozen suicide bombers which killed over forty people. More recently it has joined with Algerian and Tunisian groups to form the **Al Qaeda Organization in the Land of the Islamic Maghreb.**

Further reading
Alonso, R. and García Rey, M., 'The Evolution of Jihadist Terrorism in Morocco' *Terrorism and Political Violence* 19(4) 2007, pp. 571–92.

Kalpakian, J., 'Against Both Bin Laden and Belliraj: Lessons from Moroccan Counterterrorism' *Contemporary Security Policy* 29(3) 2008, pp. 453–76.

MOSSAD

SEE: ISRAEL INSTITUTE FOR INTELLIGENCE AND SPECIAL TASKS

MOVEMENT OF HOLY WARRIORS (Harakat ul-Mujahedeen (HuM))

Proscribed by: Australia, Canada, India, UK, UN, USA
Sometimes known as Jamiat ul-Ansar, the Harakat ul-Mujahedeen has around 400 members spread across several areas of north Pakistan and in the disputed areas of Jammu and Kashmir along the border with India. The HuM maintains connections with the Pakistani Islamist political party Jamiat Ulema-i-Islam but also with **al Qaeda**. At its inception in 1985, the group was formed to take part in the wider anti-Soviet fight in Afghanistan. But with the withdrawal of Soviet forces in 1989, its objectives shifted to the struggle to wrest the disputed Muslim-majority areas of Jammu and Kashmir from India and to establish Pakistan as an Islamic state. To these ends, it has established training camps within Pakistan itself, but also within Afghanistan. Attacks against Indian and secular Pakistani targets are principally by semi-automatic and automatic weapons, mortars and surface-to-air missiles. Supporters within Pakistan, but also in the Middle East, provide funding for these weapons. In 1998 the group hijacked an Air India flight and held passengers and crew hostage until the Indian government agreed to release a number of Islamist prisoners, including Ahmed Omar Sheik, a British-born militant who was later convicted of being involved in the kidnapping and video-taped beheading of the *Wall Street Journal* journalist Daniel Pearl in 2002. In February 2000, a transition of leadership saw the Kashmiri militant Farooq Kashmiri replace long-time leader Fazlur Rehman Khalil. Around this time, HuM also began to lose supporters to the rival **Jaish-e-Mohammed** group.

Further reading
Zahab, M. Z. and Roy, O., *Islamist Networks: The Pakistan–Afghan Connection*. London: C. Hurst and Co., 2004.

MULTILATERAL COUNTER-TERRORISM CONVENTIONS

Generally speaking, there are thirteen major multilateral counter-terrorism conventions. In chronological order these are: 1963 Convention on Offences and Certain Other Acts Committed On Board Aircraft (Aircraft Convention); 1970 Convention for the Suppression of Unlawful Seizure of Aircraft (Unlawful Seizure Convention); 1971 Convention for the Suppression of Unlawful Acts against the Safety of Civil Aviation (Civil Aviation Convention); 1973 **Convention on the Prevention and Punishment of Crimes against Internationally Protected Persons, including Diplomatic Agents** (Diplomatic Agents Convention); 1979 **International Convention against the Taking of Hostages** (Hostages Convention); 1980 Convention on the Physical Protection of Nuclear Material (Nuclear Materials Convention) (as amended); 1988 Protocol for the Suppression of Unlawful Acts of Violence at Airports Serving International Civil Aviation, supplementary to the Convention for the Suppression of Unlawful Acts against the Safety of Civil Aviation (extends and supplements the Montreal Convention on Air Safety) (Airport Protocol); 1988 Convention for the Suppression of Unlawful Acts against the Safety of Maritime Navigation (Maritime Convention) (as amended through the 2005 Protocol to the Convention for the Suppression of Unlawful Acts against the Safety of Maritime Navigation); 1988 Protocol for the Suppression of Unlawful Acts against the Safety of Fixed Platforms Located on the Continental Shelf (Fixed Platform Protocol); 1991 Convention on the Marking of Plastic Explosives for the Purpose of Detection (Plastic Explosives Convention); 1997 **International Convention for the Suppression of Terrorist Bombings** (Terrorist Bombing Convention); 1999 **International Convention for the Suppression of the Financing of Terrorism** (Terrorist Financing Convention); 2005 International Convention for the Suppression of Acts of Nuclear Terrorism (Nuclear Terrorism Convention).

Further reading

Galicki, Z., 'International Law and Terrorism' *American Behavioural Scientist* 48(6) 2005, pp. 743–57.

Martinez, L. M. H., 'The Legislative Role of the Security Council in its Fight against Terrorism' *International and Comparative Law Quarterly* 57(2) 2008, pp. 333–59.

MUNICH OLYMPIC ATTACK

At 4.30 a.m. on 5 September 1972, eight members of the **Fatah**-linked **Black September** organization forced their way into the Israeli athletes compound at the Munich summer Olympics. Two Israeli athletes were killed and another nine were taken hostage. The terrorists demanded the release of 236 prisoners from Israeli jails, as well as the release of **Andreas Baader** and **Ulrike Meinhof** from German prisons. They also insisted on safe passage to a third country. Outwardly the German government appeared to accede to the terrorists' wishes, but covert plans to infiltrate counter-terrorism police onto the aircraft that was to fly the terrorists out of Germany were foiled when the undercover police abandoned the plan. A shoot-out between the police and terrorists ensued, resulting in the deaths of all the hostages and five of the eight terrorists. The remaining terrorists were captured but were released in October in the same year after counterparts hijacked a Lufthansa flight from Damascus to Frankfurt. Israel responded to the attacks through Operation Spring of Youth – military strikes against Palestinian targets in Lebanon – and Operation Wrath of God, the targeted assassinations of the three surviving terrorists. Thirty years after the attack, a senior **al Qaeda** figure described the attacks as 'the greatest media victory and the first true proclamation to the entire world of the Palestinian resistance movement. The Munich operation was a great propaganda strike.'

Further reading

Reeve, S., *One Day in September: The Full Story of the 1972 Munich Olympics Massacre and the Israeli Revenge Operation 'Wrath of God'*. New York: Arcade Publishing, 2000.

MUSLIM BROTHERHOOD

Proscribed by: Russia

The Egyptian scholar Hassan al-Banna founded the Muslim Brotherhood (full title 'The Society of the Muslim Brothers') in 1928 as a vehicle for Muslims frustrated at the lack of economic development in the Muslim world, as well as political quiescence in the face of European colonialism. Al-Banna believed that Muslim societies had failed to develop because they had lost touch with core teachings of the Qur'an and embraced alien Western cultural practices, both of which rendered the Islamic world vulnerable to European economic and political domination. In this sense, the Muslim Brotherhood was conceived as a vanguard organization designed to recentre Islam as the key organizing principle for society and politics throughout the Muslim world. By embracing new technologies and science, and recontextualizing them within an Islamic framework, al-Banna believed that Muslims could recover those aspects of their culture that had been diluted through contact with the West, and in so doing precipitate a reflowering of Islamic civilization. The Muslim Brotherhood's connections to terrorism have always been a topic of significant disagreement. In the 1940s and 1950s, the Egyptian government alleged that the organization was behind a series of targeted assassinations and other violent acts, which led to a crackdown against members and the temporary banning of the group. Critics have argued that the allegations were fraudulent and designed to give the Egyptian government an excuse to proscribe a political movement with the potential to challenge the secular state. Supporters of the group's proscription argue that, even though it might not directly engage in acts of violence, the Brotherhood operates as a 'conveyor belt' organization that radicalizes individuals who graduate into more overtly violent groups such as **al Qaeda**. Those who subscribe to this view also point to the Brotherhood's evolution from a reformist Islamist movement into an organization that espouses a highly conservative version of Islam. They also point to the influence of former members of the Brotherhood such as **Sayyid Qutb** – whose book *Milestones* advocated the use of violence – on the development of a new generation of terrorists such as **Osama bin Laden** and **Ayman al Zawahiri**. However, critics of this view argue that the fact that some extremists have been forced to break away from the Brotherhood to form more overtly violent groups, such as Al-Gama'a al-Islamiyah and Al Takfir Wal Hijra, is evidence that the Brotherhood itself eschews violence.

Further reading
Esposito, J. L. and Mogahed, D., *Who Speaks for Islam? What a Billion Muslims Really Think*. Washington, DC: Gallup Press, 2008.
Mitchell, R. P., *The Society of Muslim Brothers*. Oxford: Oxford University Press, 1993.

NARCO-TERRORISM

Narco-terrorism refers to the nexus between the illegal narcotics trade and the act of terrorism. In its most common form it involves the sale of narcotics to procure funds needed to carry out acts of terrorism. On another level, practices inherent to the drug trade – such as trafficking routes, money laundering and the falsification of identity documents – also lend themselves to terrorism. While the practice of narco-terrorism is well developed in Colombia and some other parts of South America, there are also reports that groups linked to **al Qaeda** have become active in the Afghanistan opium trade. Meanwhile, at a micro-level, terrorist cells have been known to sell drugs on the street to finance their day-to-day activities.

Further reading

Dolan, C. J., 'United States' Narco-Terrorism Policy: A Contingency Approach to the Convergence of the Wars on Drugs and against Terrorism' *Review of Policy Research* 22(4) 2005, pp. 451–71.

Makarenko, T., 'The Crime–Terror Continuum: Tracing the Interplay between Transnational Organized Crime and Terrorism' *Global Crime* 6(1) 2004, pp. 129–45.

NARODNAYA VOLYA

Translated as 'the People's Will' or 'People's Freedom', Narodnaya Volya was a militant Russian group that was most active between 1878 and 1883. Emerging from the revolutionary Zemlya i Volya ('Land of Freedom Party') and led by Andrey Zhelyaboy and Sofya Perovskaya, the Narodnaya Volya's strategy for achieving political reform and a socialist society was based on a belief that it was possible to foment social upheaval by assassinating senior government officials. From the late 1870s and into the early 1880s, an executive committee targeted, and planned the murder of, several high-profile members of the Tsarist regime, but it was the assassination of Tsar Alexander II on 13 March 1881 that represented their most spectacular act. However, the attack quickly proved to be a pyrrhic victory as it was followed by a collapse in public support and an intensified anti-terrorism campaign that saw the capture of most of the senior leadership and the implosion of the party, rather than the Tsarist state.

Further reading
Burleigh, M., *Blood and Rage: A Cultural History of Terrorism*. London: Harper Press, 2008.
Geifman, A., *Thou Shalt Kill*. Princeton, NJ: Princeton University Press, 1995.

NASRALLAH, HASSAN
Born in Beirut on 31 August 1960, Hassan Nasrallah is the Secretary General of the Lebanese **Hezbollah**. He assumed the leadership in 1992 after the assassination of the group's former leader Abbas al-Musawi by an Israeli missile strike. His leadership of Hezbollah during the 1990s saw him play a critical role in attacks against Israeli forces in Southern Lebanon, a campaign that led to their withdrawal in 2000. Nasrallah's reputation as being a key architect in ending the eighteen-year Israeli occupation has translated into success at the ballot box, with Hezbollah emerging as a major opposition group within Lebanese politics. He has also earned kudos from across the wider Middle East for his negotiation of a 2004 prisoner exchange with Israel, an agreement that resulted in several hundred prisoners being released from Israeli jails. Although Nasrallah condemned the 9/11 attacks, he continues to adopt a belligerent stance towards Israel. He has claimed that the Holocaust is a fiction invented by Jews and he remains opposed to the existence of the state of Israel.

Further reading
Qassem, N., *Hizbullah: The Story from Within*. London: Saqi Books, 2005.
Saad-Ghorayeb, A., *Hizbu'llah: Politics and Religion*. London: Pluto Press, 2002.

NATIONAL LIBERATION ARMY (Ejercito de Liberación Nacional (ELN))
Proscribed by: Canada, USA
The Colombian National Liberation Army (ELN) emerged out of growing dissatisfaction with the endemic poverty that afflicted many Colombians in the 1960s and 1970s. Then, as now, the ELN's tactics focus on attacking representatives of the Colombian state and ruling elite, kidnapping-for-ransom, extorting money from foreign multinational companies, imposing 'revolutionary taxes' on large land-owners, and occasional partnerships with drug cartels. The group

also sets land mines to protect areas under its control. It was founded in 1964 by a group of Cuban-trained students led by Fabio Vásquez Castaño, but Father Camilo Torres Restrepo, a Catholic priest, Professor of Sociology at the National University of Colombia and early exponent of Liberation Theology, was a particular influence on its formative ideology. Restrepo sought to marry Marxism with scripture, and he viewed the ELN as a useful vehicle for putting his theories into practice and securing a fairer distribution of income and power within Colombia. For much of its existence, the ELN viewed the much larger FARC (see **Revolutionary Armed Forces of Colombia – People's Army**) as rivals, but in May 2008 it published a letter on its website inviting FARC to negotiate on the difficulties facing Marxist rebels in the face of a military campaign launched by the Uribe government and stepped-up attacks by right-wing paramilitary groups. Between 2000 and 2007, the ELN's ranks are estimated to have fallen from around 4,000 to around 2,000.

Further reading
Waldmann, P., 'Is There a Culture of Violence in Colombia?' *Terrorism and Political Violence* 19(4) 2007, pp. 593–609.

NATIONAL LIBERATION FRONT (Front de Libération Nationale (FLN)) Formed in Algeria in 1952 as an anti-colonial organization, the National Liberation Front became a lightning rod for anti-French-colonialism. Combining Arab nationalism, socialism and Islam, it played a vanguard role during the Algerian war for independence. Through its armed wing, the Armée de Libération Nationale, it carried out a series of assassinations of French colonial officials, as well as launching a bombing campaign against French settlers. Capitalizing on entrenched racism against native Algerians, by the 1960s it had evolved into a mass movement and, after independence in 1962, the FLN formed Algeria's first post-colonial government. Belying its political success, the FLN was always prone to factional infighting between its political, military and religious wings. In the years after independence, the group experienced a number of schisms with members of the religious wing breaking away to form the Islamic Salvation Front (Front Islamique du Salut – FIS) and the military effectively seizing control of the FLN's political wing and banning opposition political parties. Although widespread rioting in 1988 forced the FLN government to open-up Algerian politics to alternative parties, electoral gains by the FIS in the 1992 elections provoked the military to suspend the result and return to one-party politics. This fed the emergence of militant Islamist groups such as the Islamic Salvation Army and the Armed Islamic Group. Atrocities committed by these groups, as well as by the military, caused the deaths of between 170,000 and 200,000 civilians until a ceasefire was struck in 1997. In 1998 a number of hard-line Islamists opposed to the peace process formed the **Salafist Group for Preaching and Combat** (Groupe Salafiste pour la Prédication et le Combat – GSPC), which launched a series of attacks against government and civilian targets. The GSPC declared its support for **al Qaeda** in 2003, and several years later provided the fulcrum upon which the **Al Qaeda Organization in the Land of the Islamic Maghreb** was based.

Further reading
Horne, A., *A Savage War of Peace: Algeria 1954–1962* (illustrated edn). New York: New York Review of Books, 2006.
Stone, M., *The Agony of Algeria*. New York: Columbia University Press, 1997.

NATIONAL LIBERATION FRONT OF CORSICA (Fronte di Liberazione Naziunale di a Corsica (FLNC))
Established in 1976 out of a merger of two leftist separatist groups, Ghjustizia Paolina and the Fronte Paesanu Corsu di Liberazione, the FLNC is dedicated to securing independence for the French-controlled Mediterranean island as a way of protecting its distinct culture and language. In the 1980s, the group was responsible for hundreds of bombings, mainly against French government buildings, police stations and the properties of non-Corsican settlers. With the election of the socialist administration of François Mitterrand in 1981, the FLNC suspended its activities, but, disappointed at a lack of progress on its demands, it recommenced its campaign in 1982. In the early 1990s, the group split into two factions, the Canal Habituel ('usual channel'), which ended its separatist activities in 1997, and the Canal Historique ('historic channel'), which continued to engage in low-level terrorist violence. In 1996 the FLNC Canal Historique extended its attacks to the French mainland, although its most significant attack was when it assassinated Paris' senior administrator on the island. In 1999, FLNC Canal Historique merged with

a smaller separatist group and, soon after, declared a three-month ceasefire that was still in place ten years later. With an estimated 600 members, the group survives through robbery and extortion. The FLNC does not accept female members.

Further reading
Reid, D., 'Colonizer and Colonized in the Corsican Political Imagination' *Radical History Review* 90 2004, pp. 90–116.
Sanchez, W. A., 'Corsica: France's Petite Security Problem' *Studies in Conflict and Terrorism* 31(7) 2008, pp. 655–64.

NATIONAL REVOLUTIONARY FRONT – COORDINATE (Barisan Revolusi Nasional – Coordinate (BRN-C))
The National Revolutionary Front – Coordinate (BRN-C) is the largest of several Muslim secessionist groups operating in Thailand's southern provinces. Formed in 1963 as a vehicle for protecting the cultural and religious traditions of the region's Muslim community from increasing migration of Thais from the country's Buddhist majority, the BRN-C has traditionally focused on bombings, arson and targeted assassinations against local government officials, the police and military. Smaller insurgent groups, including BRN-Ulama and BRN-Congress (which split from BRN-C in the 1980s), and the Pattani United Liberation Organization are also active in the region, although their influence is much less than that of the BRN-C. Affirmative action policies introduced by Bangkok in the early 1990s effectively choked off support for the insurgency; however, in the early 2000s, an end to these policies under the former government of Prime Minister Taksin Shinawata saw a revival of the insurgency. The BRN-C has also capitalized on the occasionally clumsy counter-terrorism actions of the Thai military and police, whose policy of collective punishment alienated many Muslim communities. Despite rumours to the contrary, there is little evidence that the BRN-C receives support from **al Qaeda** or any other external terrorist groups, although it does receive moral and occasional financial support from sympathizers in nearby Malaysia and Indonesia.

Further reading
Askew, M., 'Thailand's Intractable Southern War: Policy, Insurgency and Discourse' *Contemporary Southeast Asia* 30(2) 2008, pp. 186–214.

Liow, J. C., 'The Security Situation in Southern Thailand: Toward an Under-standing of Domestic and International Dimensions' *Studies in Conflict and Terrorism* 27(6) 2004, pp. 531–48.

NAXALITES

'Naxalites' is a collective noun given to an informal collection of Marxist – mainly Maoist – groups operating in India's northeastern states. With their roots in the grievances of small-scale farmers and landless peasants in West Bengal, the Naxalites have expanded in influence to encompass a 'red corridor' that stretches across states such as Bihar, Orissa, Assam, Jharkhand and Andhra Pradesh. Athough Indian intelligence services assessed that, in the late 2000s, the different Naxalite groups have a collective membership of around 20,000 members under arms, other sources put the figure at 10,000 with up to 40,000 full-time unarmed cadres. After Islamist groups operating across the border from Pakistan, the Naxalites are consid-ered to pose the most significant terrorist threat to India. By the early 1980s the Naxalites had lost much of their momentum, but economic reforms initiated in the late 1990s, coupled with the growing influ-ence of Western multinationals and the undiluted power of Indian landlords, have added fresh impetus to the movement.

Further reading
Ahuja, P. and Ganguly, R., 'The Fire Within: Naxalite Insurgency Violence in India' *Small Wars and Insurgencies* 18(2) 2007, pp. 249–74.
Singh, P., *The Naxalite Movement in India*. New Delhi: Rupa & Co., 1999.

NEW PEOPLE'S ARMY

Proscribed by: EU, USA
Founded by Jose Maria Sison and Luis Jalandoni in 1969, the New People's Army (NPA) is the military wing of the Maoist Communist Party of the Philippines. It grew out of an older insurgency group, the Hukbalahap, which was the armed wing of the pro-Soviet Philip-pine Communist Party. Dedicated to overthrowing the Filipino gov-ernment and replacing it with a Marxist state, the NPA has pursued a peasant-based insurgency. Its principal targets include the police, military, and large land owners, although it is also known to assas-sinate high-profile critics of the movement. In 2002 it warned that it

would also attack any US military personnel found to be operating alongside their Filipino counterparts as part of Washington's post-9/11 counter-terrorism assistance to the Philippines government. Between 1969 and 1976 the NPA received funding from China; since then it has financed itself through kidnapping-for-ransom activities and the imposition of 'revolutionary taxes' on local and foreign businesses. Its main area of operation is the island of Luzon. At its height in the 1980s, the NPA boasted 25,000 cadres under arms, although since then its membership has shrunk to around 10,000.

Further reading
Rogers, S., 'Beyond the Abu Sayyaf' *Foreign Affairs* 83(1) 2004, pp. 15–21.
Weekley, K., *The Communist Party of the Philippines 1968–1993: A Story of its Theory and Practice*. Quezon City: University of the Philippines Press, 2001.

NEW TERRORISM

One of the enduring debates within contemporary terrorism studies concerns the extent to which groups such as **al Qaeda** constitute a new form of terrorism. Advocates of the 'new terrorism position', such as Bruce Hoffman and Walter Laqueur, define the phenomenon by focusing on three areas in particular: firstly, the extent to which new technologies such as the Internet facilitate new patterns of terrorist formation, especially through the global networking of **cells**; secondly, the role played by religion as an organizing principle that helps cohere terrorist networks while simultaneously imbuing them with a higher level of lethality; thirdly, the fact that new terrorism is often leaderless with selfgenerating cells emerging without a charismatic leader playing a dominant organizational role. In short, new terrorism is simultaneously global in nature, more deadly in its effects than the more parochial secular forms of terrorism that predominated for much of the post Second World War period, and more likely to erupt unexpectedly in the form of self-radicalized autonomous cells.

Further reading
Duyvesteyn, I., 'How New is the New Terrorism?' *Studies in Conflict and Terrorism* 27(5) 2004, pp. 439–54.

Laqueur, W., *The New Terrorism: Fanaticism and the Arms of Mass Destruction.* New York: Oxford: Oxford University Press, 2000.

Rapoport, D. C., 'The Fourth Wave: September 11 and the History of Terrorism' *Current History* December 2001, pp. 419–24.

Tucker, D., 'What is New about the New Terrorism and How Dangerous is It?' *Terrorism and Political Violence* 13(3) 2001, pp. 1–14.

OMAGH BOMBING

On 15 August 1998, the **Real Irish Republican Army** (Real IRA) carried out a car bombing attack against a hotel frequented mainly by Protestants in the small town of Omagh in Northern Ireland. The attack was designed to derail the **Good Friday Agreement**, which was viewed by the group as selling out the republican cause. However, the backlash against the attack, which killed twenty-nine people, including an eighteen-month-old child, generated a wave of cross-communal condemnation and thereby added impetus to the peace process. In June 2009, a Northern Ireland court ruled in favour of civil action brought by some of the families of victims against four convicted Real IRA members and awarded them $2.6 million in damages.

Further reading

Dingley, J., 'The Bombing of Omagh, 15 August 1998: The Bombers, Their Tactics, Strategy, and Purpose behind the Incident' *Studies in Conflict and Terrorism* 24(6) 2009, pp. 451–65.

Harnden, T., *Bandit Country: The IRA and South Armagh.* London: Hodder and Stoughton, 1999.

OPEC SIEGE

On 20 December 1975, a group of six pro-Palestinian terrorists led by **Ilyich Ramírez Sánchez ('Carlos the Jackal')** – and including supporters of the German **Baader-Meinhof Gang** – stormed a meeting of oil ministers from the Organization of Petroleum Exporting Countries (OPEC) in Vienna, killing three people in the process. Declaring themselves to be the 'Arm of the Arab Revolution' the terrorists seized seventy hostages, including eleven OPEC oil ministers. Their list of demands included a call for a declaration of war against Israel and for Arab oil-producing states to reserve a portion of their oil revenue for the Palestinians. After a twenty-hour siege, Austrian authorities acceded to the group's request for safe passage to the airport. The terrorists released some of their Austrian captives and flew to Tripoli, where they released five oil ministers and thirty-one other hostages. The group then flew to Algiers where the remaining hostages were freed after a ransom of around $5 million was paid to the terrorists.

Further reading
Follain, J., *Jackal: The Complete Story of the Legendary Terrorist Carlos the Jackal.* New York: Arcade Publishing, 1998.

OPERATION BOJINKA

In early 1995 Philippines authorities uncovered a complex three-tiered plot, Operation Bojinka (lit.: 'explosion'), involving **Khalid Sheikh Mohammed** and his nephew **Ramzi Yousef**. The first sub-plot involved the assassination of Pope John Paul II while he was on a visit to the Philippines on 15 January. The second sub-plot, and a forerunner to the **9/11** attacks, involved hijacking and exploding eleven passenger jets en route from Asia to the USA. The third involved packing a small single-engined plane with explosives before crashing it into CIA headquarters at Langley, Virginia. The plot was discovered after a fire in a Manila apartment block one week before the Pope's visit led authorities to a flat containing explosives and detonation mechanisms.

Further reading
Abuza, Z., 'Tentacles of Terror: Al Qaeda's Southeast Asian Network' *Contemporary Southeast Asia* 24(3) 2002, pp. 427–66.

OPERATION ENDURING FREEDOM

Operation Enduring Freedom was one aspect of the wider **War on Terror** announced by President George W. Bush in the wake of the attacks on **9/11**. At its core, the plan was designed to use military force to hunt down and either capture or kill terrorists and to destroy their training bases and other infrastructure. Although the focus of the operation was Afghanistan, home to **al Qaeda**'s main bases, it was also used to justify less overt military adventures in places such as the Philippines and the Horn of Africa, as well as other forms of military counter-terrorism assistance to US allies.

Further reading
Benini, A. and Moulton, L., 'Civilian Victims in an Asymmetrical Conflict: Operation Enduring Freedom, Afghanistan' *Journal of Peace Research* 41(4) 2004, pp. 403–22.
Lambeth, B. S., *Airpower against terror: America's Conduct of Operation Enduring Freedom*. Washington, DC: RAND, 2006.

OPERATION INFINITE REACH
SEE: EAST AFRICA EMBASSY BOMBINGS

OPERATION WRATH OF GOD
Also called 'Operation Bayonet', Operation Wrath of God was a covert exercise carried out by Mossad (see **Israel Institute for Intelligence and Special Tasks**), designed to hunt down and capture or kill terrorists involved in the killing of Israeli athletes during the 1972 **Munich Olympic attach**. The secret nature of the programme has made it difficult to determine the exact length of the operation or the number of people killed. Many analysts suspect the Operation lasted for more than a decade and resulted in the assassination of several dozen individuals in Europe and the Middle East.

Further reading
Hunter, T. B., 'Wrath of God: The Israeli Response to the 1972 Munich Olympics Massacre' *Journal of Counterterrorism and Security International* 7(4) 2001, pp. 16–19.
Reeve, S., *One Day in September: The Full Story of the 1972 Munich Olympics Massacre and the Israeli Revenge Operation 'Wrath of God'*. New York: Arcade Publishing, 2006.

OSLO PEACE ACCORDS ('Declaration of Principles on Interim Self-Government Arrangements')
The Oslo Peace Accords were the outcome of negotiations between the **Palestinian Liberation Organization (PLO)** and the government

of Israel. Signed by Mahmoud Abbas for the PLO and Prime Minster Shimon Peres for Israel, the principal stipulations of the Accords are that the Palestinian people in Gaza and the West Bank be granted the right to self-government and that the newly established Palestinian Authority be recognized as their legitimate governing body. In return the PLO would recognize Israel's right to exist and cease all acts of terrorism against Israeli targets. A second accord, 'The Interim Agreement on the West Bank and the Gaza Strip' (sometimes called 'Oslo Two'), was signed in September 1995, granting Palestinian self-rule in Bethlehem, Hebron, Nablus, Ramallah and over 400 other towns and villages. Although a considerable step forward in the peace process, two significant omissions were the questions of border security and the expansion of Jewish settlements in the Occupied Territories. Since then, the refusal of Israel and many other Western states to recognize **Hamas**' victory in the 2006 elections in Gaza and ongoing blockades of Palestinian townships by the Israeli military have undermined support for the Accords among many Palestinians. Meanwhile, support for the Accords among Israeli citizens has been undermined by on going attacks by Hamas and other Palestinian organizations.

Further reading

Quandt, W. B., *Peace Process: American Diplomacy and the Arab–Israeli Conflict since 1967* (3rd edn). Washington, DC: Brookings Institution Press and the University of California Press, 2005.

Said, E. W., *The End of the Peace Process: Oslo and After*. New York: Vintage, 2000.

PAKISTAN DIRECTORATE FOR INTER-SERVICES INTELLIGENCE (ISI)

The ISI is the largest intelligence agency in Pakistan with influence that permeates throughout the military and civilian spheres of government and society. At its foundation the ISI received training from the **Central Intelligence Agency** (CIA) and French intelligence services, and had a particular focus on collecting and analysing military intelligence on India – primarily in the disputed territories of Jammu and Kashmir. The ISI has a history of operating independently of its political masters and has had a hand in several coups, as well as covertly undermining initiatives taken by various civilian Pakistani governments. Its role in Pakistan's domestic politics was consolidated after the military coup of 1958 when the country's new leader, Lt-Gen. Ayub Khan, gave the ISI three additional roles: to help to ensure the longevity of military rule, to monitor the domestic opposition, and to guarantee Pakistan's wider security. From this point forward, the ISI has often conflated the idea of national security with that of regime (or military) security. During the 1980s the ISI emerged as a powerful actor in the struggle to drive the Soviet army from Afghanistan. Hundreds of millions of dollars were channelled through the ISI to the Afghan and foreign Mujahedeen, from US, Saudi and other sources. Through this role, individual ISI operatives and leaders established close working relationships with the Mujahedeen, and over time some began to sympathize with their cause. The ISI also began to expand its links to secessionist groups in Jammu and Kashmir by helping to facilitate their training at camps along the frontier with Afghanistan. It also attempted to complicate India's ability to focus its military energies in the disputed border region of Kashmir by increasing covert support for secessionist and Naxalite groups in Northeast India. After the withdrawal of Soviet forces from Afghanistan in 1989, the ISI tapped into the reservoir of former Mujahedeen and sought to direct their energies against India in the disputed territories. It was during this period that groups such as **Lashkar-e-Tayyiba** and **Jaish-e-Mohammed** were founded, with close ties to the ISI. In return for their cooperation in Kashmir, the ISI allowed these groups to proselytize within Pakistan and build on contacts with the Afghan **Taliban** and, later on, **al Qaeda**.

Further reading
Coll, S., *Ghost Wars: The Secret History of the CIA, Afghanistan, and bin Laden, from the Soviet Invasion to September 10, 2001*. New York: Penguin, 2004.
Gregory, S., 'The ISI and the War on Terrorism' *Studies in Conflict and Terrorism* 30(12) 2007, pp. 1013–31.

PALESTINE LIBERATION FRONT (PLF)
Proscribed by: Canada, EU, USA
Formed in 1959–61 by Ahmed Jibril, the Palestine Liberation Front (PLF) was one of the earliest Palestinian groups to embrace the tactic of terrorism. However, it is also known for numerous schisms that have divided the group since its inception. In 1967 Jibril joined forces with George Habash to form the **Popular Front for the Liberation of Palestine (PFLP)**. However, Habash's Marxist notion of a revolution

from below collided with Jibril's insistence on direct and immediate military action. Jibril then split from Habash and created the **Popular Front for the Liberation of Palestine – General Command (PFLP-GC)**. Jibril's ties to Damascus were so strong that he lent PFLP-GC support to assistance given by the Syrian regime to Maronite Christians fighting Palestinian guerrillas during the initial stages of the Lebanese Civil War. This support precipitated another split when, in 1977, Mohammed Zaidan (Abu Abbas) and Talat Yabub re-established the PLF along its foundational lines as an organization opposed to the state of Israel, rather than one distracted by peripheral events elsewhere in the region. The PLF launched its first terrorist attack in 1979 when a squad infiltrated the Israeli town of Nahariyah and killed a man, his daughter and an Israeli police officer. Subsequent attacks saw PLF members try to enter Israel through a variety of novel methods. In March 1981, two PLF members were captured by Israeli forces after they attempted to infiltrate Israel using hang-gliders, and in April that year Israeli forces shot down a PLF hot-air balloon. In later years, Abbas earned the nickname 'Mr Disaster'. During the mid-1980s the PLF split again, this time into three factions. The most prominent was the pro-PLO (see **Palestinian Liberation Organization**) Tunisian-based faction led by Abu Abbas. Smaller and less influential factions established bases in Lebanon and Libya. Soon after this split, Abbas became a member of the PLO executive committee, although individuals still loyal to his faction undertook operations independently. For example, in 1985, four members of the Abbas faction of the PLF hijacked the *Achille Lauro* cruise ship. This and a number of other blunders were a regular cause of embarrassment for the PLO. In 1993, the PLF officially renounced terrorism. Abu Abbas died in US custody in 2004 soon after being captured in Iraq.

Further reading
Kameel, B. N., *Arab and Israeli Terrorism: The Causes and Effects of Political Violence 1936–1993*. Jefferson: McFarland Publishers, 1997.
Tessler, M., *A History of the Israeli–Palestinian Conflict*. Bloomington: Indiana University Press, 2004.

PALESTINIAN ISLAMIC JIHAD (PIJ)
Proscribed by: Australia, Canada, EU, Israel, Japan, UK, USA
Although a number of groups around the world have adopted the label 'Islamic Jihad', one of the most significant and deadly has been

that based in the Palestinian territories. It was formed in 1982 after a militant Gaza faction led by Fathi Abd al-Aziz Shaqaqi and Abd al-Aziz Odeh broke from the Palestinian branch of the **Muslim Brotherhood**. Violence perpetrated by the PIJ's military wing, the Al-Quds Brigades, increased steadily through the 1980s, beginning with knife and gun attacks, including the assassination in August 1987 of the Commander of the Israeli Military Police in Gaza. After finding refuge in Lebanon in the late 1980s, the PIJ leadership forged closer ties with other terrorist groups such as **Hamas** and **Hezbollah** and stepped up its terrorist attacks, sometimes in cooperation with these groups, in an attempt to derail negotiations that led to the **Oslo Peace Accords**. After Shaqaqi was assassinated in Malta in 1995 (probably by Mossad agents (see **Israel Institute for Intelligence and Special Tasks**)), leadership of the PIJ passed to Ramadan Abdullah Shalah. Under Shalah, the group forged closer relations with Syria and Iran and is believed to receive funding from both. It also enhanced its relationship with Hezbollah. Unlike Hamas and Hezbollah, Islamic Jihad does not provide basic welfare services and, as a result, its ability to build a broad base of support among the Palestinian people has been limited. Even so, despite its low level of public support (compared to Hamas and **Fatah**), it has been responsible for a disproportionate level of violence. It has been especially active in launching suicide attacks and **Qassam rockets** against Israeli targets.

Further reading
Hatina, M., *Islam and Salvation in Palestine: The Islamic Jihad Movement*. Tel Aviv: The Moshe Dayan Centre for Middle Eastern and African Studies, Tel Aviv University, 2001.
Ziad, A. A., *Islamic Fundamentalism in the West Bank and Gaza: Muslim Brotherhood and Islamic Jihad*. Bloomington: Indiana University Press, 1994.

PALESTINIAN LIBERATION ORGANIZATION (PLO)

The PLO was founded in 1964 at a meeting of the Arab League in Cairo as an umbrella organization for various Palestinian resistance groups. From the outset its main purpose was to focus on the wider political dimensions of the Palestinian issue rather than the problem of refugees, which had dominated attention up until that point. Within a decade the PLO had evolved into a virtual 'government in exile', mainly through the symbolic power it generated with its attacks against Israel (which were popular among the wider Palestinian population) but also because of the wide range of welfare services it provided to displaced Palestinians. Under the leadership of **Yasser Arafat**, by 1974 the PLO was recognized by the Arab League as the sole legitimate representative of the Palestinian people. Also in 1974, Arafat addressed the General Assembly of the United Nations and the PLO was granted observer status thereafter. Operating from bases in Jordan (until 1970), Lebanon (until 1982) and Syria, as well as Gaza and the West Bank, during this period the PLO was involved in hijackings as well as gun and bomb attacks against Israeli targets around the world. On 14 December 1988 Arafat announced that the PLO would henceforth accept Israel's right to exist and that it would renounce terrorism, two preconditions which the United States had set for opening a dialogue with the PLO. However, these initiatives also corresponded with the outbreak of the first Intifada, and in this environment some saw Arafat's gestures as unacceptable concessions that compromised the Palestinian cause. On top of this, discontent with growing corruption and nepotism within the PLO fed the emergence of Islamist alternatives such as **Hamas**, making it harder for the organization to hold on to its traditional constituency. A report issued by Britain's National Criminal Intelligence Service in 1993 estimated that the PLO had accumulated between US$8 billion and US$10 billion in assets, making it the wealthiest terrorist organization in the world. In 1993, the PLO entered into talks with Israel, which led to the **Oslo Peace Accords**, with the ultimate goal of establishing the basis for a two-state solution. The outbreak of the second Intifada in September 2000 halted further peace talks between the PLO and the Israelis.

Further reading
Gelvin, J., *The Israel–Palestine Conflict: One Hundred Years of War*. Cambridge: Cambridge University Press, 2005.
Shemesh, M., 'The Palestinian Society in the Wake of the 1948 War: From Social Fragmentation to Consolidation' *Israel Studies* 9(1) 2004, p. 86.
Smith, D. C., *Palestine and the Arab–Israeli Conflict* (5th edn). New York: Bedford / St Martin's, 2004.

POPULAR FRONT FOR THE LIBERATION OF PALESTINE (PFLP)

Proscribed by: Canada, EU, Israel, USA

The Popular Front for the Liberation of Palestine (PFLP) was established in 1967 as a secular Pan-Arab Marxist organization under the leadership of George Habash, **Ahmed Jibril** and Nayif Hawatmah. However, within two years differences over ideological and military matters saw the latter two individuals split from the PFLP and form their own organizations: Jibril formed the **Popular Front for the Liberation of Palestine – General Command (PFLP-GC)** while Hawatmah formed the Popular Democratic Front for the Liberation of Palestine. Despite these setbacks, the PFLP remained steadfast to its objective to link the Palestinian issue to a wider revolution in the Arab world. In its formative years the PFLP was notorious for plane hijackings and collaboration with other left-wing terrorist groups, such as the **Japanese Red Army**. Together, both were responsible for the terrorist attack on the El Al counter at Tel Aviv's Lod airport on 30 May 1972. In September 1970 PFLP members hijacked four Western airlines, forcing three to land at an isolated airstrip outside of Amman, Jordan. Soon after the hostages were released the planes were simultaneously blown up, an event captured by media and broadcast around the world. As noted by Habash, 'We wanted to attract world attention through some action, and that was it.' The group created a military wing called the Abu Ali Mustafa Brigade during the second Intifada, and for the first time utilized the tactic of suicide terrorism. In 2001, the PFLP claimed responsibility for the assassination of Israeli Tourism Minister Rehavam Zeevi as retribution for Israel's assassination of the PFLP Secretary General earlier that year.

Further reading

Smith, D. C., *Palestine and the Arab–Israeli Conflict* (5th edn). New York: Bedford / St Martin's, 2004.

Soueid, M., 'Taking Stock: An Interview with George Habash' *Journal of Palestine Studies* 28(1) 1998, pp. 86–101.

POPULAR FRONT FOR THE LIBERATION OF PALESTINE – GENERAL COMMAND (PFLP-GC)

Proscribed by: Canada, EU, Israel, USA

The Popular Front for the Liberation of Palestine – General Command was formed in 1968 under the leadership of **Ahmed Jibril,** a former Captain in the Syrian army, after a split from the **Popular Front for the Liberation of Palestine**. It was originally a member of the PLO but left the organization in 1974 in protest at what it saw as **Yasser Arafat**'s moves towards increasing accommodation with Israel. Jibril's emphasis was on political mobilization rather than direct violence, believing that a precursor to the liberation of Palestine was the mobilization of Arabs around Pan-Arabist causes. Even so, the group was responsible for a number of high-profile terrorist attacks in the early 1970s, including placing a bomb on a Swiss Air flight that killed all forty-seven passengers and crew in 1970. On 11 April 1974, the group raided an apartment block in northern Israel, where eighteen hostages were killed during a gun battle with Israeli troops. On another front, in May 1985 Jibril negotiated the exchange of three Israeli solders (which the PFLP-GC had captured in Lebanon in 1982) for approximately 1,100 Palestinian prisoners held in Israeli jails. Throughout this period, the PFLP-GC cultivated close relations with Syria and even situated its headquarters in Damascus, although the group also received support from both Iran and Libya. More recently, the PFLP-GC has focused mainly on training Palestinian refugees in Syria and Lebanon, while sponsoring small-scale attacks in Israel.

Further reading

Laqueur, W. and Alexander, Y. (eds.) *Terrorism Reader: A Historical Anthology*. New York: Penguin, 1987.

Tessler, M., *A History of the Israeli–Palestinian Conflict*. Bloomington: Indiana University Press, 2004.

PRABHAKARAN, VELUPILLAI

Until his death in 2009, Velupillai Prabhakaran (b. 1954) was leader of the **Liberation Tigers of Tamil Eelam** (LTTE), a Sri Lankan separatist group whose extensive use of terrorism in the name of a separate Tamil nation served as a lesson for many other terrorist groups elsewhere in the world. Noted for his prowess as a military tactician and his pioneering use of suicide bombers, Prabhakaran emerged as the leader of the Tamil separatist movement after systematically eliminating his rivals in more moderate Tamil groups and uniting once-disparate organizations under the LTTE banner. He committed his first act of terrorism in 1975 when he shot and killed the Mayor of

Jaffna. Prabhakaran is especially well known for the manner in which he shaped the LTTE into a highly regimented and disciplined organization – the only terrorist group with its own navy. By tapping into the Tamil diaspora in places such as Australia, Canada, the UK and the USA, Prabhakaran built a global support network, soliciting millions of dollars in donations through front charities. Prabhakaran was killed when Sri Lankan military forces captured the LTTE's main training camp in May 2009.

Further reading
Jayatilleka, D. 'Sri Lanka's Separatist Conflict: The Sources of Intractability' *Ethnic Studies Report* 19(2) 2001, pp. 207–41.
Ramachandra, G., 'Tigers in the Alps' *World Policy Journal* 20(4) 2003, pp. 63–73.

QASSAM ROCKETS

Developed by **Hamas** in 2001, the Qassam rocket is a simple homemade device packed with impact-detonated explosives. Since their inception in 2001 there have been three different models, distinguished mainly by their range and payload, although all have lacked a precision guidance system. As Israel has hardened its borders and made it more difficult for terrorist operatives to gain access from the West Bank and Gaza Strip, the rockets have grown in their utility. Able to hit outlying Israeli settlements, the rockets killed approximately fifteen individuals during the 2000s. From the point of view of Hamas, the value of the Qassam rockets, which are named after Hamas' military wing, the Izz ad-Din al-Qassam Brigades, is in their psychological impact. On the one hand, they create fear and uncertainty among Israeli settlers. On the other hand, they have a solipsistic aspect in that they inspire fellow Palestinians by feeding the impression that the resistance is hurting Israel.

Further reading
Dolnik, A. and Bhattacharjee, A., 'HAMAS': Suicide Bombings, Rockets or WMD' *Terrorism and Political Violence* 14(3) 2002, pp. 109–28.
Richardson, D., 'IDF Hunts Qassam-II Rocket Workshops' *Jane's Missiles and Rockets* 1 April 2002.

QUTB, SAYYID

Born in Egypt in 1906, Sayyid Qutb was a high-profile member of the **Muslim Brotherhood** until his execution in 1966 by the regime of Gamal Abdel Nasser. As a young man he was given extensive instruction in Qur'anic studies before moving to Cairo where he received a secular education and graduated as a school teacher. Early in his career, Qutb spent much of his time writing fiction and poetry. A turning point occurred between 1948 and 1951 when he was awarded a scholarship for further study in the United States. Qutb was shocked by the extent of racism and by what he considered to be licentious inter-sex relationships. This shaped his view of Western societies, which he came to regard as morally debauched, and hardened his attitude against secular values. Retuning to Egypt he became active in the Muslim Brotherhood and began to develop a reputation as a staunch critic of the monarchist regime and, after the coup of 1952, of the regime of Gamal Abdel Nasser. Following an assassination attempt against Nasser in 1954 the government moved against the Muslim Brotherhood, rounding up and imprisoning hundreds of its members, including Qutb. The experience of prison inspired his most influential work, *Milestones*, which argued that the Muslim world had regressed to a state of *jahilliyah*, the condition of ignorance that existed before the Prophet Mohammed. According to Qutb, this could only be overcome through a two-pronged strategy involving preaching and revolutionary violence (an 'offensive **jihad**') against the main instruments of cultural and political repression. Qutb's later work has exerted a powerful influence within militant Islamist circles, including among some terrorist groups. The senior **al Qaeda** figure **Ayman al-Zawahiri** was a one-time student of Qutb, as were other individuals prominent in terrorist circles. In 1966 the Nasser regime implicated Qutb in a plot to assassinate Nasser and other senior Egyptian officers and overthrow the government. He was sentenced to death and was hanged on 29 August of that year.

Further reading

Bergesen, A., *The Sayyid Qutb Reader*. London and New York: Routledge, 2007.

Khatab, S., *The Political Thought of Sayyid Qutb: The Theory of Jahilliyah*. London and New York: Routledge, 2009.

RAJARATNAM, THENMULI
Thenmuli 'Dhanu' Rajaratnam was a member of the female suicide squad of the **Liberation Tigers of Tamil Eelam** (LTTE). She reached notoriety by strapping explosives to herself and assassinating Indian Prime Minister Rajiv Gandhi and killing sixteen others during an election campaign gathering near the southern Indian city of Chennai on 21 May 1991. Anecdotally, her decision to volunteer for this suicide mission was motivated by her experiences during the Indian intervention in Sri Lanka, when Indian soldiers allegedly raped her. Subsequent to her death, she become a martyr for the LTTE cause and was held up as a role model for other female volunteers.

Further reading
Friedman, M., 'Female Terrorists: Martyrdom and Gender Equality' in I. A. Karawan, W. McCormack and S. E. Reynolds (eds.) *Values and Violence: Intangible Aspects of Terrorism*. New York: Springer, 2008, pp. 43–62.

RAMÍREZ SÁNCHEZ, ILYICH ('CARLOS THE JACKAL')
Named 'Ilyich' by his father as a tribute to Lenin (whose middle name was Ilich), during the 1970s and 1980s Ilyich Ramírez Sánchez (b. 1949) was one of the world's most notorious and best-known terrorists. The nickname 'The Jackal' was appended by the media after it was reported that police found a copy of the Frederick Forsyth novel *The Day of the Jackal* in his apartment. Ramírez was born in Caracas in Venezuela on 12 October 1949. He was educated in the UK and briefly attended university in Moscow before being expelled in 1970. He then travelled to Jordan where he joined the **Popular Front for the Liberation of Palestine (PFLP)**. In the early 1970s he was involved in an aborted bomb attack against an Israeli bank in London, a failed grenade attack against El Al aircraft in Paris, and bombing attacks against pro-Israeli French newspapers in Paris. In June 1975 he was almost captured by French police in Paris, but after shooting two detectives he escaped and eventually made his way to Beirut. His first major terrorist operation occurred in December 1975 when he led a six-person team that included two individuals linked to the **Baader-Meinhoff Gang** in the **OPEC siege** in Vienna. Although still associated with Palestinian groups, by the 1980s Ramírez had become a virtual terrorist-for-hire. In the early 1980s he worked for the East German and Romanian secret police, who contracted him to

assassinate dissidents based in the West. Even so, he continued to champion Middle Eastern causes and, in the early 1980s, bombed several French trains in retaliation for French airstrikes against a PFLP camp in Lebanon. Unable to control Ramírez, a succession of Eastern European hosts withdrew their hospitality and he was forced to move to Syria and then Iraq, before being offered sanctuary in Sudan. While recuperating from an operation in 1996 he was double-crossed by his bodyguards and handed over to French agents. He was tried in Paris and sentenced to life imprisonment. However, jail did not dent his thirst for notoriety and, through his well-known legal representative (and fiancée) Isabelle Coutant-Peyre, he has continued to issue statements that inevitably attract media attention. He recently converted to Islam and, in a 2003 book authored in prison, he praised **Osama bin Laden.**

Further reading

Follain, J., *Jackal: Finally, the Complete Story of the Legendary Terrorist, Carlos The Jackal*. New York: Arcade Publishing, 2000.

REAL IRISH REPUBLICAN ARMY (REAL IRA)

Proscribed by: EU, Republic of Ireland, UK, USA

Michael McKevitt and other dissident members of the Provisional IRA (see **Irish Republican Army (Provisional)**) formed the Real IRA after leaving in protest over the signing of the **Good Friday Agreement**. Their goal remains the unification of all of Ireland's thirty-two counties within an independent Irish Republic. They remain committed to achieving this goal through armed struggle even though, in recent years, their community of support has significantly decreased. Part of the reason for their lack of support is the **Omagh bombing** in August 1998, which killed twenty-nine people. The group called a ceasefire a month later, but this was abandoned in 2000, after which the Real IRA launched a fresh wave of attacks against British military targets. That same year, it also shifted its attention to the British mainland, launching a rocket-propelled grenade attack against the MI6 (see **Secret Intelligence Service – UK**) headquarters at Vauxhall Cross and several bombings of railway and military targets. McKevitt's arrest in 2001 and subsequent twenty-year jail sentence also impacted negatively on the Real IRA and its membership is now estimated to number no more than 150. Even so, the Real IRA remains a dangerous entity, murdering two British soldiers in the town of Antrim in March 2009.

Further reading
Alonso, R., 'The Modernization in Irish Republican Thinking toward the Utility of Violence' *Studies in Conflict and Terrorism* 24(2) 2001, pp. 131–44.
McKittrick, D. and McVea, D., *Making Sense of the Troubles*. London: Penguin Books, 2001.

RED ARMY FACTION
SEE: BAADER-MEINHOF GANG

RED BRIGADES
SEE: ITALIAN RED BRIGADES

RED HAND DEFENDERS
Proscribed by: EU, Republic of Ireland, UK
An extreme offshoot of the **Ulster Defence Association** (UDA) and the **Loyalist Volunteer Force** (LVF), the Red Hand Defenders (RHD) is a loyalist group operating in Northern Ireland. There are suspicions that the group is a front organization for dissident members of the UDA and LVF who are opposed to the **Good Friday Agreement**. By joining the RHD, members of these other organizations can outwardly support the Agreement while covertly carrying out actions designed to undermine it. Using crude bombs, arson attacks and shootings, its main targets have been Catholic businesses, homes, churches and school staff. In the early 2000s, the RHD was also involved in an intramural conflict between different Loyalist organizations and has been implicated in several murders of Loyalist rivals.

Further reading
Boyce, G., *Defenders of the Union: British and Irish Unionism 1800–1999*. London: Routledge, 2001.

REID, RICHARD ('The Shoe-Bomber')

Richard Reid (b. 1973) is a British national arrested in December 2001 for planning to destroy an American Airlines flight from Paris to Miami by igniting explosive liquids concealed in the soles of his shoes. Before converting to Islam and making contact with individuals associated with **al Qaeda**, including **Khalid Sheikh Mohammed**, Reid had dropped out of secondary school and fell into a life of crime, serving a jail sentence for robbery. He converted to Islam while in prison, and after his release fell under the influence of extremist elements at the Finsbury Park Mosque in West London. On their advice, in 1999 Reid travelled to Pakistan, studying at a religious school and, from there, attended a terrorist training camp in Afghanistan. Passengers on the flight overpowered him after he was discovered trying to ignite one of his shoes. Reid was charged and convicted on three counts: attempting to use a weapon of mass destruction against US nationals outside the United States; interference with flight crew and attendants; and using a dangerous weapon. He pleaded guilty to all counts and is currently serving a life sentence in a US prison.

Further reading

Elliott, M., 'The Shoe Bomber's World' *Time* 16 February 2002.

BBC News 'Who is Richard Reid?' 28 December 2001. At http://news.bbc.co.uk/2/hi/uk_news/1731568.stm.

RESSAM, AHMED ('The Millennium Bomber')

Ahmed Ressam (b. 1967) is an Algerian-born **al Qaeda**-linked operative arrested in December 1999 while trying to smuggle a carload of explosives and bomb-making materials from Vancouver into the USA. Ressam had originally entered Canada in 1994 on a forged French passport, claiming refugee status soon after. In the late 1990s he travelled to Afghanistan on a fraudulent Canadian passport where he attended an al Qaeda training camp run by **Abu Zubaydah**. He was eventually convicted of planning to attack Los Angeles International airport and sentenced to twenty-two years in prison. According to US authorities, Ressam has cooperated with their investigations into possible terrorist networks in North America.

Further reading
Flynn, S. E., 'Beyond Border Control' *Foreign Affairs* 79(6) 2000, pp. 57–68.
Public Broadcasting Service (PBS) 'Ahmed Ressam's Millennium Plot'. At
  www.pbs.org/wgbh/pages/frontline/shows/trail/inside/cron.html.

Revolutionary Armed Forces of Colombia – People's Army

(Fuerzas Armadas Revolucionarias de Colombia – Ejército del
Pueblo (FARC-EP))
Proscribed by: Canada, EU, USA
Established in 1964 as the military wing of the Colombian Communist Party, FARC was born out of a bloody conflict between left-wing
and right-wing militias over access to land. The conflict (known locally
as 'La Violencia') lasted from 1948 to 1965 and claimed more than
200,000 lives. Pedro Antonio Marín Marín (also known as 'Manuel
Marulanda Vélez' or 'Tirofijo') served as leader of the group from its
inception until his death in early 2008. Alfonso Cano succeeded him.
At its inception, FARC's main objective was to promote the welfare
of peasants and poor labourers. Its principal modus operandi included
targeted assassinations of government officials and right-wing opponents, car bombings, kidnapping-for-ransom, extortion and the use
of land mines to protect territory under its control. Over the years, the
Marxist undertones of its justification for violence have rung increasingly hollow for many Colombians, with the FARC's actions suggesting a shift in its main objective from controlling land to protect the
welfare of its inhabitants to controlling land to help ensure its own
survival. The FARC's increasing involvement in **narco-terrorism** (with
cocaine cartels) and its use of forcibly recruited child soldiers (who
constitute up to 30 per cent of its members) have eroded much of its
moral authority among erstwhile supporters, many of whom now
view the group as little more than a crime cartel. In 2001, three
members of the Provisional IRA (see **Irish Republican Army (Provisional) (PIRA)**) were arrested for providing training in bomb-making
to the FARC. A report by a US House of Representatives Committee
in 2001 suggested that the PIRA might have been paid around $2
million in drug money in return for this training. By the mid-2000s,
anti-FARC demonstrations, sometimes drawing hundreds of thousands of people, had taken place in major cities and towns. The election of the conservative Colombian presidential candidate Álvaro
Uribe in 2002 saw an escalation in military operations against the
FARC, but his government has been slow in implementing soft-power

policies, such as improving economic and political opportunities for the rural poor, needed to choke off recalcitrant support for the FARC in some areas. By the late 2000s, FARC's membership was between 8,000 and 10,000, down from around 18,000 a decade earlier.

Further reading

Mason, A., 'Colombia's Democratic Security Agenda: Public Order in the Security Tripod' *Security Dialogue* 34(4) 2003, pp. 391–409.

Molano, A., 'The Evolution of the FARC: A Guerrilla Group's Long History' *NACLA Report on the Americas* 34(2) 2000, pp. 23–31.

Palacios, M., *Between Legitimacy and Violence: A History of Colombia, 1875–2002* (trans. Richard Stoller) (2nd edn). Durham, NC: Duke University Press, 2004.

REVOLUTIONARY ORGANIZATION 17 NOVEMBER

Proscribed by: EU, UK, USA

Usually referred to by its shorthand title 'November 17', this group takes its name from the date in 1973 when protests against the ruling military junta, by students at a university in Athens, were suppressed by the army. From its inception to the late 1990s, the group carried out a series of bank robberies and initiated more than 100 bombing and shooting attacks against US military and commercial interests, Turkish diplomats and Greek military and right-wing political targets. Embracing a Marxist–Leninist philosophy, the group's main objectives were to undermine the close bilateral relationship between Athens and Washington, end Greece's membership in NATO, and, more generally, bring about radical socio-economic change. In 2002, most of the group's leaders were arrested and given lengthy jail sentences. In 2007, a group calling itself 'Revolutionary Struggle' and claiming to be a November 17 splinter group claimed responsibility for a missile attack against the American embassy in Athens.

Further reading

Karyotis, G., 'Securitization of Greek Terrorism and Arrest of the Revolutionary Organization 17 November' *Cooperation and Conflict* 42(3) 2007, pp. 271–93.

Kassimeris, G., 'Last Act in a Violent Drama? The Trial of Greece's Revolutionary Organization 17 November' *Terrorism and Political Violence* 18(1) 2006, pp. 137–57.

RIYAD US-SALIHEYN MARTYRS' BRIGADE
Proscribed by: Russia
Also known as Riyadh-as-Saliheen, Riyadus-Salikhin Reconnaissance
and the Sabotage Battalion of Chechen Martyrs, the Riyad us-Saliheyn Martyrs Brigade is a Chechen organization dedicated to achieving independence from Moscow and establishing Chechnya and
other Muslim parts of Russia, including Dagestan, Kabardino-
Balkaria, Ingushetia, Ossetia and Tataria, as an independent Islamist
state. The organization was founded and led by Amil Basayev, who
had strong ties with individuals linked to **al Qaeda**, and in all likelihood is the result of a merger between two longer-standing secessionist groups, the Special Purpose Islamic Regiment and the
International Islamic Brigade. The organization has a female cell of
suicide bombers known as the '**Black Widows**'. The group's most
notorious attack occurred in September 2004 when thirty-two militants raided a school in the town of Beslan in North Ossetia, taking
more than 1,000 teachers and students hostage. A subsequent rescue
operation by Russian Special Forces resulted in the deaths of 331
hostages, including 171 children. Although Basayev's death in July
2006 was a setback for the group, it has not diminished the organization's ambitions or their influence within Chechnya.

Further reading
Hughes, J., *Chechnya: From Nationalism to Jihad*. Philadelphia: University
of Pennsylvania Press, 2008.
Murphy, P., *The Wolves of Islam: Russia and the Faces of Chechen Terror*.
Dulles: Brassey's Inc., 2004.

RUDOLPH, ERIC
Charged for crimes including the 1996 Centennial Olympic Park
bombing in Atlanta, 1997 bombings at a gay nightclub, an attack
against an Atlanta abortion clinic and another in Birmingham,
Alabama, in 1998, Eric Rudolph (b. 1966) was for several years
number one on the FBI's Most Wanted list. After his capture in 2005,
Rudolph justified his violence in terms of resisting what he called the
'homosexual agenda' and the 'abortion holocaust'. He eventually
pleaded guilty to multiple charges of murder and was sentenced to
five consecutive life sentences. Although claiming to be a Catholic,
Rudolph was connected to the right-wing white supremacist
Christian Identity Movement, whose ideals were imparted to the

young Rudolph by his mother. He is also thought by some to have been connected to the radical anti-abortion network **The Army of God.**

Further reading
Schuster, H. and Stone, C., *Hunting Eric Rudolph.* New York: Berkley Publishing Group, 2005.
Seegmiller, B., 'Radicalized Margins: Eric Rudolph and Religious Violence' *Terrorism and Political Violence* 19(4) 2007, pp. 511–28.

SAEED, SHEIKH OMAR
Omar Saeed (b. 1973) was one of the first of the contemporary British-born homegrown terrorists to come to the notice of international counter-terrorism agencies. Born into an upper-middle-class family and educated at some of Britain's exclusive educational institutions, Saeed became radicalized while a student at the London School of Economics. While still a university student he travelled to Bosnia and then to Pakistan, the birthplace of his parents, where he was introduced to members of **Harakat ul-Mujahedeen (HuM)**. While in HuM he became closely acquainted with Maulana Masood Azhar, who later left the group to form **Jaish-e-Mohammed** (JeM). Saeed was eventually charged with being involved in the kidnapping and videotaped execution of the *Wall Street Journal*'s South Asia correspondent, Daniel Pearl. According to Henri Bernard Levi, Saeed set out to make Pearl's acquaintance by offering to introduce him to some militant figures who would help the journalist with a story he was writing. Pearl was captured, held for several weeks and then beheaded, with his death posted on the Internet as a warning to other Westerners. Saeed was arrested in Pakistan in 2002 and sentenced to death for his role in Pearl's execution. He appealed against the sentence.

Further reading
Levi, H. B., *Who Killed Daniel Pearl?* Brooklyn: Melville House, 2003.

SALAFIST GROUP FOR PREACHING AND COMBAT (Groupe Salafiste pour la Prédication et le Combat (GSPC))
Proscribed by: UK
An offshoot of the **Armed Islamic Group**, the Algerian Salafist Group for Preaching and Combat (GSPC) is now a pivotal component of the

al Qaeda Organization in the Land of the Islamic Maghreb. Active since 1996, it adheres to an extremist Sunni ideology and aims to establish Algeria as an Islamist state. Initially, the GSPC's targets were exclusively Algerian, specifically government and military personnel. Indeed, in 1998, when the GSCP publicly (somewhat hypocritically) pleaded for the avoidance of civilian casualties in battles against the secular Algerian government, the group attracted a considerable amount of support from the general populace, exceeding that enjoyed by the Armed Islamic Group (GIA). The GSPC also managed to tap into the Algerian diaspora and build extensive logistical and support networks in Western Europe. However, the GSPC has also suffered several major splits. Since 2004, the northern faction of the group has been led by Abdelmalek Droukdal (also known as Abu Abdul Wadoud), after its previous leader, Nabil Sahrouki, was killed during a battle with government forces. Meanwhile, the southern faction is led by Mokhtar Belmokhtar (also known as 'One-Eye') and Ammar Saifi (also known as 'El Para'). Although both factions experienced further schisms in the late 2000s, the GSPC remains a highly dangerous organization. In what has been considered by some as an attempt to enhance the group's recruitment and financial position, in 2003 the GSPC declared its allegiance to **al Qaeda**. In 2006, **Ayman al-Zawahiri** publicly approved the merger in a videotaped message, after which the GSPC changed its name to the Al-Qaeda Organization in the Land of the Islamic Maghreb and set about trying to bring other North African groups into its orbit. Since then, the group has played a considerable role in funnelling foreign fighters into Iraq and has extended its financial and logistical networks. In 2007, five of its members were arrested by Nigerian authorities for allegedly plotting a terrorist attack against a US government building in the country. On 11 April 2007, the group carried out simultaneous suicide bombings near a government building, killing twenty-three people. That same day, the group detonated a bomb at a police station in the capital, Algiers, killing eight people.

Further reading

Hunt, E., *Islamist Terrorism in North-Western Africa: A 'Thorn in the Neck' of the United States, Policy Focus No.65.* Washington, DC: The Washington Institute for Near East Policy, 2007.

Steinberg, G. and Werefels, I., 'Between the "Near" and the "Far" Enemy: Al-Qaeda in the Islamic Maghreb' *Mediterranean Politics* 12(3) 2007, pp. 407–13.

SANDS, ROBERT ('BOBBY')

In 1981, PIRA (see **Irish Republican Army (Previsional)**) member Robert 'Bobby' Sands (b. 1954) died in prison after a hunger strike designed to force the British government of Margaret Thatcher to recognize Irish Republican inmates as political prisoners rather than criminals. Five core demands were associated with this objective: the right not to wear the prison uniform; the right not to participate in prison work; the right to associate freely with other inmates; the right to receive one visit, one letter and one parcel per week; and, lastly, restoration of remission lost during the hunger strike. Sands joined the republican movement at the age of eighteen. In 1972 he was convicted for possessing handguns. He was released in 1976; however, the following year he was again convicted and sentenced to fourteen years for possessing a revolver that had been used in a shoot-out with police. Sands also participated in the first hunger strike that commenced on 27 October 1980; however, shortly afterward the PIRA commander inside the prison, Brendan Hughes, called off the strike after the British government offered some concessions. Nonetheless, many prisoners deemed London's concessions unacceptable and consequently Sands commenced another strike on 1 March 1981. During his strike, Sands was elected MP for the constituency of Fermanagh and South Tyrone in Northern Ireland. Sands died on 5 May 1981 in the prison hospital, after sixty-six days without food. Nine other hunger strikers died after him.

Further reading
Adams, G., *Bobby Sands: Writings from Prison.* Cork: Mercier, 2001.
Dingley, J. and Marcello, M., 'The Human Body as a Terrorist Weapon: Hunger Strikes and Suicide Bombers' *Studies in Conflict and Terrorism* 30(6) 2007, pp. 459–92.

SECRET INTELLIGENCE SERVICE – UK (MI6)

With its origins in a 1909 decision to combat the rise of German naval power, the Secret Intelligence Service – or MI6 as it is more popularly known – has developed into the United Kingdom's principal foreign-intelligence-gathering organization. Focusing on the collection of human intelligence, but working closely with electronic and signals intelligence organizations such as the Government Communication Headquarters (GCHQ), it plays a front-line role in counter-terrorism activities. The focus on terrorism, along with the proliferation of weapons of mass destruction, grew out of an inquiry conducted in the 1990s designed to reassess MI6's operations in a post-Cold-War world. Like its domestic counterpart MI5 (see **Security Service – UK**) the organization also exchanges intelligence with a wide array of foreign intelligence partners.

Further reading
Davies, P., *MI6 and the Machinery of Spying: Structure and Process in Britain's Secret Intelligence*. London and New York: Routledge, 2004.
Dorril, S., *MI6: Inside the Covert World of Her Majesty's Secret Intelligence Service*. New York: Free Press, 2002.

SECURITY SERVICE – UK (MI5)

MI5 is the UK's domestic intelligence agency and is mandated to protect the country from threats to national security, including those posed by 'terrorism, espionage and proliferation of weapons of mass destruction'. It carries out this role by both collecting intelligence and analysing that collected by other UK agencies such as MI6 (see **Secret Intelligence Sevice – UK**) and signals intelligence organizations such as the Government Communications Headquarters (GCHQ). MI5 also works closely with the police Special Branch and maintains a diverse collection of partnerships with foreign agencies such as the **Federal Bureau of Investigation (FBI)** in the USA, ASIO in Australia, and counterparts in the EU.

Further reading
Hollingsworth, M. and Fielding, N., *Defending the Realm: Inside MI5 and the War on Terrorism*. Glasgow: Andre Deutsch, 2004.
Thomas, G., *Secret Wars: One Hundred Years of British Intelligence inside MI5 and MI6*. London: Thomas Dunne Books, 2009.

SHABAK, THE
SEE: ISRAEL SECURITY AGENCY

SHIGENOBU, FUSAKO

Fusako Shigenobu (b. 1945) was leader of the ultra-leftist **Japanese Red Army** (JRA). Having previously been a member of the Japanese Communist League – Red Army Faction, Shigenobu came into contact with members of the **Popular Front for the Liberation of Palestine (PFLP)** while travelling in Europe. In 1971 she moved to Beirut where, along with Tsuyoshi Okudaira, she established the Japanese Red Army. Okudaira was subsequently killed during an attack on Lod Airport in Tel Aviv by three JRA members acting on behalf of the PFLP. Shigenobu is best known for the key role she played in the JRA's 1974 assault on the French embassy at The Hague, where the French ambassador, along with ten other people, was held hostage. Under her leadership, the JRA also engaged in a number of other hijackings and hostage-taking exercises. Shigenobu was finally arrested in 2000 in the Japanese city of Osaka, soon after she had entered the country using a false passport. She was convicted for her role in the French embassy seige and given a twenty-year prison sentence. An appeal against the severity of the sentence was rejected in 2006. In 2001, Shigenobu issued a statement from prison disbanding the JRA and claiming that the armed struggle was over.

Further reading

Gonzalez-Perez, M., *Women and Terrorism: Female Activity in Domestic and International Terror Groups*. London: Routledge, 2008.

Steinhoff, G. P., 'Three Women Who Loved the Left: Radical Women Leaders in the Japanese Red Army Movement', in A. E. Imamua (ed.) *Re-Imaging Japanese Women*. Berkeley: University of California Press, 1996, pp. 301–23.

SHIN BET
SEE: ISRAEL SECURITY AGENCY

SHINING PATH (Sendero Luminoso)
Proscribed by: Canada, EU, USA
Sendero Luminoso (an abbreviation of 'Partido Comunista de Peru – Sendero Luminoso ('The Communist Party of Peru – Shining Path')) emerged in the late 1960s as a Marxist–Maoist group under the leadership of **Abimael Guzmán**. In its early years, membership was made up mainly of academics and students from San Cristóbal of Huamanga National University in Ayacucho, where Guzmán was a professor of philosophy. Initial activities consisted of study groups that critiqued government reforms on issues that impacted on the peasantry, such as regional subsistence farming. However, Shining

Path's activities soon expanded to include self-help projects for local peasant communities, which enhanced its grass-roots support. By the mid-1970s, the group began developing clandestine military units that aimed to topple Peru's pro-Western government. The group's first act of violence occurred in 1980 when they burned a number of ballot boxes. By the mid-1980s, the group further expanded its activities to include assassination and kidnapping, targeting in particular government officials and wealthy business owners. Shining Path also targeted local peasants who resisted the group's policy of 'starving the cities' by interrupting the delivery of food from rural areas. Anti-Shining-Path paramilitary groups, known as the Rondas, emerged in the 1980s, killing suspected Shining Path members and supporters. This led to a cycle of violence whereby tit-for-tat killings became commonplace. Some estimates suggest that between 1980 and 1993 – the most deadly part of this cycle of violence – over 10,000 people were killed in and around the city of Ayacucho alone. De-escalation occurred after the 1992 capture of Guzmán. Following his arrest, Guzmán made several television appearances, and it was during one of these in 1993 that he declared an end to hostilities. After Guzmán's statement, around 6,000 cadres accepted an offer of a government amnesty and surrendered. The arrest of more leaders precipitated a schism which saw the emergence of a break-away group – Sendero Rojo ('Red Path'). The early 2000s saw a revival of violence by Sendero Luminoso, now under the leadership of an individual with the *nom de guerre* 'Comrade Artemio', with a series of attacks against the US embassy in Lima and Peruvian infrastructure and military targets.

Further reading

Osborn, R., 'On the Path of Perpetual Revolution: From Marx's Millenarianism to Sendero Luminoso' *Totalitarian Movements and Political Religions* 8(1) 2007, pp. 115–36.

SIDDIQUE KHAN, MOHAMMAD

Mohammad Siddique Khan (1974–2005) was the one of the British-born suicide bombers who attacked the London transport system on 7 July 2005. Born in Leeds, he was the oldest of the bombers and the ringleader. Like those of two of his accomplices, **Shezhad Tanweer** and Hasib Hussain, Khan's parents had emigrated from Pakistan to Britain. After graduating from Leeds Metropolitan University, Khan started work at a local primary school as a learning mentor for special-needs children. That same year, 2004, Khan married and had a daughter. As stated in the official report into the London bombings, it is unclear when the process of Khan's radicalization started. In hindsight, his colleagues stated that he became more introverted twelve months after commencing work at the primary school. By this time, Khan was viewed as a mentor in the community; however, his speeches at community talks became increasingly aggressive, especially after the UK's involvement in the invasion of Iraq. In a video prepared by Khan prior to his death, he stated,

> Our driving motivation doesn't come from tangible commodities that this world has to offer . . . *Your* democratically elected governments continually perpetuate atrocities against *my* people all over the world. And *your* support of them makes you directly responsible . . . And until you stop the bombing, gassing, imprisonment and torture of *my* people we will not stop this fight. We are at war and I am a solider.

Although investigators searched for tangible evidence of an external support network by focusing on Khan's multiple trips to Pakistan during 2003, 2004 and 2005, the official report into the bombings stated: 'There is as yet no firm evidence to collaborate this claim or the nature of the **al Qaeda** support, if there was any. But the target and mode of the attack of the 7 July bombings are typical of al Qaeda and those inspired by its ideologies.'

Further reading

House of Commons, *Report of the Official Account of the Bombings in London on 7th July 2005*. London: The Stationery Office, 11 May 2006.

Kirby, A., 'The London Bombers as "Self-Starters": A Case Study in Indigenous Radicalization and the Emergence of Autonomous Cliques' *Studies in Conflict and Terrorism* 30(5) 2007, pp. 415–28.

SINGH BHINDRANWALE, JARNAIL

Jarnail Singh Bhindranwale (1947–84) was a Sikh holy man before becoming a militant leader of a violent campaign for a Sikh homeland in northern India. He was born in India's Punjab region and was sent to study under a respected Sikh scholar and teacher at a Sikh religious school at a young age. After the teacher's death in 1977, Bhindranwale became the school's principal. During his later years at the school his views became increasingly militant and, in 1978, his followers were involved in an assault against a group of Niran-karis, a small sect of former Sikhs who follow their own guru. Violence triggered by the attack escalated, and in 1980 the leader of the Nirankaris was assassinated. Although Bhindranwale was charged with ordering the murder he was eventually acquitted. In 1981, he was arrested once again for being involved in the killing of the Niran-kari publisher of a newspaper that had printed several articles criticiz-ing Bhindranwale. This time he was released due to insufficient evidence. The experience marked a turning point in his life and, henceforth, he dedicated himself to forging an independent Sikh homeland called Khalistan where Sikhs would no longer be at risk of losing their identity due to secularism and resurgent Hinduism. By this period, Bhindranwale's power had grown to such a level that the then Prime Minister, Indira Gandhi, suspended the Punjab state government on the grounds that it had become hostage to Bhindran-wale's supporters. Bhindranwale responded by setting up a de facto government in the holiest of Sikh shrines, the Golden Temple in Amritsar. In June 1984 the failure of negotiations designed to coax the group from the temple led Prime Minister Gandhi to order the army to use force, an assault given the name 'Operation Blue Star'. Two days of fighting in and around the temple left more than 700 dead, including Bhindranwale. On 31 October 1984, Prime Minister Ghandi was assassinated by two of her Sikh bodyguards as retaliation for the assault on the temple. Even so, Bhindranwale's memory remains a rallying point for militant Sikhs, such as those associated with the **International Sikh Youth Federation.**

Further reading
Joshi, C., *Bhindranwale: Myth and Reality*. New Delhi: South Asia Books, 1985.
Juergensmeyer, M., *The New Cold War? Religious Nationalism Confronts the Secular State*. Delhi: Oxford University Press, 1994.

SIPAH-E-SAHABA PAKISTAN (SESP)
SEE: LASHKAR-I-JHANGVI

SIRHAN SIRHAN
On 5 June 1968, Sirhan Sirhan (b. 1944) assassinated US Senator Robert Kennedy Jr, who was campaigning in the Democratic Party

primaries. Sirhan was born a Palestinian Christian in the British Mandate for Palestine, and his family immigrated to the United States when he was an adolescent. Sirhan justified his attack against Kennedy on Arab nationalist grounds, particularly the Senator's support for Israel during the 1967 Six Day War. Sirhan was tackled to the ground immediately after the incident and arrested by police. He is currently serving a life sentence. As with the assassination of his brother President John F. Kennedy, a myriad of conspiracy theories surround Robert Kennedy's murder, with some authors questioning the findings of the Los Angeles police that Sirhan acted alone.

Further reading
Ayton, M., *The Forgotten Terrorist: Sihan Sirhan and the Assassination of Robert F. Kennedy*. Dulles: Potomac Books Inc., 2007.
Diamond, B., 'Interview regarding Sirhan Sirhan' *Psychology Today* September 1969, pp. 48–55.

STATE-SPONSORED TERRORISM

Although most terrorism-related scholarship focuses on non-state actors, it has been estimated that, even when deaths in wars are excluded, state-sponsored terrorism is greater than non-state terrorism by a ratio of 260 : 1. On one level, state-sponsored terrorism can be defined as the use or threatened use of violence for political purposes by a government against its own citizens, or against the citizens of another nation state. In many instances, terrorism by non-state actors is a response to violence perpetrated by governments. However, debates about state-sponsored terrorism are complicated by the issue of sovereignty, whereby a state has the right to use measured violence to defend itself against illegal or unwarranted forms of aggression. This opens up a complex set of legal questions about when the alleged threats are exaggerated or real, and therefore when state-sanctioned violence is either legitimate or illegitimate. By declaring their opponents as illegal or illegitimate or by depicting them as agents of foreign powers, governments can avoid the opprobrium associated with having its actions labelled as terrorist. On another level, the issue of state-sanctioned terrorism is more clear-cut. This is the case when governments actively sponsor designated terrorist groups. Libya's past support for terrorist groups as diverse as the Provisional IRA (see **Irish Republican Army (Provisional)**) and the **Palestinian Liberation Organization**, the US government's support for right-wing paramilitary groups in South and Central America in the 1970s and 1980s, and Iran's ongoing support for **Hezbollah** are all examples of this type of state-sponsored terrorism.

Further reading
Byman, D., *Deadly Connections: States that Sponsor Terrorism*. Cambridge: Cambridge University Press, 2005.
Rummel, R. J., *Death by Government*. New Brunswick: Transaction Publishers, 1996.

STERN GANG

The 'Stern Gang' (more correctly 'Lehi' – an acronym of Lohamei Herut Israel, Hebrew for 'Fighters for the Freedom of Israel') was an underground Zionist group operating in the 1940s in the British Mandate of Palestine. Led by Avraham Stern, the group's primary goals were to drive the British from the area, to establish an independent Jewish homeland and to allow for the unrestricted immigration of Jews – in the wake of the Holocaust, mainly from war-ravaged Europe. To achieve its goals the group carried out a series of terrorist attacks against British and Arab targets. Amongst these operations were the attack on the British Minister of State in the Middle East, Lord Moyne, who was assassinated in Cairo in November 1944; the truck bombing of a British police station in 1947; a massacre of around 120 unarmed Palestinian villagers in the town of Deir Yassin in 1948; the assassination of UN mediator Folke Bernadotte in 1948; the murder of several British soldiers in 1948; and the **King David Hotel bombing**. Despite outrage among many Jewish groups at the violence of the Stern Gang, in 1949 its members were granted a general amnesty, while in 1980 the government commemorated its actions by creating a military decoration in its name, the Lehi ribbon, which was awarded to former members. The Stern Gang's better-known members include Yitzhak Shamir, Prime Minister from 1983 to 1984 and again from 1986 to 1992.

Further reading
Brenner, Y. S., 'The "Stern Gang" 1940–1948' *Middle Eastern Studies* 2(1) 1965, pp. 2–30.
Heller, J., *The Stern Gang: Ideology, Politics and Terror*, 1940–1949. London: Routledge, 1995.

STOCKHOLM SYNDROME

'Stockholm Syndrome' refers to a psychological process whereby a hostage comes to identify with his or her captors. At its core, Stockholm Syndrome is 'an automatic, often unconscious, emotional response to the trauma of victimization' and is not the result of rational choice by the victim, who calculates, rightly or wrongly, that the most advantageous and safe form of behaviour is to befriend their captor. The term was coined in 1973 when four bank employees were taken hostage in Stockholm. On their release the victims evinced no negative feelings towards the hostage-takers, despite being held in a bank vault for 131 hours but they did express hostility towards the police who ended the ordeal. One of the most infamous cases of Stockholm Syndrome occurred during the kidnapping of **Patty Hearst** by the **Symbionese Liberation Army** in February 1974. Although having numerous chances to escape, Hearst became involved with the group and participated in two bank robberies before being arrested by authorities.

Further reading

Cantor, C. and Price, J., 'Traumatic Entrapment, Appeasement and Complex Post-Traumatic Stress Disorder: Evolutionary Perspectives of Hostage Reactions, Domestic Abuse and the Stockholm Syndrome' *Australian and New Zealand Journal of Psychiatry* 41(5) 2007, pp. 377–84.

de Fabrique, N., Van Hasselt, V. B., Vecchi, G. M. and Romano, S. J., 'Common Variables Associated with the Development of Stockholm Syndrome: Some Case Examples' *Victims & Offenders* 2(1) 2007, pp. 91–8.

Fuselier, G. D., 'Placing the Stockholm Syndrome in Perspective' *FBI Law Enforcement Bulletin* 68 1999, pp. 22–5.

STUDENTS ISLAMIC MOVEMENT OF INDIA (SIMI)

Formed in the Indian state of Uttar Pradesh in 1977, the Students Islamic Movement of India (also known as Al-Arbi and Al-Hindi) was initially established as the student wing of an Indian Muslim organization, the Jamaat-e-Islami Hind, which was dedicated to promoting the rights of Muslim students in particular, but of India's minority Muslim community more generally. Over the years, SIMI has developed a more militant edge, with some members promoting violent **jihad** as a way to purge India of un-Islamic influences and establish an Islamic state. Indian authorities suspect that SIMI receives covert support from Pakistani intelligence and from Pakistan-based terrorist groups such as **Jaish-e-Mohammed** and **Lashkar-e-Tayyiba**. Some government officials have even suggested that **al Qaeda** has penetrated SIMI, but these claims have not been verified. On the basis of these suspicions, in 2002 the Indian government banned SIMI. However, SIMI appealed against the banning and, in 2008, a special judicial tribunal ordered the ban be lifted, only for it to be reinstated several months later by the Indian Supreme Court. Indian officials also believe that some members of SIMI now operate covertly under the title 'Indian Mujahedeen', a group that claimed responsibility for a series of 2008 bomb attacks in New Delhi, Jaipur and Ahmedabad.

Further reading

Ahmad, I., 'Between Moderation and Radicalization: Transnational Interactions of Jamaat-e-Islami' *Global Networks: A Journal of Transnational Affairs* 5(3) 2005, pp. 279–99.

Sikand, Y., 'Countering Fundamentalism: Beyond the Ban on SIMI' *Economic and Political Weekly* 36(40) 2001, pp. 3803–4.

SUICIDE TERRORISM

According to Robert Pape, suicide terrorism (which involves an individual having prior knowledge that their actions will not only kill their target but lead to their own death in the process) is most likely to occur when the perpetrator believes that he or she is acting in the name of national liberation, hence its use in places such as Iraq against US forces, Palestine against Israeli targets, Sri Lanka by Tamils in the name of a separate state, and Chechnya against Russian interests. This theory needs to be nuanced by the spread of suicide terrorism to places such as Indonesia, where **Jemaah Islamiyah** has used the tactic in an attempt to force the government in Jakarta to abandon its secular orientation in favour of a rigid form of Islamism. However, even in cases such as Indonesia, or that of the 7/7 bombings in the UK, it is possible to discern an element of national liberation. In the case of Indonesia, suicide bombers have acted partly out of a feeling that the secular regime operates as an agent for the spread of Western values and culture, while in the UK it is clear from the video statements of two of the 7/7 bombers that they had developed a bifurcated view of the world, in which Muslims ('we') were oppressed by and needed to be liberated from non-Muslims ('you'). For some scholars, suicide terrorism is a uniquely modern phenomenon, but, while this is the case for suicide bombing, suicide terrorism has a much longer pedigree. Violence perpetrated by groups such as **The Assassins** and **The Zealots** often carried little or no chance of escape for the terrorist, leading some to argue that the actions of such groups were effectively suicide attacks.

Further reading

Gambetta, D., 'Can we Make Sense of Suicide Missions?' in Diego Gambetta (ed.) *Making Sense of Suicide Terrorism.* Oxford: Oxford University Press, 2006, pp. 259–300.

Pape, R., 'The Strategic Logic of Suicide Terrorism' *American Political Science Review* 97(3) 2003, pp. 343–61.

Silke, A., 'The Role of Suicide in Politics, Conflict and Terrorism' *Terrorism and Political Violence* 18(1) 2006, pp. 35–46.

SYMBIONESE LIBERATION ARMY

Formed in 1973 in Oakland, California, the Symbionese Liberation Army (SLA) was a small left-wing urban guerrilla group that comprised the radical element of the student revolutionary and black-liberation movements of the 1960s. Although Donald DeFreeze, a black prison escapee, led the group, most of its members were white, middle-class and college-educated. The SLA advocated the overthrow of what they believed to be a corrupt federal government. The group's first attack was the murder of Marcus Foster, Oakland's black superintendent of schools, whom the SLA condemned as a 'fascist'. Two SLA members, Joe Remiro and Russ Little, were convicted for the murder, although Little's conviction was subsequently overturned. The most significant act undertaken by the SLA was the February 1974 kidnapping of **Patty Hearst**, granddaughter of the media baron Randolph Hearst. Even though the Hearst family acceded to most of the SLA's hostage demands, Hearst was not released, and two months later a security camera filmed her taking part in a bank raid. Hearst was captured later that year and was convicted for bank robbery. Soon after, remaining SLA members retreated from violence and went underground. In the early 2000s, US authorities gradually caught up with remaining SLA members who were sentenced to jail sentences ranging from four to fourteen years. All those convicted eventually had their sentences reduced, and the last of the SLA inmates was released from prison in 2009.

Further reading
McLellan, V. and Avery, P., *The Voices of Guns: The Definitive and Dramatic Story of the Twenty-Two-Month Career of the Symbionese Liberation Army, One of the Most Bizarre Chapters in the History of the American Left*. New York: Putnam, 1977.
Pearsall, R. B., *Symbionese Liberation Army – Documents and Communications*. Amsterdam: Rodopi NV, 1974.

TALIBAN

The Taliban (from the Arabic root word for 'student') is generally equated with the fundamentalist Islamist government that controlled Afghanistan from 1996 until the US-led invasion of 2001. Educated mainly in religious schools in Pakistan, the Afghan Taliban introduced a highly austere public code which forbade women from attending school and most other social activities unless accompanied by a male relative, and mandated the wearing of the burkah. At the same time, men were obliged to grow their beards, and music and other forms of electronic entertainment were banned. In terrorism circles, the Taliban government, led by Mullah Omar, a reclusive cleric who lost an eye fighting the Soviets during the 1980s, is perhaps most notorious for hosting **Osama bin Laden** and several **al Qaeda** training camps from the late 1990s until 2001, when the camps were destroyed by the USA and its allies. It was at these camps that the **9/11** plot was planned. With the toppling of the Afghan government in 2001, the remnants of the Taliban retreated to the mountainous areas of Afghanistan and began to wage an insurgency against the US and NATO forces, as well as the new military and police force of the post-Taliban government led by Hamid Karzai. By 2009, the insurgency had grown stronger as an increasing number of individuals disillusioned with the pace of change and the reemergence of traditional warlords were driven back into the arms of the Taliban. It is important to note, however, that in the post-2001 period the Taliban are far from a unified group. There are various Taliban factions, although most are united by a single cause, the removal of the USA and its allies from Afghanistan.

Further reading
Mandaville, P., *Global Political Islam*. New York: Routledge, 2007.
Marsden, P., *The Taliban: War and Religion in Afghanistan*. New York: Zed
   Books Ltd, 2002.

TANWEER, SHEHZAD

Shehzad Tanweer (1982–2005) was the one of the four British-born
suicide bombers who attacked the London transport system on 7 July
2005. Tanweer himself targeted the eastbound underground Circle
Line train, detonating the bomb in close proximity to Liverpool Street
station, killing 8 people (including himself) and injuring more than
170 others. Born in Bradford, Tanweer was the eldest of two children
born to Pakistani immigrants. As a teenager, he performed well aca-
demically and was a gifted sportsman, especially in cricket and athlet-
ics. He was popular with his peers at school, taking particular pride
in his appearance – often wearing designer clothes. In his late teens,
he dropped out of Leeds University and began to devote himself to
religious studies. He also began to attend a local gymnasium where
he met two fellow bombers, **Mohammad Siddique Khan** and Hasib
Hussain. From November 2004 to February 2005, Tanweer, along
with Khan, travelled to Pakistan for further Islamic studies. During
this period, it has been alleged that Tanweer met members of militant
groups who might have accelerated his embrace of suicide
terrorism.

Further reading
Burke, J., *Al-Qaeda: The True Story of Radical Islam*. (3rd edn). London:
   Penguin, 2007.
House of Commons, *Report of the Official Account of the Bombings in London
   on 7th July 2005*. London: The Stationery Office, 11 May 2006.

TERRORIST PSYCHOLOGY

Until the early 1980s it was commonly assumed that terrorists suffered from one of a variety of psychopathological illnesses. The two
most common maladies associated with terrorism were narcissistic
personality disorder or paranoid personality disorder. Beginning in
the early 1980s, a growing number of scholars began to challenge

this view. Based on extensive fieldwork and interviews with terrorists, it soon became clear that, far from being 'mad', terrorists were often 'frighteningly sane', and capable of unimpaired rational decision-making. In short, terrorists were normal people behaving in an abnormal manner. Since then, a growing field of terrorist psychology has focused on the pathways to terrorism, looking at how a mix of socio-political conditions impacts on individual and group psychologies to trigger the urge to violence. For scholars such as John Horgan, terrorism is therefore best regarded as a process: unlike people suffering from impaired reasoning abilities at birth, terrorists evolve a violent mindset over time. This evolution is shaped by a combination of the way in which the psychology of the individual concerned responds to external social stimuli and the internal psycho-social dynamics of the group that he or she joins.

Further reading

Horgan, J., 'The Social and Psychological Characteristics of Terrorism and Terrorists' in T. Bjørgo (ed.) *Root Causes of Terrorism*. London and New York: Routledge, 2005, pp. 44–53.

Moghaddam, F., 'The Staircase to Terrorism' *American Psychologist* 60(2) 2005, pp. 161–9.

Silke, A., 'Becoming a Terrorist' in Silke (ed.) *Terrorists, Victims and Society: Psychological Perspectives on Terrorism and its Consequences*. New York: Wiley, 2003, pp. 29–53.

TOKYO CONVENTION (ON OFFENCES AND CERTAIN OTHER ACTS COMMITTED ON BOARD AIRCRAFT)

The Tokyo Convention was ratified in 1963 and is designed to deal with jurisdiction issues while a hijacked commercial aircraft is in flight. It covers any act that jeopardizes the in-flight safety of the aircraft and/or its passengers. Under the terms of the Convention, responsibility for prosecuting breaches falls upon the country within which the aircraft is registered. Other countries can only undertake punitive measures when its territory, citizens or residents are threatened by the actions of certain passengers. The Convention also allows the aircraft captain to restrain forcibly any passenger whose actions might reasonably be deemed as posing a danger to the security of the aircraft or the safety of its passengers.

Further reading
Abeyratne, R. I. R., 'Attempts at Ensuring Peace and Security in International Aviation' *Transportation Law Journal* 24(1) 1996, pp. 27–72.

TORTURE

The United Nations Convention against Torture (ratified 26 June 1987) defines torture as 'any act by which severe pain or suffering, whether physical or mental, is intentionally inflicted on a person for such purposes as obtaining from him or a third person information or a confession'. The use of torture as a device for countering terrorism has generated heated debate. On the one hand, advocates of the use of limited forms of torture (practices that fall short of causing permanent physical disability or death) usually fall back upon the 'ticking bomb scenario', a utilitarian argument that suggests that, if torture can solicit vital information that prevents an imminent terrorist attack and thereby prevent the deaths of innocent people, then not only is it an appropriate course of action but there exists a moral imperative upon governments to utilize the practice. On the other hand, opponents of torture argue that the ticking bomb scenario is an abstraction from reality and that, in actual practice, terrorists rarely know all the details of a planned attack, or, alternatively, they are trained to withstand torture long enough for their contemporaries to accelerate any attack or abandon it and camouflage their tracks. Other critics of torture argue that in an atmosphere of panic there is a significant possibility that innocent people might be tortured on the basis of incomplete information or even mistaken identity. In the latter case, torture constitutes not just the brutalization of the individual but of society as a whole, and as such it can spread anti-government sentiment and thereby assist terrorist recruiting efforts. It has also been pointed out that even though torture might generate temporary physical discomfort, debilitating psychological effects can last a lifetime. Writers such as Dershowitz have attempted to steer a middle ground by proposing the introduction of 'torture warrants', whereby officials are required to present evidence of complicity to a judge or judicial panel who will decide whether or not limited forms of torture are to be allowed.

Further reading
Dershowtiz, A. M., *Why Terrorism Works*. New Haven: Yale University Press, 2002.

Foot, R., 'Torture: The Struggle over a Peremptory Norm in a Counter-Terrorist Era' *International Relations* 20(2) 2006, pp. 131–51.

Lukes, S., 'Liberal Democratic Torture' *British Journal of Political Science* 36(1) 2005, pp. 1–16.

TRANS-ATLANTIC AIRLINE PLOT

In mid-2006 British police discovered an **al Qaeda**-linked plot to blow-up simultaneously ten aircraft as they flew from Britain to different parts of the United States and Canada. It was alleged that operatives disguised as passengers, using liquid explosives contained in innocuous containers such as baby formula jars and hair products, would detonate the planes at a predetermined time, an act that would have been the largest terrorist strike since the **9/11** attacks. In many parts of the world, but especially the UK and USA, the discovery of the plot was the catalyst for the introduction of onerous airport security procedures, including restrictions on passengers taking liquids onto aircraft. Twenty-four people were arrested in connection with the plot, although only eight were charged. At their trials in 2008 the eight accused claimed that pre-prepared videos and the small amount of explosives found in their possession had only been designed to cause a public nuisance and not destroy aircraft. The jury found that there was insufficient evidence to link the men to the targeting of an aircraft, although two were convicted of conspiracy to murder. The court was unable to reach verdicts on five of the men and acquitted another of all charges. Most of those arrested for being involved in the plot were British-born Muslims who had become radicalized after attending mosques controlled by extremist factions and/or after being introduced to terrorist individuals linked to al Qaeda or other groups, such as **Jaish-e-Mohammed**, on visits to Pakistan. It was alleged that they had been put in contact with al Qaeda by extremist Rashif Rauf, born in Birmingham (UK), who was at that time residing in Pakistan. UK attempts to extradite Rauf in connection with the murder of his uncle and for questioning over the airline plot faltered when he escaped from Pakistani custody under what UK authorities called 'questionable circumstances'. Media reports in late November 2008 suggested Rauf might have been killed along with several other al Qaeda operatives in a US missile strike earlier that same month.

Further reading

Corera, G., 'Bomb Plot – the al Qaeda Connection' *BBC News* 9 September 2008. At: http://news.bbc.co.uk/2/hi/uk_news/7606107.stm.

Parkes, R., 'What Limits for Government Control? Civil Liberties and Anti-Terror Measures after the Heathrow Bomb Plot' *The Political Quarterly* 78(2) 2007, pp. 272–81.

TÚPAC AMARU REVOLUTIONARY MOVEMENT (Movimiento Revolucionario Túpac Amaru (MRTA))

The Túpac Amaru Revolutionary Movement is a Peruvian organization founded in 1983 with two main aims – to purge the country of US economic and political influence and, secondly, to turn Peru into a Marxist–Leninist state. Its strength peaked in the early 1990s when, in terms of membership and national reach – including small pockets of land controlled by MRTA cadres – it sat just behind the **Shining Path** as Peru's second-largest insurgency group. Unlike Shining Path, which, under the influence of its founder **Abimael Guzmán**, developed a reputation for a condescending approach to the poor folk it claimed to be fighting for, the MRTA focused on establishing familial-like links with the peasantry and urban poor. In late 1996, fourteen MRTA terrorists launched an audacious attack on the Japanese embassy in Lima and took hostage several hundred diplomats and officials attending a function to celebrate the birthday of the Japanese emperor. The MRTA's demands included the release of MRTA cadres in Peruvian jails and a reversal of the government's neo-liberal economic reforms. The MRTA cadres gradually released most of the hostages so that, by the time Peruvian Special Forces stormed the embassy in April 1997, there were just seventy-two hostages. The military assault killed the fourteen MRTA terrorists, with the loss of only one hostage and two commandos.

Further reading

Baer, S., *Peru's MRTA: Túpac Amaru Revolutionary Movement*. New York: Rosen Publishing Group, 2003.

McCormick, G. H., *Sharp Dressed Men: Peru's Túpac Amaru Revolutionary Movement*. Santa Monica: RAND, 1993.

ULSTER DEFENCE ASSOCIATION (Also: Ulster Freedom Fighters)

Proscribed by: EU, UK

The Ulster Defence Association (UDA) is a paramilitary organization based in Northern Ireland dedicated to upholding union with the

United Kingdom. UDA violence has typically been perpetrated under the banner of a group calling itself the Ulster Freedom Fighters (UFF), even though it was not always clear that the UDA leadership sanctioned all attacks by the UFF. In 2007, the UDA ordered the UFF to disband – a gesture consistent with the **Good Friday Agreement**. Between the late 1960s and 2007, the UDA carried out more than 250 killings, the victims of which were mainly Catholic civilians. However, internecine fighting between different Protestant groups also saw the group implicated in the killing of more than 30 Protestant loyalists.

Further reading
Lister, D., *Mad Dog: The Rise and Fall of Johnny Adair and 'C Company'.* Edinburgh: Mainstream Publishing, 2005.
Wood, I. S., *God, Guns and Ulster: A History of Loyalist Paramilitaries.* London: Caxton Editions, 2003.

ULSTER VOLUNTEER FORCE (UVF)

Proscribed by: Republic of Ireland, UK
Like their counterparts in the **Ulster Defence Association** (UDA), the Ulster Volunteer Force (UVF) is a Loyalist paramilitary group in Northern Ireland. Formed in the late 1960s, the UVF acted mainly in County Armagh and Belfast's Shankill Road, carrying out targeted assassinations of Catholics and republican paramilitaries and/or their families. In the 1970s and 1980s the UVF often collaborated with the UDA in some of its campaigns, allegedly receiving covert assistance from the Royal Ulster Constabulary and rogue elements of the British army. Indeed, there were a significant number of individuals who joined both the UVF and the UDA, and because of this it was sometimes difficult to identify the real culprits for a given attack. By the late 1980s the UVF's capacity to wage a sustained campaign against republicans had been undermined by the arrest of senior members, facilitated by help from police informers. In June 1994, UVF paramilitaries opened fire on a group of civilians watching the Irish Republic football team playing in the World Cup, killing six people and injuring five others. Public outrage at this act led the UVF leadership to agree to a ceasefire in October 1994. However, there remained a hard-core group, led by Billy Wright, who opposed the ceasefire and broke from the group to form the **Loyalist Volunteer Force**. Tensions caused by this schism precipitated intramural con-

flict between Loyalist groups and led to the deaths of around ten people. In May 2007, the UVF leadership officially declared that it was decommissioning its weapons, although it stopped short of formally disarming.

Further reading
Edwards, A., 'Abandoning Armed Resistance? The Ulster Volunteer Force as a Case Study of Strategic Terrorism in Northern Ireland' *Studies in Conflict and Terrorism* 32(2) 2009, pp. 146–66.
Wood, I. S., *God, Guns and Ulster: A History of Loyalist Paramilitaries*. London: Caxton Editions, 2003.

Umkhonto we Sizwe (Spear of the Nation)
See: African National Congress

Unabomber

Theodore 'Ted' Kaczynski (b. 1942), a former university mathematics professor, carried out a letter-bombing campaign that caused three deaths and twenty-two injuries and lasted from 1979 until his capture in 1995. His targets included airlines and academics, hence the acronym 'Unabomber' (*UN*iversity and Airline *BOMBER*). In April 1995, Kaczynski promised to end his campaign if the *New York Times* and *Washington Post* published his manifesto, 'Industrial Society and its Future' – a rambling diatribe against the spread of new technologies and their deleterious impact on society, particularly in terms of the diminution of freedom. Working from a secluded cabin in the forests of Montana, he generated one of the most expensive manhunts in US history, although it was Kaczynski's brother who alerted authorities after he recognized his turn of phrase and beliefs in the published manifesto. Kaczynski was sentenced to life in prison in return for a guilty plea.

Further reading
Chase, A., *Harvard and the Unabomber: The Education of an American Terrorist*. New York: W. W. Norton and Co., 2003.
Oleson, J. C., ' "Evil the Natural Way": The Chimerical Utopias of Henry David Thoreau and Theodore John Kaczynski' *Contemporary Justice Review* 8(2) 2005, pp. 211–28.

UNITED LIBERATION FRONT OF ASSAM (ULFA)
Proscribed by: India
Founded in April 1979, the United Liberation Front of Assam's aims are to secede from India and establish an independent socialist state. Its use of terrorism as a tactic began in 1986 and, since then, it has launched attacks against Indian government officials, security forces, local infrastructure and migrant workers from other states such as Bihar. New Delhi proscribed the ULFA as a terrorist organization in 1990. Its failure to rally mass support has seen the group drift into criminal activities such as extortion and drug trafficking. There have also been unsubstantiated claims by Indian officials that the ULFA has received assistance from Pakistani intelligence. Tentative peace talks with New Delhi began in 2005.

Further reading
Cline, L. E., 'The Insurgency Environment in Northern India' *Small Wars and Insurgencies* 17(2) 2006, pp. 126–47.

UNITED NATIONS SECURITY COUNCIL COMMITTEE 1267
The United Nations Security Council established the United Nations Security Council Committee 1267, also known as the Al-Qaeda and Taliban Sanctions Committee, on 15 October 1999. The committee maintains a consolidated list of individuals and organizations that serves as a guide for implementing sanctions against **al Qaeda** and the **Taliban**. The resolution obliges UN member states to freeze funds and other financial assets of designated individuals and entities, prevent the entry into or transit through their territories by designated individuals, and prevent the direct or indirect supply, sale and transfer from their territories of any materials that can be used in military-style activities by individuals and organizations included on the designated terrorist list.

Further reading
Greenwood, C., 'International Law and the War against Terrorism' *International Affairs* 78(2) 2002, pp. 301–16.

UNITED NATIONS SECURITY COUNCIL RESOLUTION 1373

United Nations Security Council Resolution 1373 was adopted on 28 September 2001. Binding on all UN members, it emphasizes the importance of international cooperation in the fight against terrorism. The Resolution calls on member states to amend domestic laws so that they are consistent with international counter-terrorism conventions. The Resolution also emphasizes the importance of member states developing better intelligence-sharing and law-enforcement procedures as mechanisms for more effectively combating the threat of terrorism.

Further reading
Rosand, E., 'Security Council Resolution 1373, the Counter-Terrorism Committee and the Fight Against Terrorism' *American Journal of International Law* 97(2) 2003, pp. 333–41.

UNITED SELF DEFENCE FORCES OF COLOMBIA (Autodefensas Unidas de Colombia (AUC))

Proscribed by: Canada, EU, USA
Established in Colombia in 1997 in response to the targeting of wealthy land owners by Marxist terrorist groups such as the FARC (see **Revolutionary Armed Forces of Colombia**) and ELN (see **National Liberation Army**), the United Self Defence Forces of Colombia is an umbrella organization of right-wing paramilitary groups committed to protecting the interests of large landholders and corporations from sabotage by leftist groups. At the height of its power in the early 2000s it boasted almost 20,000 militia under arms; however, the 2002 election of the Uribe administration and its relatively successful military offensive against the FARC and ELN have satisfied many erstwhile AUC supporters and, as a result, by the late 2000s its influence was diminishing. The AUC uses assassination, kidnapping and torture in an effort to dissuade peasants from supporting or cooperating with groups such as FARC. Like FARC, a large part of the AUC's operations are funded through links with Colombia's cocaine cartels.

Further reading
Human Rights Watch, *Breaking the Grip? Obstacles to Justice for Paramilitary Mafias in Colombia*. New York: Human Rights Watch, October 2008.

James, M., *DEA Congressional Testimony. House International Relations Committee, Subcommittee on the Western Hemisphere*, 16 July 1997. At: www.usdoj.gov/dea/pubs/cngrtest/ct970716.htm.

USA PATRIOT ACT

The USA PATRIOT Act is an Act of the US Congress signed into law by President George W. Bush on 26 October 2001, just forty-five days after the attacks of 9/11. The phrase 'USA PATRIOT' is an acronym for the Act's actual title, the 'Uniting and Strengthening America by Providing Appropriate Tools Required to Intercept and Obstruct Terrorism Act of 2001'. In essence, the Act widens substantially the authority and powers of US intelligence and law enforcement organizations for the purposes of combating the threat of terrorism to the USA, both at home and overseas. Areas where these powers have been widened considerably include the right to intercept and monitor medical, financial, telephone, Internet and even library borrowing records for terrorism suspects. The Act also removed some of the restrictions on overseas intelligence-gathering efforts, widened the powers of the Treasury Department to monitor suspicious financial transactions and enhanced the powers of the immigration service to detain, deport, or refuse entry to the USA of, any person suspected of potential terrorism-related activities. Despite the Act receiving comfortable approval in both houses of Congress, it generated widespread condemnation from civil liberties groups. Criticisms of the Act centred on the significantly enhanced powers conferred upon intelligence and other law enforcement agencies to intrude into the private affairs of ordinary Americans, as well as those staying in the USA as temporary workers or students. According to the American Civil Liberties Union, different sections of the Act are at odds with at least six provisions of the US Bill of Rights – the First, Fourth, Fifth, Sixth, Eighth and Fourteenth Amendments. The targeting of immigrants from Muslim countries also generated widespread opprobrium, especially in light of the apparently random detention of several thousand students and workers on what appeared to be purely religious and cultural grounds. A sunset clause of four years obliged Congress and the President to review the provisions of the Act in late 2005. After a difference of opinion between the Senate and House of Representatives was reconciled, President Bush signed a revised bill into law in February 2006. Even so, civil rights groups such as the American Civil Liberties Union have successfully challenged the constitutionality of some provisions of the PATRIOT Act through the courts. At the international level, the Act has served as a template for US efforts to export counter-terrorism policies to other parts of the world. This has proved problematic in countries that already labour under authoritarian and/or semi-authoritarian regimes, where the US model has been used as an excuse to crack down on dissidents under an artificial pretext of countering terrorism.

Further reading
Baker, S. A. (ed.), *Patriot Debates: Experts Debate the USA Patriot Act.* Washington, DC: The American Bar Association, 2005.
Etzioni, A., *How Patriotic is the Patriot Act? Freedom versus Security in the Age of Terrorism.* New York and Abingdon: Routledge, 2005.
Farrier, J., 'The Patriot Act's Institutional Story: More Evidence of Congressional Ambivalence' *PS: Political Science and Politics* 40(1) 2007, pp. 93–7.
Whitaker, B. E., 'Exporting the *Patriot Act?* Democracy and the "War on Terror" in the Third World' *Third World Quarterly* 28(5) 2007, pp. 1017–32.

VIGOROUS BURMESE STUDENT WARRIORS

Founded in 1999, the Vigorous Burmese Student Warriors (VBSW) is an anti-government group opposed to the military regime in Burma (Myanmar). Although little is known about the VBSW, a number of like-minded radical student groups have formed in neighbouring Thailand since the Burmese military took power in the late 1980s after a military coup. The military regime (at that time known as the State Law and Order Restoration Council) allowed elections to take place in 1990 that led to the victory of the National League for Democracy, led by Nobel Peace Prize winner Aung San Suu Kyi. The regime subsequently placed Suu Kyi under house arrest and nullified the election result. Despite nearly a decade of peaceful political opposition by democracy groups in Thailand, the Burmese military's hold on power had scarcely been weakened and this process of cumulative frustration led to the formation of the VBSW. The group's most significant act took place in October 1999 when members attacked the Burmese embassy in Bangkok, taking fifty-one Burmese and a number of Western tourists as hostages. The group demanded the release of political prisoners in Burma, that dialogue commence between the Democratic Party of Suu Kyi and the Burmese military government, and the convening of an elected parliament. Shortly afterward, the VBSW backed down from their initial demands and freed the hostages, two days after receiving guarantees of free passage to the Thai–Burma border.

Further reading
Kurlantzick, J., 'Fear Moves East: Terror Targets the Pacific Rim' *Washington Quarterly* 24(1) 2001, pp. 19–29.
Skidmore, M., 'Scholarship, Advocacy, and the Politics of Engagement in Burma (Myanmar)' in V. Sanford and A. Angel-Ajani (eds.) *Engaged Observer: Anthropology, Advocacy and Activism*. Piscataway, NJ: Rutgers University Press, 2006, pp. 42–59.

WAAGNER, CLAYTON LEE

Clayton Lee Waagner (b. 1956) is a prominent US anti-abortion terrorist responsible for sending to abortion clinics hundreds of letters claiming to contain anthrax. A supporter of the **Army of God**, Waagner describes himself as an 'anti-abortion warrior' and claims that God has told him to assassinate abortion doctors. In October 2001, the father of nine sent hundreds of letters marked 'Time Sensitive' and 'Urgent Security Notice Enclosed', and displaying return addresses from the US Marshals Service and Secret Service, to abortion clinics across the USA. Waagner emerged as a suspect after escaping from an Illinois jail in February 2001 while awaiting sentencing on firearm and motor vehicle charges. He was recaptured in December 2001 and sentenced to nineteen years in prison.

Further reading
Juergensmeyer, M., *Terror in the Mind of God: The Rise of Religious Violence*. Berkeley: University of California Press, 2003.
Levitas, D., 'The Radical Right after 9/11' in G. Martin (ed.) *The New Era of Terrorism: Selected Readings*. Thousand Oaks: Sage Publications Inc., 2004.

WAR ON TERROR

The phrase 'War on Terror' was coined by the Administration of President George W. Bush and refers to a complex array of domestic and foreign policies designed to help the USA and its friends and allies to combat the threat of terrorism. From the outset, the term attracted a significant amount of scepticism. In particular, it was pointed out that, as an abstract noun, terrorism is a process and the result of rational decision-making by individuals. As such, it cannot be dealt with through the concept of 'war', since a war inevitably results in a victor and a loser. In short, it is not possible to defeat a tactic. Because of this, critics argued that the term 'War on Terror' implied an open-ended conflict in which the curtailment of civil liberties and other deleterious aspects of counter-terrorism imposed in the immediate aftermath of the 9/11 attacks were at risk of becoming a permanent feature of post-9/11 society. It is partly for this reason, but also because of the perception that the measures taken by the USA and other countries were targeted mainly at Muslims, that, by the mid-2000s, the term began to disappear from official US government rhetoric. Nevertheless, under the auspices of the War on Terror a series of policies were enacted simultaneously at the military, political, cultural and legal levels, both domestically and internationally. The purpose of these policies was to protect better the US homeland, but also its citizens and assets overseas, by destroying or disrupting terrorist networks. At the military level this included the invasions of Afghanistan and Iraq as well as the establishment of the detention facility at Guantánamo Bay. At the international policy level it included the expansion of intelligence-gathering and sharing activities with traditional allies, but also with governments not traditionally involved in the US intelligence-sharing circle. At the cultural level it included a public relations campaign across the Muslim world designed to dispel negative images of the USA. Meanwhile, at the US domestic level, the War on Terror included legislative initiatives such as the **USA PATRIOT Act** and associated legislation, and, at the foreign policy level, a range of initiatives covering terrorist financing as well as more vigorous customs and shipping regulations.

Further reading
Gordon, P. H., 'Can the War on Terror be Won?' *Foreign Affairs* 86(6) 2007, pp. 53–66.
Hoge, J. F. and Rose, G. (eds.) *Understanding the War on Terror*. Washington, DC: Foreign Affairs, 2005.
Lustick, I. S., *Trapped in the War on Terror*. Philadelphia: University of Pennsylvania Press, 2006.

WEAPONS OF MASS DESTRUCTION (WMD)

Capturing the theatrical nature of most terrorist violence, the scholar Brian Jenkins once observed that 'Terrorists want lots of people watching, not lots of people dead.' Against the backdrop of the **9/11** attacks, the **Bali bombings**, the **7/7** bombings in London and, among other events, **Aum Shinrikyo**'s sarin gas attack on the Tokyo subway system, this aphorism has been increasingly called into question. Given the difficulties involved in constructing or procuring a nuclear bomb, most attention has focused on the potential use of chemical, biological or radiological (CBR) devices. On the one hand, there are those who argue that the gradual escalation in the deadly character of terrorist violence reflects both the terrorists' capacity to adapt to new and increasingly destructive technologies and the psychological need to maintain the attention of the media and governments by designing attacks that are progressively more spectacular. Hence, for some scholars, there exists a 'logic of escalation' that will eventually lead to the use of CBR weapons. On the other hand, there are scholars who argue that terrorists will continue to confine themselves to the use of conventional tactics and weapons. First, CBR weapons are typically complex and hard to manufacture and there is a high likelihood that any attempt to use them for terrorist purposes will fail. Second, terrorists do not commit random violence; they calibrate their violence against two factors, the need to intimidate their enemy while at the same time inspiring their potential supporters. Should their violence be too violent, or kill too many innocent people, as could be the case with a CBR attack, there is a risk the terrorists will alienate their support base and bring down upon themselves and their supporters a counter-terrorist response that could threaten their existence.

Further reading
Laqueur, W., *The New Terrorism: Fanaticism and the Arms of Mass Destruction*. Oxford and New York: Oxford University Press, 1999.
Sprinzak, E., 'The Great Superterrorism Scare' *Foreign Policy* 112 Fall 1998.

THE WEATHER UNDERGROUND

A break-away faction of the Students of Democratic Society (SDS), the Weather Underground was one of the most infamous domestic terrorist groups in the United States. The organization was heavily influenced by opposition to the Vietnam War and inspired by the Civil Rights Movement. Describing themselves as the 'Action Faction', their use of violence began in 1969, referred to by the group as the 'days of rage', during which time they fomented violence at anti-war rallies, vandalizing cars and property and attacking those who tried to protect their belongings. By the early 1970s the group had retreated underground and launched a bombing campaign against police stations, government buildings and banks. The group 'declared war' on the US government and established a network based on 'affinity cells', controlled at the apex by the 'Weather Bureau'. In 1970, members of a New York cell were killed while attempting to manufacture explosives. Soon after, the Chicago cell was compromised and its members arrested. These events, coupled with the group's failure to cultivate a wider community of support and the withdrawal of US troops from Vietnam in 1973, contributed to the gradual disintegration of the group, so that, by 1977, it had ceased to operate altogether.

Further reading
Gentry, C., 'The Relationship Between New Social Movement Theory and Terrorism Studies: The Role of Leadership, Membership, Ideology and Gender' *Terrorism and Political Violence* 16(2) 2004, pp. 274–93.

Sprinzak, E., 'The Psychopolitical Formation of Extreme Left Terrorism in a Democracy: The Case of the Weatherman' in Walter Reich (ed.) *Origins of Terrorism: Psychologies, Ideologies, Theologies, States of Mind*. Washington, DC: Woodrow Wilson Center Press, 1998, pp. 65–85.

WORLD ISLAMIC FRONT FOR COMBAT AGAINST JEWS AND CRUSADERS
SEE: AL QAEDA

WRIGHT, BILLY
SEE: LOYALIST VOLUNTEER FORCE

XINJIANG
Comprising one-sixth of China's territory, the Xinjiang Uighur Autonomous Region is located in western China and has a

population of approximately 20 million people made up of thirteen major ethnic groups. The largest ethnic group are the Uighur, a Turkic-speaking Muslim people. Government-sponsored migration of Han Chinese to Xinjiang has in recent years given rise to the growth of Uighur nationalism and the gradual emergence of groups willing to use terrorism as a tactic for asserting their cultural auton-omy and securing independence from Beijing. The most prominent of these groups is the East Turkestan Liberation Organization (ETLO). Uighur independence movements have existed for many decades, yet the fall of the Soviet Union and the establishment of independent Turkic states along the west Chinese border has inspired the move-ment and raised its struggle to a new level. Some experts have ques-tioned the real extent of the threat posed by Uighur independence groups such as the ETLO, pointing out that terrorist attacks commit-ted by such groups lack any clear pattern and occur on a small scale in an apparently spontaneous manner. Others, however, have pointed to the existence of Uighur at **al Qaeda** training camps in Afghanistan and argue that, after the US-led invasion of that country in 2001, these individuals returned to Xinjiang to continue the fight against Beijing. The ETLO is listed by the UN as an al Qaeda-linked entity and is proscribed by the EU and Pakistan.

Further reading
Clarke, M., 'China's "War on Terror" in Xinjiang: Human Security and the Cause of Violent Uighur' *Terrorism and Political Violence* 20(2) 2008, pp. 271–301.

YASSIN, AHMED

Sheikh Ahmed Yassin (1929–2004) was the co-founder and spiritual leader of **Hamas**. In this position he wielded significant influence over those Palestinians who had become disillusioned with the peace process and with the increasingly corrupt **Palestinian Liberation Organization (PLO)** and its political wing **Fatah**. Born in the British Mandate of Palestine, Yassin and his family became refugees in the Gaza Strip after the establishment of the state of Israel in 1948. Despite a childhood accident leaving him nearly blind, paralysed and confined to a wheelchair, Yassin remained mentally alert and highly active in the Palestinian resistance movement. At a time when most Palestinians subscribed to the secular socialism of Fatah and the

PLO, Yassin stood out as an advocate of a different ideology, that of political Islam. His views had been shaped by an early exposure to the **Muslim Brotherhood**, an organization he joined while a student in Egypt. By the late 1960s Yassin had began to use his position as a teacher to encourage greater religious observance among Palestinian youth in Gaza and, by the 1970s, his activities broadened to include the provision of welfare services for Palestinians. One of the first manifestations of Yassin's welfare initiatives was the establishment in 1970 of the al-Mujamma' al-Islami (Islamic Center) which oversaw the Muslim Brotherhood's benevolent activities – such as the provision of healthcare and education – in the Gaza Strip. With the outbreak of the first Intifada in 1987 Yassin demonstrated deft skill in tapping into the anger and frustrations of Palestinian youth. It was during this tumultuous period that he played a key role in forming Hamas. In 1989, Yassin was arrested by Israeli authorities and sentenced to life imprisonment for ordering an attack on Israeli soldiers, but he was released in 1997 in exchange for two Mossad (see **Israel Institute for Intelligence and Special Tasks**) agents captured in Jordan. On his release, Yassin resumed the leadership of Hamas and continued to approve terrorist attacks against Israel, including suicide operations. Yassin was killed by an Israeli missile strike on 22 March 2004. More than 200,000 supporters attended his funeral.

Further reading
Levitt, M., *Hamas: Politics, Charity, and Terrorism in the Service of Jihad*. New Haven: Yale University Press, 2007.
Milton-Edwards, B., *Islamic Politics in Palestine*. London: Tauris Academic Studies, 1996.

YOUSEF, RAMZI
Born in Kuwait in 1968 into a Pakistani family, Ramzi Yousef (also known as Abdul Basit Mahmoud Karrem, among other aliases) is best-known as the master bomber in the 1993 World Trade Center attacks in New York. As a young adult, Yousef studied electrical engineering in Britain, but in 1989 he travelled to Pakistan where he made contact with militant Islamist groups and used his technical skills to teach bomb-making. In 1991 Youself made contact with Abdurajak Abu Bakr Janjalani, the leader of the Philippines-based **Abu Sayyaf Group**, and is believed to have trained militants in the

Philippines for a short period. In 1992 Yousef returned to Pakistan before travelling to New York, where he cooperated with his uncle **Khalid Sheikh Mohammed** and others in beginning preparations for the World Trade Center bombing on 26 February 1993. Yousef flew back to Pakistan almost immediately after the attack and was soon involved again in extremist activity, being charged in absentia in 1994 for a failed assassination attempt against the then Pakistani Prime Minister Benazir Bhutto. By late 1994, Yousef was back in the Philippines working on another terrorist attack, **Operation Bojinka**. This ambitious plot included simultaneously blowing up eleven US aeroplanes in mid-flight over the Pacific and assassinating Pope John Paul II on a visit to Manila. In December 1994, he tested a prototype bomb by placing it under a seat of a Japanese Airlines flight from the Philippines to Japan, with the ensuing explosion killing one passenger and injuring approximately ten others, but it did not bring down the aircraft. Soon after returning to Manila to complete Operation Bojinka, Yousef was forced to flee back to Pakistan after an accidental fire in his safe house attracted the attention of the Philippines police. Shortly after his return, Yousef was arrested in Islamabad in a joint US–Pakistani intelligence operation on 7 February 1995. He was extradited to the USA, tried and found guilty for his role in the Bojinka plot and the 1993 World Trade Center bombing, and is currently serving a life sentence.

Further reading
Reeve, S., *The New Jackals: Ramzi Yousef, Osama bin Laden and the Future of Terrorism*. Boston: Northeastern University Press, 2002.
Burke, J., *Al-Qaeda: The True Story of Radical Islam* (3rd edn). London: Penguin, 2007.

ZASULICH, VERA

Vera Zasulich (1849–1919) was a Russian revolutionary whose notoriety rests in an 1878 assassination attempt against the Tsarist police chief in St Petersburg, General Theodore Trepov. So reviled was Trepov that a sympathetic jury found Zasulich not guilty, after which she fled Russia temporarily to avoid re-arrest. Zasulich's assassination attempt against Trepov was undertaken at a time when she was actively involved with the Russian anarchist movement led by Mikhail Bakunin. However, after being acquitted in the Trepov case she drifted away from anarchism towards Marxism, becoming the Editor of a communist newspaper that was much respected in revolutionary circles. After a split in the Russian Social Democratic Labour Party in 1903, she sided with the more moderate Mensheviks against the alternative Bolshevik faction headed by Lenin.

Further reading
Siljak, A., *Angel of Vengeance: The 'Girl Assassin', the Governor of St. Petersburg, and Russia's Revolutionary World*. London: St Martins Press, 2008.

THE ZEALOTS
Motivated by a combination of scriptural fundamentalism and nationalism, the Zealots emerged around the year 60CE in the Ludaea province of Judea in opposition to Roman occupation and the forced introduction of aspects of Roman culture that were inimical to Jewish practice – including enforced deference to Roman gods and icons. Most of what is known about the Zealots comes from the book *The Jewish War*, written by Josephus, a one-time sympathizer who turned to siding with the Romans. From being peripheral players in Jewish affairs, by 66CE the Zealots had emerged as a vanguard movement opposed to Roman rule. In particular, they took the lead in the 'Great Jewish Revolt' (66–70CE) against Roman rule, going so far as to capture and hold Jerusalem until Titus, the son of the Roman Emperor Vespasian, retook the city. During their insurgency against the Romans, the Zealots adopted a series of tactics that have earned them the terrorist label, including the poisoning of wells used by Roman families and other groups suspected of collaborating with the occupation and the kidnapping for ransom of the servants of wealthy Jews. A parallel group at this time were the 'Sicarii' (lit. 'dagger men'), based mainly in Galilee, who would cut the throats of suspected Jewish collaborators, Greek merchants and Roman officials, using a long knife.

Further reading
Brandon, S. G. F., *Jesus and the Zealots: A Study of the Political Factor in Primitive Christianity*. Manchester: Manchester University Press, 1967.
Josephus, F., *The Jewish War* (trans. G. A. Williamson, intro. E. Mary Smallwood). London: Penguin Classics, 1981.

ZUBAYDAH, ABU

The US government described Abu Zubaydah as a high-level **al Qaeda** member and part of the select al-Qaeda inner core. He is alleged to have directed logistical matters and was one of very few members who had an overview of terrorist operations. However, US media reports in early 2009, citing military officials, suggest that this might be an exaggeration of his actual role within the organization. Few facts are known about Zubaydah, though he is believed to be a Palestinian born in Saudi Arabia in 1971. He was also known under numerous aliases, such as Zayn al-Abidin Muhammad Husain and Abd Al-Hadi Al-Wahab. It was initially alleged that by the early 1990s he had become a chief recruiter and logistics co-ordinator in al Qaeda-affiliated training camps in Afghanistan and Pakistan. It was also claimed that Zubaydah was involved in various al Qaeda-sponsored attacks, such as the millennium plots to bomb the Radisson Hotel in Jordan and **Ahmed Ressam**'s attempt to bomb Los Angeles International airport. For his part in the Radisson Hotel plot, Zubaydah was sentenced to death in absentia in Jordan. It was also alleged that he played a considerable role in planning the **9/11** attacks and in recruiting terrorists to bomb the US embassy in Paris. He is also said to have had discussions with the 'Shoe-Bomber', **Richard Reid**. US and Pakistani forces captured Zubaydah in Pakistan in 2002. Since then he has been held in US detention at Guantánamo Bay. A report released by the CIA (see **Central Intelligence Agency**) in 2009, under a freedom-of-information suit filed by the American Civil Liberties Union, suggests that Zubaydah might have been subjected to waterboarding, a form of **coercive interrogation** widely condemned as **torture**, more than eighty times.

Further reading
Bergen, P., *Holy War Inc.: Inside the World of Osama bin Laden*. London: Weidenfeld and Nicolson, 2001.
Finn, P. and Tate, J., 'CIA Mistaken on "High-Value" Detainee, Document Shows' *The Washington Post* 16 June 2009. At: www.washingtonpost.com/wp-dyn/content/article/2009/06/15/AR2009061503045.html.

Bibliography

Arendt, H. (2006 [1963]) *Eichmann in Jerusalem: A Report on the Banality of Evil*. London: Penguin Books.

Atran, S. (2009 [2003]) 'Genesis of Suicide Terrorism' in J. Victoroff and A. W. Kruglanski (eds.) *Psychology of Terrorism: Classic and Contemporary Insights*. New York: Psychology Press, pp. 145–56.

Bandura, A. (1990) 'Mechanisms of Moral Disengagement' in W. Reich (ed.) *Origins of Terrorism: Psychologies, Ideologies, Theologies, States of Mind*. Washington, DC: The Woodrow Wilson Center.

Bandura, A., Barbaranelli, C., Vittorio Caprara, G. and Pastorelli, C. (1996) 'Mechanisms of Moral Disengagement in the Exercise of Moral Agency' *Journal of Personality and Social Psychology* 71(2):364–74.

BBC (2004) 'Five Live Survey Suggests Ethnic Minority Applicants Still Discriminated Against in UK Job Market', 12 July. Available at www.bbc.co.uk/pressoffice/pressreleases/stories/2004/07_july/12/minorities_survey.shtml (accessed 12 March 2005).

— (2005) 'London Bomber: Text in Full', 1 September. Available at http://news.bbc.co.uk/2/hi/uk_news/4206800.stm (accessed 3 September 2005).

Beck, U. (2005) *Power in the Global Age* (trans. K. Cross). Cambridge: Polity.

Bowden, B. and Davis, M. T. (eds.) (2008) *Terror: From Tyrannicide to Terrorism*. St Lucia: The University of Queensland Press.

Bowen, J. R. (2006) *Why the French Don't Like Headscarves: Islam, the State, and Public Space*. Princeton: Princeton University Press.

Brighton, S. (2007) 'British Muslims, Multiculturalism, and UK Foreign Policy: "Integration" and "Cohesion" in and beyond the State' *International Affairs* 83(1):1–17.

Brown, C., and Gay, P. (1985) *Racial Discrimination: 17 Years after the Act*. London: Policy Studies Institute.

Burleigh, M. (2008) *Blood and Rage: A Cultural History of Terrorism*. London: Harper Press.

Chase, A. (2003) *Harvard and the Unabomber: The Education of an American Terrorist*. New York: W. W. Norton and Co.

Christian Science Monitor (2005) 'Deep Roots of Paris Riots', 4 November 2005. Available at www.csmonitor.com/2005/1104/p06s02-woeu.html (accessed 7 November 2005).

Coogan, T. P. (2002) *The IRA* (revised edn). New York: Palgrave.

Crenshaw, M. (1992) 'How Terrorists Think: What Psychology can Contribute to Understanding Terrorism' in L. Howard (ed.) *Terrorism: Roots, Impacts and Responses*. London: Praeger, pp. 71–80.

— (2000) 'The Psychology of Terrorism: An Agenda for the Twenty-First Century' *Political Psychology* 21(2):405–20.

Currie, E. (1985) *Confronting Crime: An American Challenge*. New York: Pantheon.

Daniel, W. W. (1968) *Racial Discrimination in England*. Harmondsworth: Penguin.

Dartnell, M. Y. (1995) *Action Directe: Ultra Left Terrorism in France 1979–1987*. London: Frank Cass Publishers.

Della-Porta, D. (2008) *Social Movements, Political Violence, and the State: A Comparative Analysis of Italy and Germany*. Cambridge: Cambridge University Press.

Dingley, J. (2009) 'The Bombing of Omagh, 15 August 1988: The Bombers, Their Tactics, Strategy, and Purpose behind the Incident' *Studies in Conflict and Terrorism* 24(6):451–65.

Elias, N. (1996 [1989]) *The Germans*. Cambridge: Polity.

Elias, N. and Scotson, J. L. (1965) *The Established and the Outsiders: A Sociological Enquiry into Community Problems*. London: Frank Cass.

Esenwein, G. R. (1989) *Anarchist Ideology and the Working Class Movement in Spain, 1868–1898*. Berkeley: University of California Press.

European Training Foundation (2005) *Unemployment in Jordan*. Turin: European Training Foundation.

Fetzner, J. S. and Soper, J. C. (2004) *Muslims and the State in Britain, France, and Germany*. Cambridge: Cambridge University Press.

Fishman, B. (2006) 'After Zarqawi: The Dilemmas and Future of al Qaeda in Iraq' *The Washington Quarterly* 29(4):19–32.

Follain, J. (2000) *Jackal: Finally, the Complete Story of the Legendary Terrorist, Carlos The Jackal*. New York: Arcade Publishing.

Geertz, C. (1973) 'Thick Description: Toward an Interpretive Theory of Culture' in *The Interpretation of Cultures: Selected Essays*. New York: Basic Books, pp. 3–30.

Gerges, F. A. (2005) *The Far Enemy: Why Jihad Went Global*. Cambridge: Cambridge University Press.

Gilligan, J. (2000) *Violence: Reflections on Our Deadliest Epidemic*. London: Jessica Kingsley Publishers.

— (2003) 'Shame, Guilt and Violence' *Social Research* 70(4):1149–80.

Gough, H. (2008) 'The Terror in the French Revolution' in B. Bowden and M. T. Davis (eds.) *Terror: From Tyrannicide to Terrorism*. St Lucia: University of Queensland Press, pp. 77–91.

Guelke, A. (2006) *Terrorism and Global Disorder*. New York: I. B. Tauris.

Gunning, J. (2007) 'A Case for Critical Terrorism Studies?' *Government and Opposition* 42(3):363–93.

Haaretz (2007) 'UN Report: At 45%, Gaza Unemployment is Highest in the World', 28 July. Available at www.haaretz.com/hasen/spages/1006282. html (accessed 1 August 2007).

Haque, R., Dustmann, C., Fabbri, F., et al. (2002) *Migrants in the UK: Their Characteristics and Labour Market Outcomes and Impacts*, RDS Occasional Paper No. 82. London: Development and Statistics Directorate, The Home Office. Available at www.homeoffice.gov.uk/rds/pdfs2/occ82migrantuk. pdf (accessed 12 October 2004).

Hardy, R. (2006) 'Unemployment, the New Saudi Challenge'. BBC News, 4 October. Available at http://news.bbc.co.uk/2/hi/business/5406328.stm (accessed 6 October 2006).

Hoffman, B. (2006) *Inside Terrorism* (revised edn). New York: Columbia University Press.

Horgan, J. (2005) *The Psychology of Terrorism*. London: Routledge.

Horne, A. (2006) *A Savage War of Peace: Algeria 1954–1962*. New York: New York Review of Books Classics.

Ikram, K. (2005) *The Egyptian Economy: Performance Policies and Issues*. Abingdon: RoutledgeCurzon.

Iviansky, Z. (2008 [1977]) 'Individual Terror: Concept and Typology' in J. Victoroff and A. W. Kruglanski (eds.) *Psychology of Terrorism: Classic and Co-temporary Insights*. New York: Psychology Press, pp. 9–22.

Jaynes, G. D. (2000) 'Identity and Economic Performance' *Annals* 568:128–39.

Jenkins, R. (1986) *Racism and Recruitment*. Cambridge: Cambridge University Press.

Josephus (1981) *The Jewish War*. London: Penguin Classics.

Juergensmeyer, M. (2003) *Terror in the Mind of God: The Global Rise of Religious Violence* (3rd edn). Berkeley: University of California Press.

Kelman, H. C. (1973) 'Violence without Moral Restraint: Reflections on the Dehumanization of Victims and Victimizers' *Journal of Social Issues* 29:25–61.

Kepel, G. and Milelli, J. (2005) *Al Qaeda in its Own Words*. Cambridge, Mass: The Belknap Press of Harvard University.

Kinnvall, C. (2004) 'Globalization and Religious Nationalism: Self, Identity, and the Search for Ontological Security' *Political Psychology* 25(5):741–67.

Laqueur, W. (2000) *The New Terrorism: Fanaticism and the Arms of Mass Destruction*. Oxford and New York: Oxford University Press.

— (2004) *No End to War: Terrorism in the Twenty-First Century*. New York: Continuum International Publishing Inc.

Lewis, B. (2003 [1967]) *The Assassins*. New York: Basic Books.

Lofors, J. and Sundquist, K. (2007) 'Low-linking Social Capital as a Predictor of Mental Disorders: A Cohort Study of 4.5 Million Swedes' *Social Science and Medicine* 64(1):21–34.

Maleckova, J. (2005) 'Impoverished Terrorists: Stereotype or Reality?' in T. Bjorgo (ed.) *Root Causes of Terrorism*. London: Routledge, pp. 33–43.

Marmot, M. and Wilkinson, R. G. (eds.) (2005) *Social Determinants of Health* (2nd edn). New York: Oxford University Press.

Mason, D. (2000) 'Ethnicity' in G. Payne (ed.) *Social Divisions*. Basingstoke: Palgrave.

McCauley, C. (2006) 'Psychological Issues in Understanding Terrorism and the Response to Terrorism' in B. Bongar, L. M. Brown, L. E. Beutler and J. N. Breckenridge (eds.) *Psychology of Terrorism*. Oxford and New York: Oxford University Press, pp. 13–31.

Mennell, S. (1994) 'The Formation of We-Images: A Process Theory' in Craig Calhoun (ed.) *Social Theory and the Politics of Identity*. Oxford, and Cambridge, Mass.: Blackwell, pp. 175–97.

Merkl, P. H. (2001 [1995]) 'West German Left-Wing Terrorism' in Martha Crenshaw (ed.) *Terrorism in Context*. University Park: The Pennsylvania State University Press, pp. 160–210.

Moghaddam, F. M. (2005) 'The Staircase to Terrorism: A Psychological Exploration' *American Psychologist* 60(2):161–9.

New York Times (2005) 'Inside French Housing Project, Feelings of Being the Outsiders', 9 November 2005 p. A1.

— (2007) 'Terror Officials See Al Qaeda Chiefs Regaining Power', 19 February 2007. Available at www.nytimes.com/2007/02/19/world/asia/19intel.html (accessed 1 March 2007).

Noon, M. (1993) 'Racial Discrimination in Speculative Applications: Evidence from the UK's Top 100 Firms' *Human Resource Management Journal* 3(4):35–47.

The Observer (2006) 'Extracts of Tanweer's Speech', 15 October. Available at http://observer.guardian.co.uk/uk_news/story/0,,1922641,00.html (accessed 21 October 2006).

Pedahzur, A., Perliger, A. and Weinberg, L. (2003) 'Altruism and Fatalism: The Characteristics of Palestinian Suicide Terrorists' *Deviant Behaviour* 24:405–23.

Phillips, J. and Evans, M. (2008) *Algeria: Anger of the Dispossessed*. New Haven: Yale University Press.

Piazza, J. A. (2006) 'Rooted in Poverty? Terrorism, Poor Economic Development, and Social Cleavages' *Terrorism and Political Violence* 18:159–77.

Rapoport, D. (2001) 'The Four Waves of Rebel Terror and September 11' *Current History* 100(650):419–24.

Rasch, W. (1979) 'Psychological Dimensions of Political Terrorism in the Federal Republic of Germany' *International Journal of Law and Psychiatry* 2(1):79–85.

Reich, W. (1998) 'Understanding Terrorist Behaviour: The Limits and Opportunities of Psychological Inquiry' in W. Reich (ed.) *Origins of*

Terrorism: Psychologies, Ideologies Theologies, States of Mind. Washington, DC: Woodrow Wilson Center Press, pp. 261–80.

Richardson, L. (2006) *What Terrorists Want: Understanding the Terrorist Threat.* London: John Murray Publishers.

Rummel, R. J. (1996) *Death by Government.* New Brunswick, NJ: Transaction Publishers.

Sageman, M. (2008) *Leaderless Jihad: Terror Networks in the Twenty-First Century.* Philadelphia: University of Pennsylvania Press.

Saggar, S. (2006) 'The One Per Cent World: Managing the Myth of Muslim Religious Extremism' *The Political Quarterly* 77(3):314–27.

Sarraj, E. E. and Butler, L. (2002) 'Suicide Bombers: Dignity, Despair and the Need for Hope: An Interview with Eyad El Sarraj' *Journal of Palestinian Studies* 31(3):71–6.

Sidanius, J. and Pratto, F. (1999) *Social Dominance: An Intergroup Theory of Social Hierarchy and Oppression.* Cambridge: Cambridge University Press.

Siljak, A. (2008) *Angel of Vengeance: The 'Girl Assassin', the Governor of St. Petersburg, and Russia's Revolutionary World.* London: St Martins Press.

Silke, A. (2008) 'Holy Warriors: Exploring the Pyschological Processes of Jihadi Radicalization' *European Journal of Criminology* 5(1):99–123.

Sonn, R. (1989) *Anarchism and Cultural Politics in Fin de Siècle France.* Lincoln: University of Nebraska Press.

The Times (2006) 'Foiled Transatlantic Bomb Plot "Was Ready to go in Days"' *The Times Online* 10 August. Available at www.timesonline.co.uk/tol/news/uk/crime/article605120.ece (accessed 12 August 2006).

Toolis, K. (1995) *Rebel Hearts: Journey's Within the IRA's Soul.* New York: Thomas Dunne.

Victoroff, J. (2009 [2005]) 'The Mind of the Terrorist: A Review and Critique of Psychological Approaches' in J. Victoroff and A. W. Kruglanski (eds.) *Psychology of Terrorism: Classic and Contemporary Insights.* New York: Psychology Press, pp. 55–86.

Waller, James E. (2007) *Becoming Evil: How Ordinary People Commit Genocide and Mass Killing* (2nd edn). Oxford: Oxford University Press.

Washington Post (2007) 'Terrorist Networks Lure Young Moroccans to War in Far-Off Iraq', 20 February 2007 p. A01.

Weinberg, L. (2006) 'Democracy and Terrorism' in L. Richardson (ed.) *The Roots of Terrorism.* London and New York: Routledge, pp. 45–55.

Wieviorka, M. (2004) 'The Making of Difference', *International Sociology* 19(3):281–97.

Wilkinson, R. G. (2004) 'Why is Violence More Common where Inequality Is Greater?' *Annals of the New York Academy of Science* 1036:1–12.

— (2005) *The Impact of Inequality: How to Make Sick Societies Healthier.* New York: The New Press.

Winslow, D. and Woost, M. D. (2004) *Economy, Culture and Civil War in Sri Lanka.* Bloomington: Indiana University Press.

Index

7/7 xviii, xxiv, xxix, xxxvi, 3, 8, 66
9/11 xviii, xxxii, xxxvi, 4–6, 14, 15;
  and 9/11 Commission 6–7;
  and Saif al-Adel 16;
  and al Ghurabba 18;
  and Abu Faraj al-Libi 20;
  and al Qaeda 23;
  and Ayman al-Zawahiri 29;
  and Army of God 37;
  and Mohammed Atta 41;
  and Axis of Evil 43;
  and Osama bin Laden 51, 52;
  and Mohammed Bouyeri 55;
  and Central Intelligence Agency
     60;
  and Coercive Interrogation 62;
  and Council of Europe
     Convention on the Prevention
     of Terrorism 66;
  and Counter-Terrorism 68;
  and US Department of
     Homeland Security 73;
  and East Africa Embassy
     Bombings 76;
  and Federal Bureau of
     Investigation 84;
  and First of October Anti-Fascist
     Resistance Group (GRAPO)
     87;
  and Adam Yahiye Gadahn 89;
  and Muammar Gaddafi 90;
  and Hambali 98;
  and International Convention for
     the Suppression of the
     Financing of Terrorism 104;
  and Khalid Sheikh Mohammed
     126;
  and Lashkar-e-Tayyiba 129;
  and Libyan Islamic Fighting
     Group 133;
  and Hassan Nasrallah 150;
  and New People's Army 155;
  and Operation Bojinka 157;
  and the Taliban 188;
  and Trans-Atlantic Airline Plot
     192;
  and USA PATRIOT Act 198;
  and War on Terror 201;
  and Weapons of Mass
     Destruction 202;
  and Abu Zubaydah 208;
9/11 Commission 6–7

Abu Hafs al-Masri Brigades 3, 7
Abu Nidal Organization 8, 81
Abu Sayyaf Group 9, 142, 205
Achille Lauro hijacking 10
Action Directe xii, 11, 46
Adams, Gerry 12, 110, 137
African National Congress xxxiii,
     13, 70
Agca, Mehmet 14
airline hijackings 14–15
al-Adel, Saif 16

Al Aqsa Martyrs Brigades (al-Shaid
Yasser Arafat Brigades) 16–17,
82
Al-Banna, Hassan 17
Algerian Group for Preaching and
Combat (GSPC) 23, 25
Al Ghurabaa 18
Al Ittihad al Islamia 18–19
Al Jihad 19
Al-Libi, Abu Faraj 20
Al-Manar 20
Al-Maqdisi, Abu Muhammad 21
Al-Masri, Abu Ayyub 21, 25
al Qaeda xii, xiv, xv, xxiv, xxxii,
xxxiii, xxxxiv, 22–24;
and 7/7;
and 9/11 4;
and Abu Hafs al-Mazri Brigades
7;
and Saif al-Adel 16;
and Al Ittihad al Islamia 18;
and alJihad 19;
and Abu Faraj al-Libi 20;
and Abu Ayyub al-Masri 21;
and al Qaeda in Iraq 24–25;
and al Qaeda Organization in the
Land of the Islamic Maghreb
25–26;
and Fadl al-Sharif 27;
and Abu Musab al-Zarqawi 28;
and Ayman al-Zawahiri 28–29;
and Ansar al-Islam 32;
and Armed Islamic Group 36;
and Mohammed Atta 41;
and Abdullah Yusuf Azzam 44;
and Bali Bombings 47;
and Beheading 49–50;
and Osama bin Laden 51–53;
and Decolonization 71;
and East Africa Embassy
Bombings 76;
and Fatwa 83;
and Abdullah Mohammed Fazul
84;

and Adam Yahiye Gadahn 89;
and Hambali 98;
and Hezb-e-Islami Gulbuddin
100;
and Islamic Army of Aden 111;
and Islamic Movement of
Uzbekistan 112;
and Jemaah Islamiyah 120;
and Jihad 122;
and Khalid Sheikh Mohammed
126;
and Lashkar-e-Tayyiba 129;
and Libyan Islamic Fighting
Group 133;
and Madrid Bombings 136;
and Media and Publicity 139;
and Moro Islamic Liberation
Front 142;
and Moroccan Islamic
Combatant Group 144;
and Movement of Holy Warriors
145;
and Munich Olympic Attack
147;
and Muslim Brotherhood 148;
and Narco-Terrorism 149;
and National Liberation Front
152;
and National Revolutionary Front
– Coordinate 153;
and New Terrorism 155;
and Operation Enduring
Freedom 157;
and Pakistan Directorate for
Inter-Services Intelligence
160;
and Sayyid Qutb 167;
and Richard Reid 171;
and Riyad us-Saliheyn Martyrs'
Brigade 174;
and Salafist Group for Preaching
and Combat 176;
and Mohammed Siddique Khan
181;

al Qaeda (cont.)
  Students Islamic Movement of
    India 186;
  and the Taliban 188;
  and Trans-Atlantic Airline Plot
    192;
  and United Nations Security
    Council Committee 1267 196;
  and Xinjiang 204;
  and Abu Zubaydah 208;
al Qaeda in Iraq 21, 23, 24–25, 32,
  40
al Qaeda Organization in the Land
  of the Islamic Maghreb 23,
  25–26, 36, 144, 152, 176
al Qaedaism xxiv, 26
Al-Sharif, Fadl 27
Al-Zarqawi, Abu Musab xxxiv, 21,
  24, 27–28, 32, 50
Al-Zawahiri, Ayman 3, 19, 21, 22,
  25, 26, 27, 28–30, 38, 44, 52,
  76, 77, 78, 148, 167, 176
Anarchist terrorism 30
Animal Liberation Front 30–31, 75,
  77
Ansar al-Islam 32
Ansar al-Sunna 32–33
Anti-Terrorist Operational
  Coordination Unit of France
  (UCLAT) 33
Arab Convention on the
  Suppression of Terrorism
  33–34
Arafat, Yasser 16, 34–36, 81, 163,
  165
Armed Islamic Group (GIA) 33,
  36, 175
Army of God 37, 56, 175, 200
As-Sahab xxxiv, 23, 38, 89, 139
Asahara, Shoko 38–39, 41, 42
Asbat al-Ansar 39–40
Assassins, The xv, xxxiii, xxxiv, 40,
  187
Atta, Mohammed 41

Aum Shinrikyo 38, 39, 41–42, 202
Axis of Evil 43
Azzam, Abdullah 22, 44, 51

Baader, Andreas xxxiv, 44–45, 46,
  139, 147
Baader-Meinhof Gang xii, 11, 44,
  45–46, 87, 139, 140, 156, 168
Babbar Khalsa 46–47, 105
Bali bombings 47–48, 2002
Baluchistan Liberation Army 48–49
Beheading 49–50
Beirut bombings 50
Bin Laden, Osama xv, xxiii, xxxiii,
  5, 7, 9, 19, 21, 22, 26, 27, 28,
  29, 38, 41, 44, 47, 76, 78, 82,
  83, 98, 100, 111, 113, 117, 169,
  188
Black September 53–54, 90
Black Widows 54, 174
Booth, John Wilkes 54–55
Bouyeri, Mohammed 55, 102
Bray, Michael 37, 56

Canadian Security Intelligence
  Service (CSIS) 56–57
car bomb 57
Carlos the Jackal, see Ramírez
  Sánchez, Ilyich
Cells 31, 58–59, 155
Central Directorate of Interior
  Intelligence 59
Central Intelligence Agency (CIA)
  5, 6, 13, 59–60, 62, 84, 98, 159,
  208
Christian Identity Movement 61,
  174
Coalition of the Willing 61–62
coercive interrogation 62–63, 208
Communist Party of Nepal (Maoist)
  63–64
Communist Party of the
  Philippines, see New People's
  Army

community of support 64–65,
    67
Continuity Irish Republican Army
    65–66
Convention on the Prevention and
    Punishment of Crimes Against
    Internationally Protected
    Persons, Including Diplomatic
    Agents 66, 146
Council of Europe Convention on
    the Prevention of Terrorism
    66–67
counter-terrorism 67–68
cyber-terrorism 68–69
Czolgosz, Leon xxxiii, 30, 69–70

Decolonization 70–71
Defence Intelligence Staff (DIS)
    71–72; 123
Defense Intelligence Agency (DIA)
    71, 72
Democracy 72–73
Department of Homeland Security
    5, 73–74
Dhanu, see Rajaratnam, Thenmuli
Directorate-General for External
    Security 74–75

Earth Liberation Front 75, 77
East Africa embassy bombings 16,
    18, 22, 23, 29, 52, 76, 84
East Turkestan Liberation
    Organization, see Xinjiang
eco-terrorism 77
Egyptian Islamic Jihad 16, 19, 21,
    22, 29, 52, 76, 77–78
Ejercito de Liberación Nacional, see
    National Liberation Army
EU Framework Decision on
    Countering Terrorism 78
Euskadi Ta Askatasuna (ETA)
    (Basque Fatherland and
    Liberty) xxxiii, 79–81, 87, 110,
    135

Fatah 35, 53, 81–82, 121, 147, 162,
    204
Fatwa 82
Fawkes, Guy xiv, 83
Fazul, Abdullah Mohammed 84
Federal Bureau of Investigation
    5, 6, 31, 59, 84–85, 89, 126,
    178
Feinians 85
Figner, Vera 85–86
First of October Anti-Fascist
    Resistance Group (GRAPO)
    86–87
Front de Libération du Québec
    (Quebec Liberation Front)
    87–88
Fronte di Liberazione Naziunale di
    a Corsica, see National
    Liberation Front of Corsica
Fuerzas Armadas Revolucionarias
    de Colombia – Ejército del
    Pueblo (FARC-EP), see
    Revolutionary Armed Forces of
    Colombia – People's Army

Gadahn, Adam Yahiye 23, 89
Gaddafi, Muammar 89–90, 133
al-Gama'a al-Islamiyah, see Islamic
    Group
Godse, Nathuram Vinayak 90–91
Goldstein, Baruch 91–92, 97, 125
Good Friday Agreement 12, 92–93,
    106, 110, 135, 137, 155, 169,
    170, 194
Groupe Islamique Combattant
    Morrocain, see Moroccan
    Islamic Combattant Group
Grupo de Resistencia Anti-Fascista
    Primero de Octubre (GRAPO),
    see First of October Anti-fascist
    Resistance Group
Guevara, Ernesto ('Che') 93, 125
Guzmán, Abimael 94, 179, 180,
    193

Haganah 94–95
Hague Convention (Convention for
    the Suppression of Unlawful
    Seizure of Aircraft) 15, 95–96
Hamas xxxi, 17, 35, 71, 82, 96–98,
    115, 121, 159, 162, 163, 166,
    204
Hambali 98–99, 121
Harakat ul-Mujahedeen, see
    Movement of Holy Warriors
Harkat-ul-Jihad-al-Islami –
    Bangladesh, see Islamic
    Struggle Movement –
    Bangladesh
Hearst, Patty 99, 185, 187
Hezb-e-Islami Gulbuddin 100
Hezbollah xxxii, 20, 33, 50, 71,
    100–101, 150, 162, 184
Hofstaad Group 55, 101–102
hostage taking 102

International Convention against
    the Taking of Hostages 103,
    146
International Convention for the
    Suppression of Terrorist
    Bombings 103–104, 146
International Convention for the
    Suppression of the Financing
    of Terrorism 104–105, 146
International Sikh Youth
    Federation 46, 105–106, 182
Irish National Liberation Army
    106, 109, 135
Irish Republican Army xxiii, xxxi,
    xxxiii, xxxvi, 65, 68, 70, 106,
    107
Irish Republican Army (Official)
    107–109
Irish Republican Army
    (Provisional) 12, 65, 90, 92,
    108, 109–110, 134, 137, 169,
    172, 177, 183
Islamic Army of Aden 110–111

Islamic Group 19, 77, 111–112
Islamic Movement of Uzbekistan
    112
Islamic Struggle Movement 113,
    118
Israel Institute for Intelligence and
    Special Tasks – Mossad 114,
    158, 162, 205
Israel Security Agency – The
    Shabak (Shin Bet)
    114–115
Italian Red Brigades xii, 11, 87,
    115–116, 141
Izz ad-Din al-Qassam Brigades, see
    Hamas

Jaish-e-Mohammad 113, 116–118,
    129, 130, 131, 145, 160, 175,
    186, 192
Jamatul Mujahedeen Bangladesh
    (JMB) 118–119
Jamiat ul-Ansar, see Movement of
    Holy Warriors
Japanese Red Army 15, 46,
    119–120, 164, 178, 179
Jemmah Islamiyah 15, 47, 48, 98,
    120–121, 142, 186
Jibril, Ahmed 121, 164, 165
Jihad 27, 122, 167, 185
Joint Intelligence Committee
    122–123

Kach 123–124, 125
Kaczynski, Theodore, see
    Unabomber
Kahane Chai 124
Khaled, Leila 125–126
Khalid Sheikh Mohammed 4, 5,
    10, 20, 41, 52, 89, 98, 126–127,
    157, 171, 206
King David Hotel bombing
    127–128, 184
Kongra-Gele (KGK – formerly PKK)
    128

Lashkar-e-Tayyiba (LeT) 113, 117, 129–130, 160, 186
Lashkar-I-Jhangvi (LiJ) 117, 130–131
Lehi, see Stern Gang
Liberation Tigers of Tamil Eelam (LTTE) xv, xxiii, 131–132, 165, 166, 168
Libyan Islamic Fighting Group (al Jamaa al Islamiyah al Muqatilah) 132–133
Lockerbie 9, 90, 133–134
London Bombings, see 7/7
Loyalist Volunteer Force 106, 134–135, 170, 194

Madrid bombings xxxvi, 8, 66, 135–136, 144
Marighella, Carlos 136–137
McGuinness, Martin 110, 137
McVeigh, Timothy 138
media and publicity 138–139
Meinhof, Ulrike 45, 46, 139–140, 147
MI5, see Security Service – UK
MI6, see Secret Intelligence Service – UK
Montreal Convention (Convention for the Suppression of Unlawful Acts against the Safety of Civil Aviation) 140–141
Moretti, Mario 141–142
Moro Islamic Liberation Front (MILF) 142–143, 144
Moro National Liberation Front (MNLF) 9, 70, 142, 143–144
Moroccan Islamic Combatant Group (GCIM) 144–145
Mossad, see Israel Institute for Intelligence and Special Tasks
Movement of Holy Warriors 117, 145, 175

multilateral counter-terrorism conventions 68, 146
Munich Olympics attack 53, 102, 103, 147, 158
Muslim Brotherhood 17, 29, 35, 96, 147–148, 162, 167, 205

narco-terrorism 149, 172
Narodnya Volya ('Narodniks') xii, xiii, xiv, 86, 149–150
Nasrallah, Hassan 101, 150
National Liberation Army (Ejercito de Liberación Nacional (ELN) 150–151, 197
National Liberation Front (Front de Libération Nationale (FLN) xiii, 71, 151–152
National Liberation Front of Corsica (Fronte di Liberazione Naziunale di a Corsica (FLNC)) 152–153
National Revolutionary Front – Coordinate (Barisan Revolusi Nasional – Coordinate (BRN-C)) 153–154
Naxalites 154
New People's Army 154–155
New Terrorism 51, 155–156

Omagh bombing xxxiv, 156, 169
OPEC siege 156–157, 168
Operation Bojinka 10, 93, 126, 157, 206
Operation Enduring Freedom 23, 157
Operation Infinite Reach, see East Africa embassy bombings
Operation Wrath of God 53, 158
Oslo Peace Accords 121, 126, 158–159, 162, 163

Pakistan Directorate for Inter-Services Intelligence (ISI) 105, 129, 159–160

Palestine Liberation Front (PLF) 125, 160–161
Palestinian Islamic Jihad (PIJ) 35, 82, 161–162
Palestinian Liberation Organization (PLO) 8, 10, 44, 52, 81, 96, 125, 158, 159, 161, 162–163, 183, 204
Popular Front for the Liberation of Palestine 15, 45, 46, 53, 119, 121, 125, 160, 164, 165, 168, 179
Popular Front for the Liberation of Palestine – General Command 121, 161, 164, 164–165
Prabhakaran, Velupillai xv, 131, 132, 165–166

Qassam rockets 17, 97, 162, 166
Qutb, Sayyid 18, 29, 148, 167

Rajaratnam, Thenmuli 168
Ramírez Sánchez, Ilyich ('Carlos the Jackal') xx, 103, 156, 168–169
Real Irish Republican Army (Real IRA) xxxiv, 155, 169–170
Red Army Faction, see Baader-Meinhof Gang
Red Brigades, see Italian Red Brigades
Red Hand Defenders 170
Reid, Richard ('The Shoe Bomber') 171, 208
Ressam, Ahmed ('the Millenium Bomber') 171–172, 208
Revolutionary Armed Forces of Colombia (FARC) 151, 172–173, 197
Revolutionary Organization 17 November 173
Riyad us-Saliheyn Martyrs Brigade 174
Rudolph, Eric 37, 174–175

Saaed, Sheikh Omar 175
Salafist Group for Preaching and Combat (Groupe Salafiste pour la Prédication et le Combat (GSPC) 152, 175–176
Sands, Robert ('Bobby') 12, 177
Secret Intelligence Service – UK (MI6) 123, 133, 169, 177–178
Security Service – UK (MI5) 123, 178
Shabak , see Israel Security Agency
Shigenobu, Fusako 119, 178–179
Shin Bet , see Israel Security Agency
Shining Path (Sendero Luminoso) 94, 179–180, 193
Siddique Khan, Mohammad xviii, 3, 180–181, 189
Singh Bhindranwale, Jarnail 105, 181–182
Sipah-e-Sahaba Pakistan (SeSP), see Lashkar-i-Jhangvi (LiJ))
Sirhan Sirhan 182–183
state-sponsored terrorism 183–184
Stern Gang 70, 95, 184
Stockholm Syndrome 185
Students' Islamic Movement of India (SIMI) 185–186
suicide terrorism 186–187
Symbionese Liberation Army 99, 185, 187–188

Taliban 52, 100, 112, 113, 118, 160, 188–189, 196
Tanweer, Shezad xviii, 3, 4, 180, 189
terrorist psychology 189–190
Tokyo Convention 15, 190–191
Torture 191–192, 208
trans-Atlantic airline plot 15, 20, 117, 192–193
Túpac Amaru Revolutionary Movement (MRTA) 193

Ulster Defence Association (also known as Ulster Freedom Fighters) 170, 193, 194
Ulster Volunteer Force 134, 194–195
Umkhonto we Sizwe (MK), see African National Congress
Unabomber xx, xxxiii, 195
United Liberation Front of Assam (ULFA) 196
United Nations Security Council Committee 1267 133, 196
United Nations Security Council Resolution 1373 197
United Self Defence Forces of Colombia 197–198
USA PATRIOT Act 5, 68, 198–199, 201

Vigorous Burmese Student Warriors xx, 199–200

Waagner, Clayton Lee 37, 200
'War on Terror' xv, 47, 157, 200–201

Weapons of Mass Destruction 202
The Weather Underground 202–203
World Islamic Front for Combat against Jews and Crusaders, see al Qaeda
Wright, Billy (also see Loyalist Volunteer Force) 134, 194

Xinjiang 112, 203–204

Yassin, Ahmed 96, 97, 115, 204–205
Yousef, Ramzi 10, 52, 98, 126, 157, 205–206

Zasulich, Vera xiii, 206–207
Zealots, The xiii, xiv, xv, xx, xxxiii, 187, 207
Zubaydah, Abu 171, 208